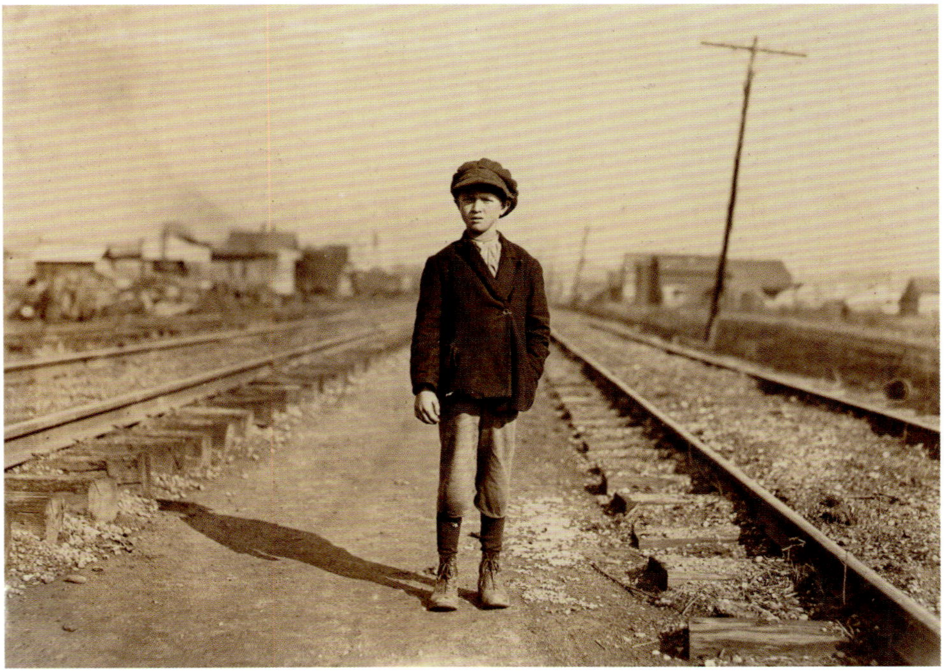

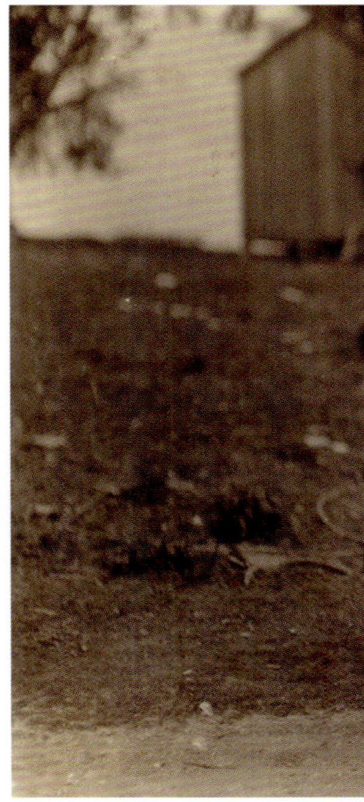

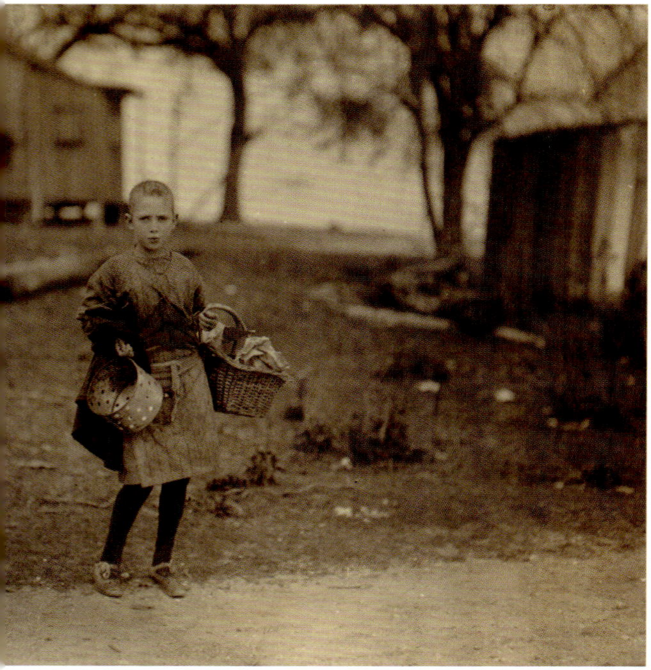

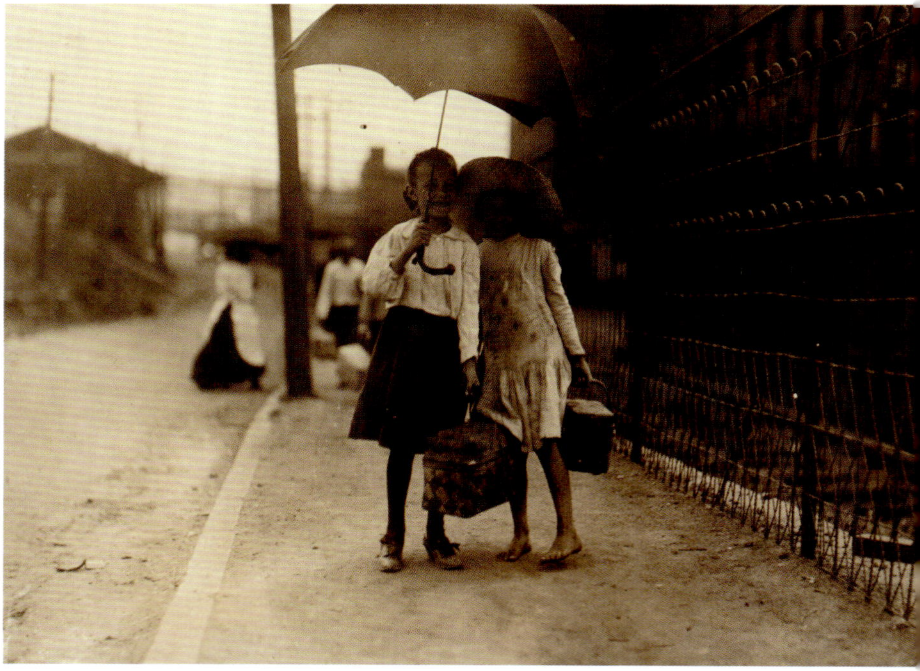

ALEXANDER NEMEROV

SOULMAKER

The Times of Lewis Hine

Princeton University Press
Princeton and Oxford

In memory of Brock Brower (1931–2014)

Published by Princeton University Press
41 William Street
Princeton, New Jersey 08540

In the United Kingdom:
Princeton University Press
6 Oxford Street
Woodstock, Oxfordshire OX20 1TW

press.princeton.edu

Jacket illustrations: (*front*) One of the spinners in Whitnel Cotton Mfg. Co. N.C. December 1908. Library of Congress, Prints and Photographs Division. (*back*) Whitnel Cotton Mfg. Co., Whitnel, N.C. Running at night. Out of 50 employees there, 10 were about 12 years old, and some surely under that. December 1908. Library of Congress, Prints and Photographs Division.

Library of Congress Cataloging-in-Publication Data
Nemerov, Alexander.
Soulmaker : the times of Lewis Hine / Alexander Nemerov.
pages cm
Includes bibliographical references and index.
ISBN 978-0-691-17017-6 (hardcover : alk. paper)
1. Hine, Lewis Wickes, 1874–1940. 2. Working class—United States—Pictorial works. 3. United States—Social conditions—Pictorial works. I. Title.
TR681.W65N46 2016
770.973—dc23
2015022259

British Library Cataloging-in-Publication Data is available

Designed by Jeff Wincapaw
Typeset in Adobe Garamond Pro by Jeff Wincapaw

Printed on acid-free paper. ∞
Printed in China
10 9 8 7 6 5 4 3 2 1

CONTENTS

Our faith comes in moments; our vice is habitual. Yet there is a depth in those brief moments which constrains us to ascribe more reality to them than to all other experiences.

—*Ralph Waldo Emerson*

ACKNOWLEDGMENTS

My long-standing attraction to Lewis Hine's photographs finally got a strong push forward when I met Connie Wolf, who encouraged me to pursue an exhibition at the Cantor Arts Center at Stanford University—an exhibition (and book) I decided would be on Hine. From there I went to meet with Tom Beck, curator of special collections at the University of Maryland–Baltimore County, repository of one set of Hine's child labor photographs. Beck, deeply knowledgeable about Hine, gave me further encouragement and practical help to continue this project. Then I went to Oshkosh, spending delightful September days working with Deb Daubert of the Oshkosh Public Museum. Working up my courage, I next contacted Joe Manning, the person who knows more about the people Hine photographed than anyone else, and to my delight, found Joe to be a kind and generous person and an ideal colleague. Then I spoke with Jason Francisco, the accomplished photographer and writer, contacting him because he wrote a great essay on photography—"The Prismatic Fragment," on Alfred Stieglitz's *The Steerage* (in *The Steerage and Alfred Stieglitz* [Berkeley: University of California Press, 2012]). I sensed that Hine was Jason's kind of person, and I was right. Jason drove thousands of miles to photograph in the places Hine had been, and some of the photographs he took at those sites are included in this book.

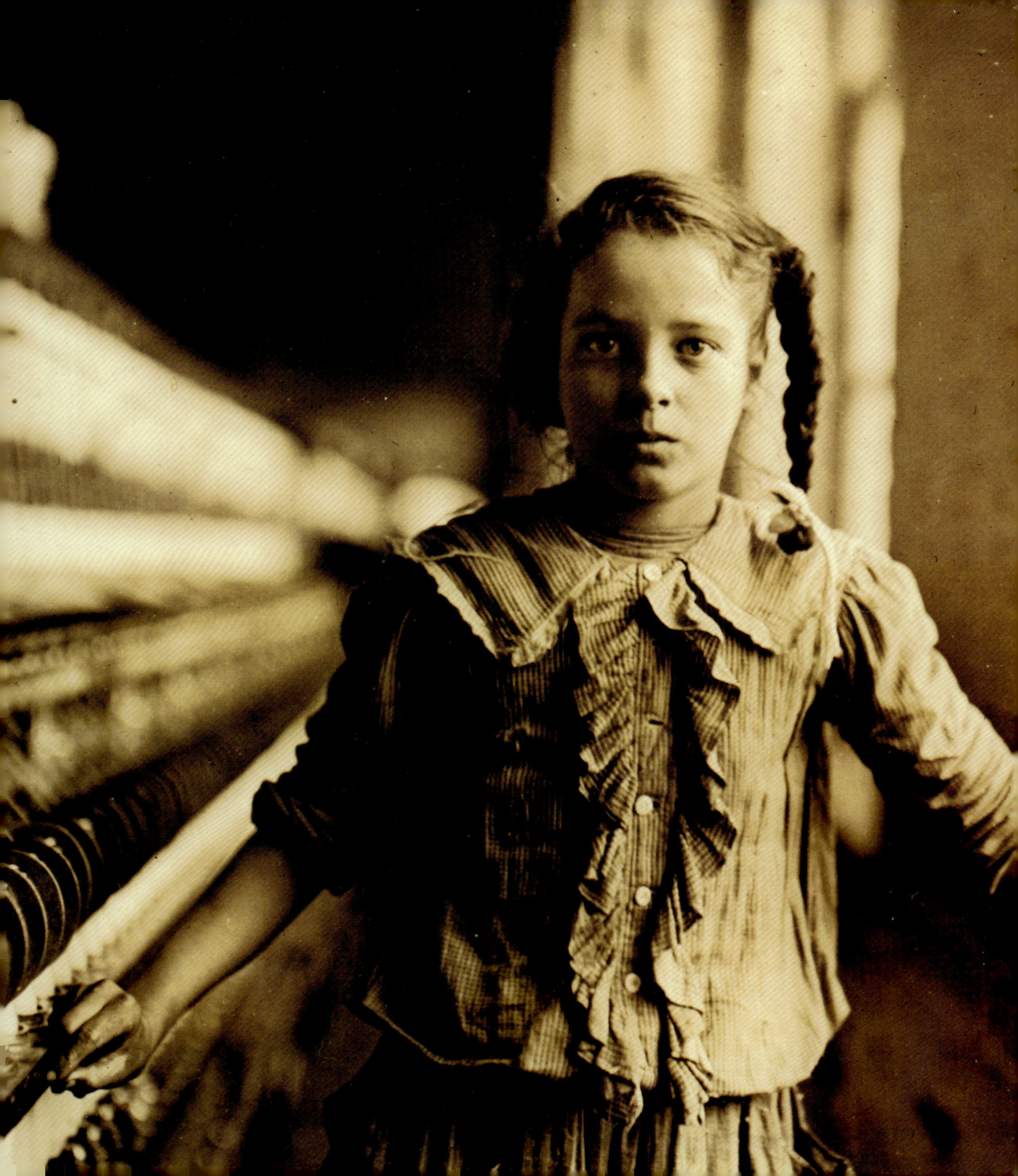

1 SOULMAKER

The look on the girl's face is difficult to know (fig. 1). She stares at us as if the directness of her gaze would reveal all there is to see, but the longer we look, the less we feel certain of. Drawn down the middle, her pretty face is shaded on the left and lit on the right, the light side brought out by the stiff braided ribboned tail of hair that hangs to one side in the brightness . . . the pursed lips, the dirty paired frills on the front of her pinstriped dress, the missing button between those frills . . . the buttonhole winking as her eyes do not.

The hands, both dirty, the left one resting on the coarse stone ledge of the window—fingers extended, the forearm lit to a porcelain smoothness—the right one bent so that middle and index fingers and thumb gather in an escutcheon shape, as if the girl were holding some knob-topped cane, the filigree of an invisible lineage. No cane but a long row of bobbins supports her, keeping her aright, folded in the narrow flow of a day's work.

Lewis Hine, a socialist working for the National Child Labor Committee, made the photograph in December 1908. That year Hine's acquaintance and friend, the tireless socialist writer John Spargo, wrote that "the liberation of the soul" is the highest aim of socialism. "To free the wage-worker from economic exploitation is indeed the primary object, the immediate aim, of socialism," Spargo said, "but it is not the sole object. It is not the end, but the means to an end that is higher, the liberation of the soul." This was *The Spiritual Significance of Modern Socialism*, the title of Spargo's book. Hine probably heard Spargo's lectures on the topic in the winter of 1907/8 at Cooper Union in New York. He knew Spargo's detailed and passionate condemnation of child labor practices, *The Bitter Cry of the Children*, published in 1906. It seems he portrays the little North Carolina spinner in a moment of spiritual awakening.

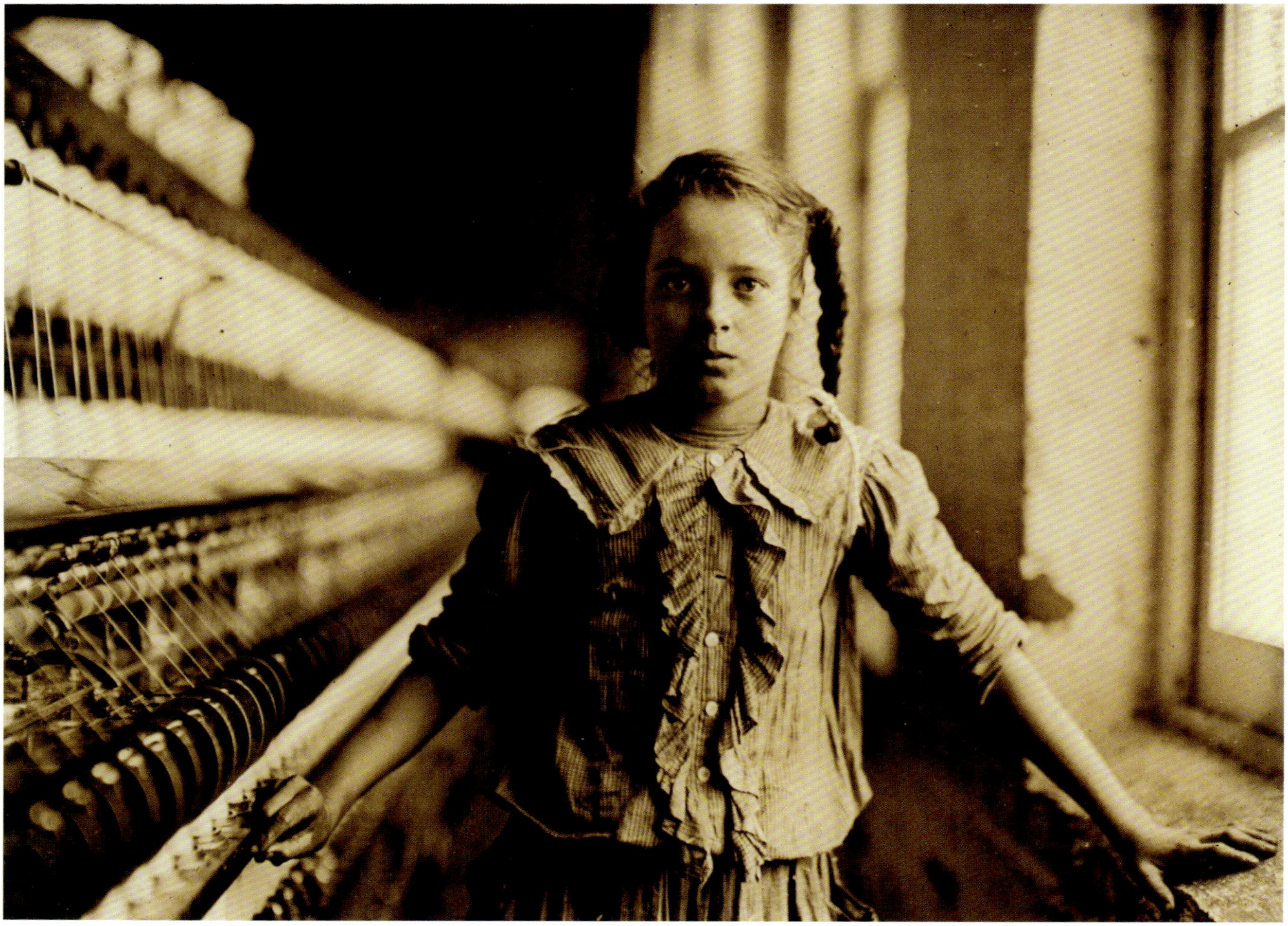

But still she is difficult to know. What quickens the girl to her vulnerable alertness? Something beyond or before what she represents, some sense that she is *in time*, or out of time. What is the nature of this time? The long row of bobbins shows the repetitive labor she is accustomed to—the factory time that governs her days. She handles this "side" of bobbins, as the rows were called, repairing broken threads up and down the line of whirring spools. Sherwood Anderson, in his later book about the mills, *Beyond Desire* (1932), described what such work was like:

Fig. 1
One of the spinners in Whitnel Cotton Mfg. Co. N.C. December 1908.

> Thousands of separate threads came down from up above somewhere to be wound, each thread on its own bobbin, and if it broke the bobbin stopped. You could tell how many had stopped at one time just by looking. The bobbin stood still. It was waiting for you to come quickly and tie the broken thread in again. There might be four bobbins stopped at one end of your side, and at the same time, at the other end, a long walk, there might be three more stopped.

When a bobbin was full, a doffer boy would take it, load it into a cart with other full bobbins, and replace the full one with an empty bobbin. He would take his loaded cart of full bobbins to the loom room. Being a spinner, like the little girl, or a doffer, as many young boys were, was not complicated work. There was a reason why children got these jobs—someone needed to supervise the spinning bobbins, and someone needed to "doff" them to the next stage of the process. Children were the definition of cheap labor, and their employment could readily be cast as a form of social uplift. Around Whitnel, North Carolina, where Hine's spinner girl stands, previous generations lived and worked on mountain farms, struggling in dire poverty and squalor: "At the mills, children over 12 years old, after they learn their job, can make more than men can make on farms," ran a testimonial distributed around the western North Carolina town of Clyde in 1907. Even the sallow appearances of the spinners and doffers, mill apologists claimed, owed more to their lives *before* the mill than in it, where medical care, daily bread, and a living wage were newly the norm for these poor folk.

But the job was hard, requiring long hours of repetitive action and the pure boredom of standing around day after day. Hugo Münsterberg, a Harvard psychologist of those years, noted that some workers enjoyed repetitious tasks while others loathed them, depending on temperament. A person comforted by routine, for example, "will experience the repetition itself with true satisfaction." But Hine's girl does not seem to be one of these people. Hine makes the infinity of her labor stretch to the vanishing point. The uniformity of the perspective is her unchanging mental world. Chained to the traces like Buck, the dog hero of Jack London's novel *The Call of the Wild* (1903), she sleds in a mill of fluff, a heroine who would be at home in a naturalist novel, mired in the long avenues marked No Way Out. Her blur is the lost focus of boredom and weariness, a panorama in which every scene is the same, forever.

All the moments drown into one another, an empty sea of time. "Yesterday or last year were the same as a thousand years—or a minute," London wrote in his short story of child labor, "The Apostate," published in 1908. "Nothing ever happened. There were no events to mark the march of time. Time did not march. It stood always still. It was only the whirling machines that moved, and they moved nowhere—in spite of the fact that they moved faster." Likewise, in his account of his visit to the United States, *The Future in America* (1906), London's fellow socialist H. G. Wells quotes Spargo's *Bitter Cry of the Children*: "for ten or eleven hours a day children of ten and eleven stoop over the chute and pick out the slate and other impurities from the coal as it moves past them." An illustration shows the chute-children bent like penitents at a confession. Instead of being pelted with stones, their punishment—the true measure of horror—is to *look* at rocks (fig. 2). The coal coming down the chutes is like the river Wells describes gathering to fall at Niagara—"a limitless ocean pouring down a sloping world," a sign of America both majestic and terrifying, "so broad an infinitude of splash and hurry."

The Niagara of endless work—the horizontal fall of the bobbin row—the cascade of labor, pitching forth and over in a strict level, ruled and regulated in a mind-numbing noise, a crescendo that makes the cotton thread like the plucked strings of a grotesque elongated harp—this is the stripped mental world where the punishment seems to be that the child will see and hear, even asleep, the sounding picture of what America is. Says one of Anderson's mill girls, her eyes closed at night, "I got thread in my brain."

But this naturalist detailing is only a baseline in Hine's photograph. It is not the kind of time he most wants to show. Factory time is the machinery that gets the photograph into operation—the power of thrumming naturalist storytelling (victimized worker, nefarious machinery, endless hours, pointless labor)—but all of this is only a grease works allowing a more important time to emerge as a puff of inexplicable steam. Who knows but that the catatonic dreariness, the loud noise of the spindles, is even a requirement for the school-less child to be sufficiently

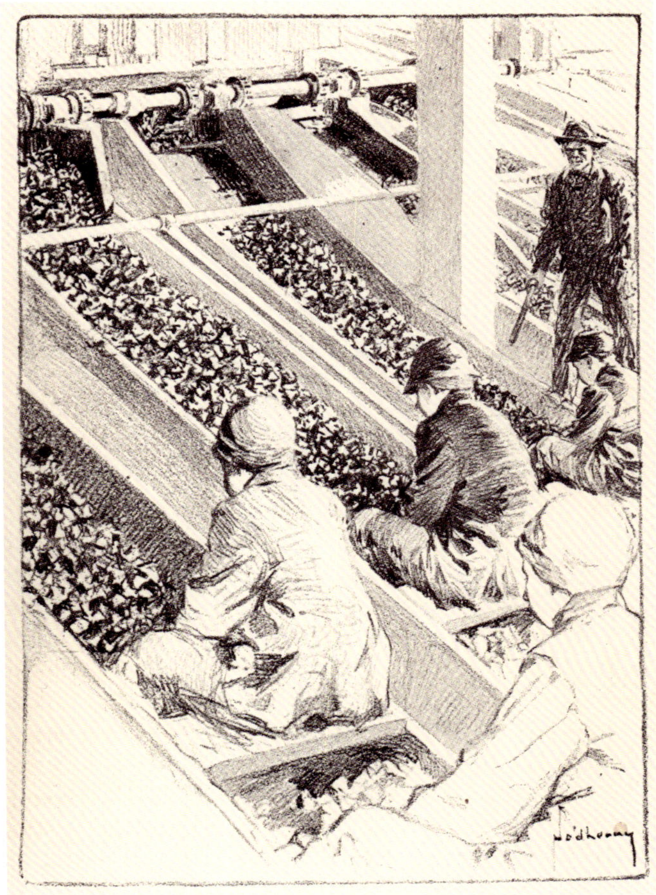

Fig. 2
Breaker Boys at a Pennsylvania Colliery, from H. G. Wells, *The Future in America*, 1906.

instructed in weariness, sufficiently lost or disoriented, to allow some other and more mystical time to flitter into the scene.

That other time is a pause. The girl stops her work. The kindly stranger with a camera walking into the mill and taking her photograph is an extraction from her day, a ceremonial ceasefire. What happens is not just a rest, or a break. It is something made by the photograph, made, too, by the photographer and the little girl as well. Neither of them knows what it will look like, but the time they conspire to create together is a *moment*—just the moment of the photograph itself, what it will be *then*. It has no backstory and no predetermined look. It may need to be sprung from the routinized time of the mill, where the hours are quantified, theorized, overseen—as if only in a place where time is so thick, so ceremonially extolled, might this more elusive form of time, almost imperceptible on its wings, appear.

That moment is not guaranteed to emerge. It is not synonymous with the click of the camera button. A photograph Hine took on the same occasion of the

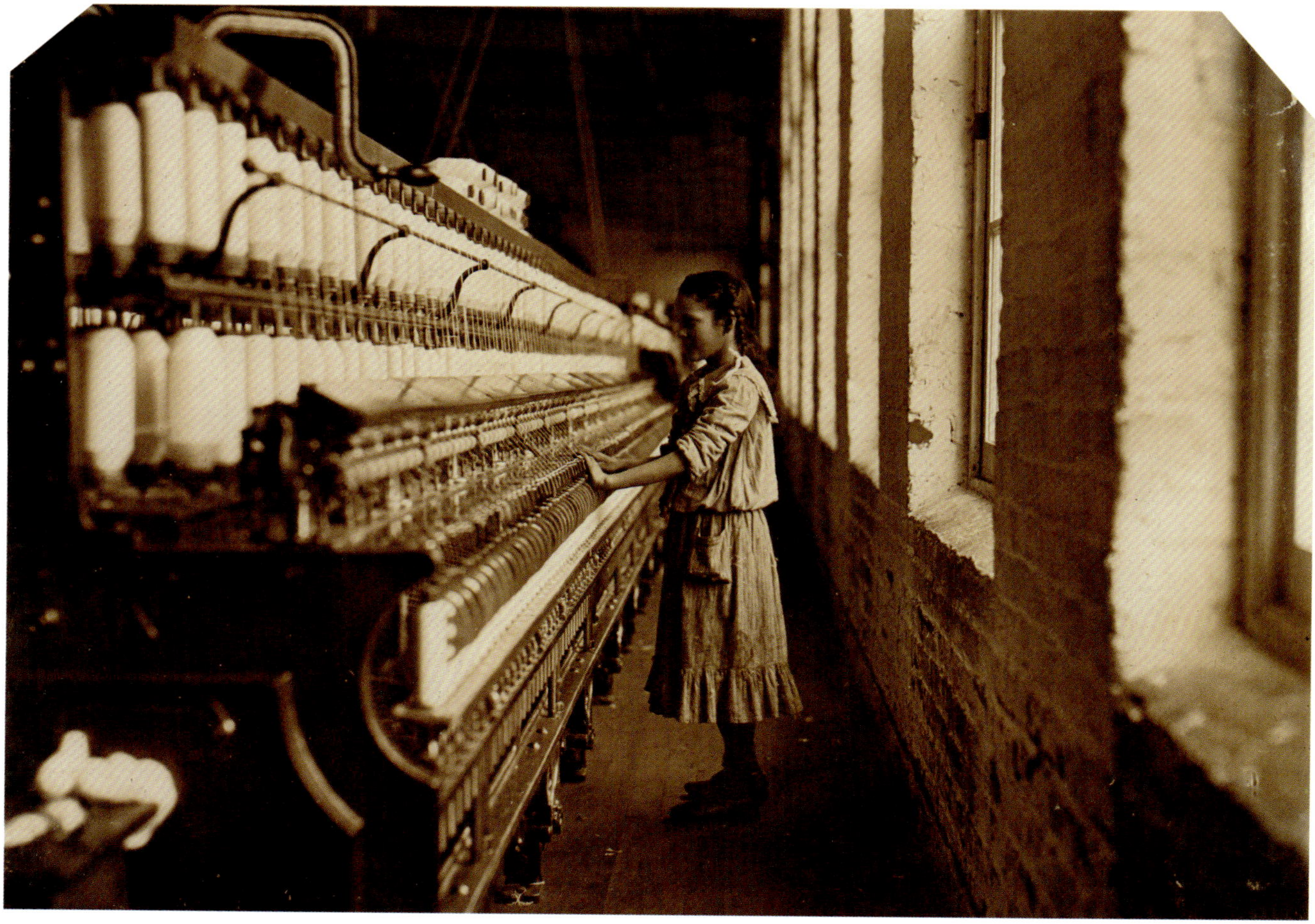

Fig. 3
One of spinners in Whitnel Cotton Mfg. Co. (N.C.) December 1908.

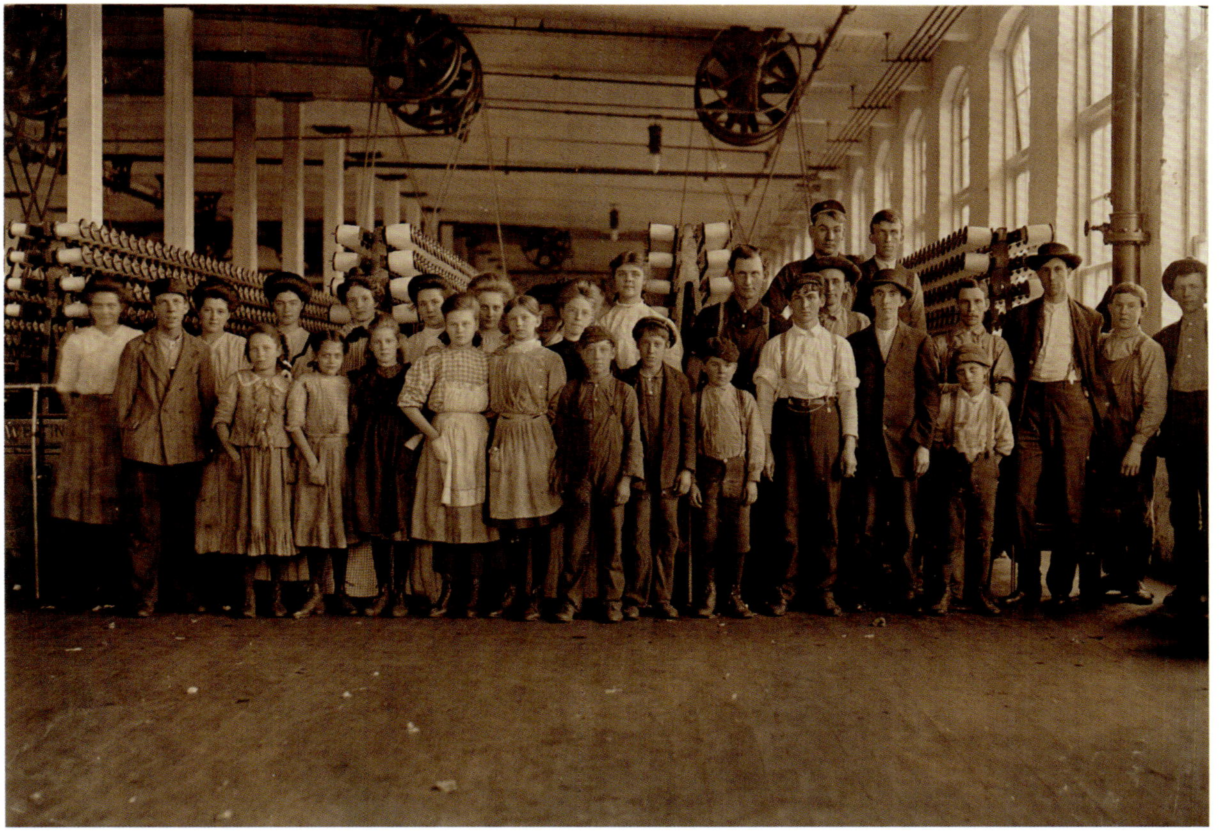

same little girl in the same place (fig. 3)—note the same chipped white paint on the windowsill behind her—is too frozen to emit the vibrating poise of the front-facing image. Likewise, still another photograph he took on this occasion, this one a group picture of child workers in which she appears as the first girl on the left in the front row (fig. 4), may contain a pathos of its own—it may mark time clearly enough—but it too lacks the elusive and unintentional feeling, the feeling one cannot plan for, wherein some weird temporal sensation makes itself felt.

Cinderella is a by-word for this other time, this timeless time—the attenuated moment—that makes itself felt in Hine's Whitnel photograph. Felix Adler, the educational theorist and the rector of the Ethical Culture School in New York, where Hine taught from 1901 to 1907, wrote that the two white doves alighting on Cinderella's shoulders are "the loveliest picture to be found in all fairy lore." The value

Fig. 4
This shows the number of small children on the day shift (50 employees in all) Whitnel, (N.C.) Cotton Mfg. Co. Nearly as many small ones on night shift. This is a new up-to-date mill. Whitnel, North Carolina. December 1908.

of fairy tales, Adler went on, "is that they are instantaneous photographs, which, reproduce, as it were, in a single flash of light, some one aspect of human nature."

Hine, who took up photography at the Ethical Culture School, learned that lesson well. His Whitnel spinner, not to mention other young girls he photographed toiling at their machines in the Carolinas in 1908 (fig. 5), steps out of folklore. We can all but imagine the evil stepmother and stepsisters lurking in the wings, or out having fun, while the drudge in her dirty dress labors the day long, her case all the more piteous for how beautiful she is. The photograph becomes a supercondensed story, "a single flash of light," the fairy tale crystallized to a moral truth, the unfairness of being cooped up, deprived of even the doves that would alight on one's shoulders.

The instant of the Whitnel spinner photograph is "Once upon a time," but it is also outside of time. The moment unfolds to tell a story, a fable, though it is not clear what the moral is. The long row of bobbins, yes, is some nightmare version of the enchanted avenues down which a dreaming princess might stroll. In Hine's picture there is an overabundance of pumpkins and not enough carriages. Everything is constantly turning back to, and never changing back from, the pure drudgery of slops and mops that beautiful slippers were supposed to redeem. If a strong feeling is identifiable in the photograph of the Whitnel spinner, it belongs to the emotion-world of these fables, where right is right and wrong is wrong, but the look on the girl's face is again so difficult to know. To fix her as sad, as in a pitiful state, as Hine's humanist admirers have long done with so many of his pictures, is to arrest the photograph's exquisitely fluid invention of momentariness.

That moment is nameless, like the little girl. Hine did not bother to record what her name was. This is not to say that her name is not now known. In 2008 a man named Joe Manning—not long after starting a passionate quest to learn the identities of the children in Hine's photographs—discovered that the Whitnel spinner was named Cora Lee Griffin, that she was born on July 12, 1896, and that the 1920 census lists her still as a spinner at the mill and married with two children. She died on June 3, 1985, age eighty-eight, survived by "two sons, three daughters, eight grandchildren, eight great-grandchildren, one brother and one sister." Manning's research is extraordinary, his motivations earnest. He has now discovered the identities and life stories of many of Hine's subjects, using pragmatic deduction and simple methods such as asking newspaper editors in the towns in which Hine photographed to post the pictures he made there. That is how he found out

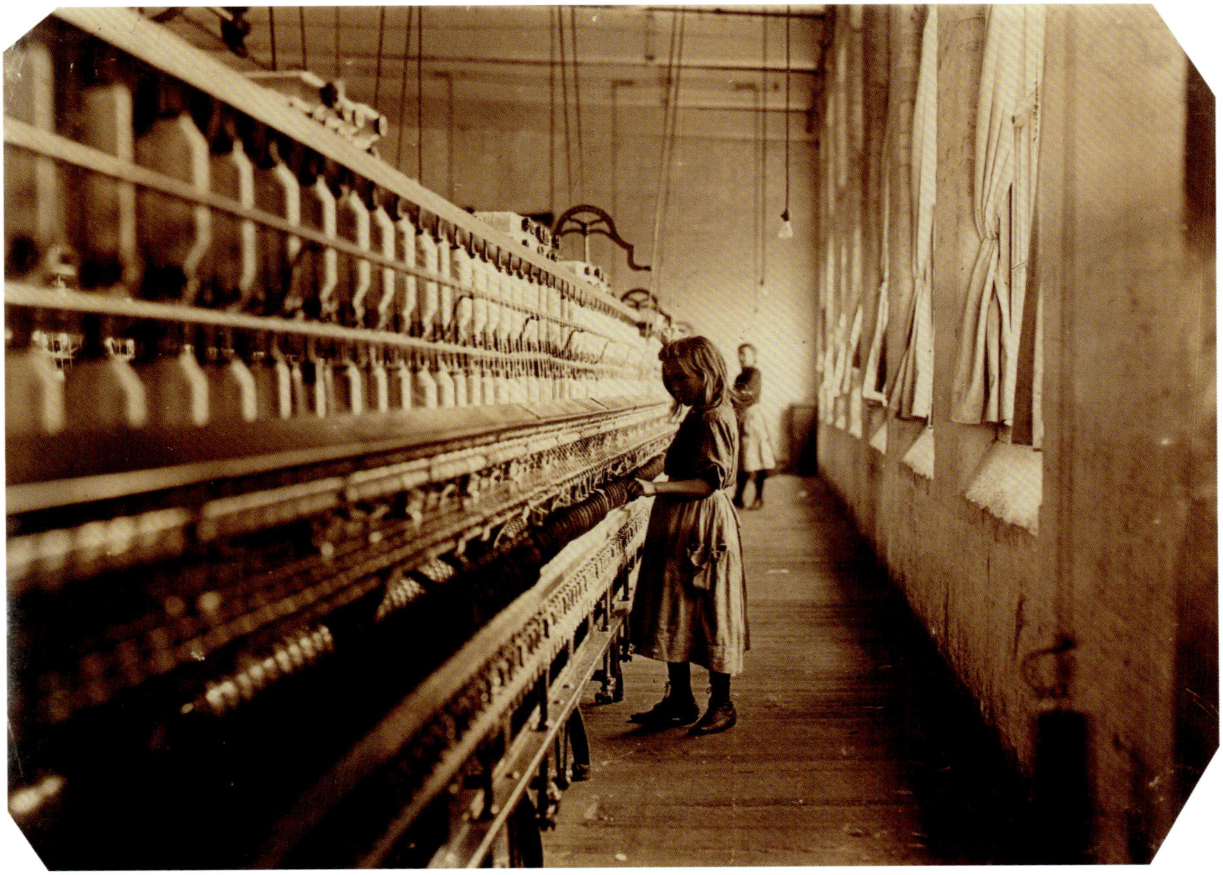

Fig. 5
Sadie Pfeifer, 48 inches high, has worked half a year. One of the many small children at work in Lancaster Cotton Mills. Nov. 30, 1908. Lancaster, South Carolina. November 30, 1908.

who Cora Lee Griffin was. Manning's way of repatriating Hine's photographs with descendants who often had no idea that their grandmother or grandfather or other relative had been photographed at so young an age has made him a humble guest of honor at family reunions where the Hine photograph he has solved has become nearly a sacred icon. As well it might. As well it should.

But Manning's methods and focused passion seem at odds with Hine's way of working. Sometimes in his captions Hine names the child correctly, other times he gets the name wrong, and still other times (as at Whitnel) he gets no name at all. But often something that cannot be identified hovers at the scene of these photographs. Looking at them is like going into a field to search for coins with a metal detector only after carefully disabling the metal detector beforehand—removing the batteries or bashing the metal-finding disc against a rock. Anything so that

Fig. 6
Edvard Munch, *Puberty*, 1894.
Oil on canvas, 149 × 112 cm.

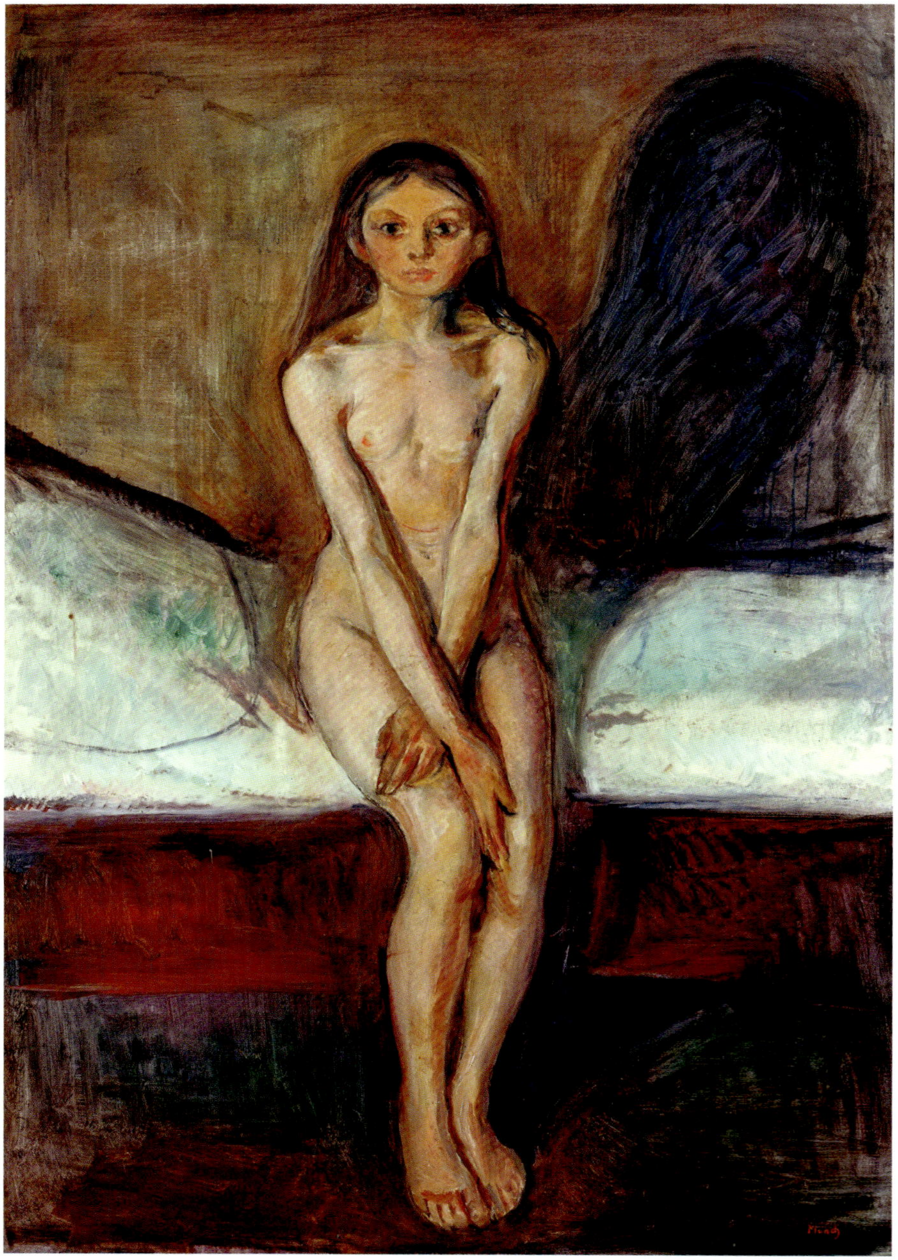

the device won't work. The aim is to make one's ignorance like that of the person within the moment herself. The Whitnel spinner may or may not read—socialists such as Spargo and Hine himself focused on rates of literacy and illiteracy among child workers—but what is clear is that, within the photograph, she cannot decipher the moment in any way. Wide-eyed, she is blind to how she appears, the knob-headed cane I've imagined that she holds a figure for that blindness, that feeling of feeling-of-one's-way. Fingers on the coarse ledge—that is the look of a moment when beheld from within (by her and by Hine, who sees more than she does but also feels his way). The wide eyes betoken their mutual burst of not-seeing. The eyes are merely the starting point for all that they, at this moment, can never know: the future Manning has discovered for her, the husband, the children, the old age, the lineage of descendants who will recollect her. That dizzying array of times is not absent in the photograph—implicit futurities are part of what makes a photograph such as this so eerie, even terrifying—but, again, she cannot know any of this. Blind, feeling her way, holding her cane (even that is not there), she and the man taking her picture do not know each other and will never encounter each other again.

Somewhere out there one of Munch's puberty-stricken vampires is the Whitnel spinner's cousin (fig. 6). The likeness does not concern puberty and adolescence but a kind of staring vulnerability. Each girl is given an existential awareness: being alive, being in time, emotions changeable in the moment. Fredric Jameson, writing of the sense of time in realist literature, describes "a temporality specific to affect . . . in which each infinitesimal moment differentiates itself from the last by a modification of tone and an increase or diminution of intensity." Different from the old emotional registers, where sadness to anger to joy might all be portrayed on a fixed chart, *affect* flows on "a sliding scale of the incremental," changing even as we look. Like the dark wing of gauzy shadow behind her, moods pass across Munch's girl in temporary patterns.

The nameless affect of the Whitnel spinner is likewise no readily identifiable emotion. Hine's admirers and detractors miss this mutability when they assume that his pictures portray legible feelings. Instead, without knowing it, but somehow responding to it as the deepest impulse of his work, Hine intuited the momentariness of affect as an important part of what, for him, it was to be human. He may have created the basis for every UNICEF poster child a fatigued liberal has seen in the last forty years, but that does not mean that his own photographs are anywhere near as clear. The humanists are not wrong in their estimation of Hine's goal. But they miss what the human was for him.

"I have come to think that the true history of life is but a history of moments," wrote Sherwood Anderson in his memoir *A Story Teller's Story* (1924). "It is only at rare moments that we live." The great literary critic Alfred Kazin elaborates: "Anderson did not merely live for the special 'moments' in experience; he wrote, by his own testimony, by sudden realizations, by the kind of apprehension of a mood, a place, a character, that brought everything to a moment's special illumination and stopped short there, content with the fumbling ecstasy it brought."

Fumbling ecstasy is a good term for Hine's special illuminations, too. The epiphanies in Anderson's *Winesburg, Ohio* (1919) take place at crossroads to nowhere, and whatever's the weather at that second is the emotional meteorology of the indelible event that happens there. A boy and a girl have their first sexual experience: "He took hold of her hand that was also rough and thought it delightfully small. . . . They crossed a bridge that ran over a tiny stream and passed another vacant lot in which corn grew." A little man haunted by his past, picking crumbs off the floor, is revealed in a moment to be doing an infinite penance in the private religion of his pain for a crime he did not commit: "In the dense blotch of light beneath the table, the kneeling figure looked like a priest engaged in some service of his church." Coaching baseball, a frenetic man with an evangelical sense of purpose screams instructions to his players from the first-base box: "'Now! Now! Now! Now!' . . . 'Watch me! Watch me! Watch my fingers! Watch my hands! Watch my feet! Watch my eyes! Let's work together here! Watch me! In me you see all the movements of the game! Work with me! Work with me! Watch me! Watch me! Watch me!'"

Kazin calls Anderson's focus on the moment a "left-handed mysticism." Anderson was "groping for the unnamed and realized ecstasy immanent in human relations, that seemed the sudden revelation of the lives Americans led in secret." Kazin goes on, using words so good for Hine's mystic photographs:

> A certain sleepy inarticulation, a habit of staring at faces in wondering silence, a way of groping for words and people indistinguishably, also crept into his work; and what one felt in it was not only the haunting tenderness with which he came to his characters, but also the measureless distances that lay between these characters themselves. They spoke out of the depths, but in a sense they

did not speak at all; they addressed themselves, they addressed the world around them, and the echoes of their perpetual confession were like sound-waves visible in the air.

The Whitnel spinner is the subject of the photographer's wondering stare and silence. Uncertainty, tentativeness, fumbling ecstasy—these are the touchstones for an encounter between photographer and subject, two strangers, that will elicit a confession, some soulful revelation "out of the depths," a momentary connection, you could call it, that is yet wordless, a confession made possible only by the haunting tenderness with which Hine approached the task. The moment that appears is so vivid it colonizes the long row of machinery, the weary length of industrial time, until the grand perspective itself becomes the infinite elongation of a mystical moment such as Anderson and his kindred spirit Hine envisioned it. "Life was a dream to him," Kazin writes of Anderson, "and he and his characters seemed always to be walking along its corridors."

It is all made possible by Hine's lack of training. The social workers knew what they were talking about when they initially told him he could not visit the mills and factories to photograph child laborers because he was not sufficiently trained in social work. If there is one thing Hine's photographs are remarkable for, it is the unschooled way he came into a town he did not know, into a factory he did not know, and photographed people he did not know, all with the knowledge that he would be leaving quickly, that he would never see any or almost any of these places ever again. But the brevity of all this was essential—any tarrying or delaying or dutiful consideration, beyond what the exigencies of the situation required, would dispel the urgency of his pictures.

Diligence was disastrous. Knowing the backstory of the mills—how they had begun emerging in the South around 1880, part of a progressive new economy offering regular employment to the region's poor whites—had no place when one's business was the momentary encounter itself. The successive waves of mill historiography—praise for the new southern entrepreneurs, condemnation of the same men, then fine-grained exploration of mill workers' lives—alike pass across Hine's photographs with a kind of irrelevance. Likewise knowing something about the complex racial displacements in the new mill economy is beside the point. If southern apologists such as the National Child Labor Committee's own Alexander McElway excoriated the mills for dehumanizing white children—"the depreciation

Fig. 7
Addie Card, 12 years. Spinner in North Pownal Cotton Mill. Vt. August 1910.

of our racial stock has already begun," he put it in 1907—and if the Indiana senator Albert Beveridge, in his three-day oration against child labor on the Senate floor in 1907, emphasized bitterly that the victims of the nation's current labor laws were "*white* children, 6 and 7 years of age," this was no business of Hine's.

He could not afford to show something so cumbersome as ideas, his own or anyone else's, not if his touch was to be light and true to the moment. His photographs trail a vast sociological story, yes, one that licenses people understandably to this day to misread his pictures as documents, but the real import of their "once upon a time" is the dream that theirs is no time, another time, a flicker of affect, reams of social history and attitude condensed to the flare of a fable, a dream, a moment so true it could scarcely be real. "Now! Now! Now! Now!" yells Sherwood Anderson's baseball coach at the game, and no one, not even his own players, understands his strange urgency.

Hine sought the moment—this is the hardest part to articulate—even if he intended to do otherwise. Having such a sovereign power in his work, the moment drowned out anything resembling an opinion or "statement" (at least in the most successful photographs)—even the statements that conscientious Hine himself intended to make. The very act of making the photograph—burdened with different expectations concerning labor history, race relations, public policy—somehow vanquished these topical attitudes and exhortations. As a result, each truly momentary picture became not so much a statement of the times as a curious departure from them. Quickness was all.

This was true north and south. Hine might have wondered anywhere about how briefly he was around his subjects, about the effect of that brevity on his pictures. Consider his photograph of Addie Card, taken in August 1910 in North Pownal, Vermont, along the Vermont-Massachusetts border, not far from Williamstown, Massachusetts, and Bennington, Vermont (fig. 7).

The girl stands with her right arm slack, hanging straight down. The one pocket of her stained smock slouches to the left. The fuzzy white threads from the spools stick to her front like she's walked through a spiderweb. Her left arm, resting on the row of spindles, strangely diminishes, as if stunted, a twig-arm, hand cupped, fingers extended, whereas the fingers of the hanging right arm curl. Each arm of this eventually long-lived girl—Joe Manning has found that she lived to be ninety-four—matches the thinness of the cylindrical bobbins ranged behind her. Not for nothing Hine's critics' sense of the plaintive emotional appeal of kids

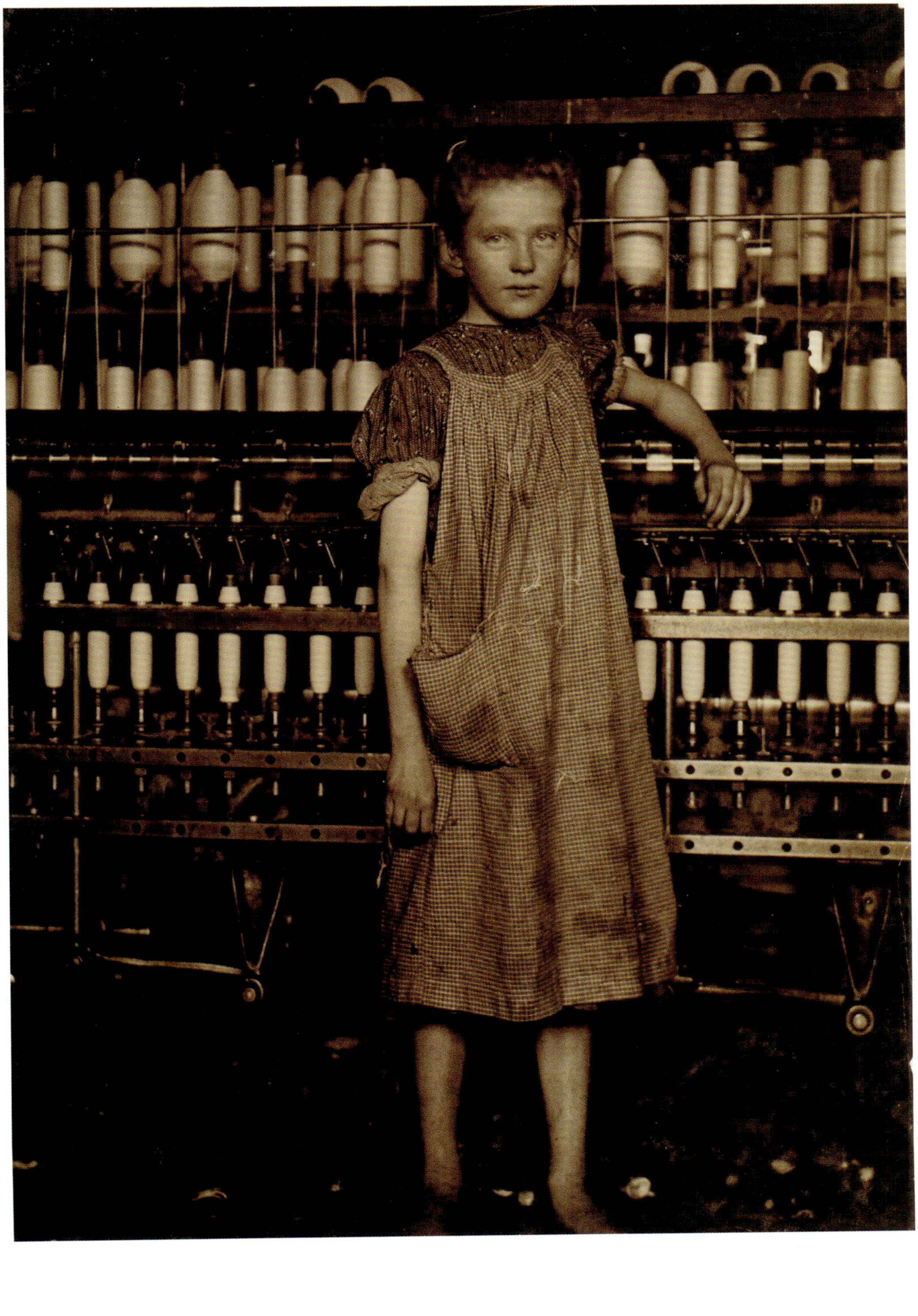

like this one. The spindly legs, the pocket sewn onto her right hip like a kangaroo's pouch reattached by an incompetent surgeon—she is a virgin of asymmetry, her crippled thinness swelling to a plaintive demand on the viewer. Pretty gaze as burnished as the shining spindles, she is a machine of sentiment, whirring with emotional intensity, a saint in chains, a girl visionary.

We get the picture. But what of the moment she and Hine confronted each other? How does the photograph unmoor their encounter from ordinary time, and from resolutions of sentimental meaning and social purpose? A New England contrast brings out the feeling of Hine's momentary muse. About a hundred miles from North Pownal is Cornish, New Hampshire, where Hine's contemporary, the well-known artist and illustrator Maxfield Parrish, lived with his wife and children at their custom-built estate house, The Oaks. Around 1905 a teenage girl named Susan Lewin came to work as a nanny there. Born in 1889, Lewin had attended nearby Quechee High School until the age of fourteen, when she became a wage earner to support her family. Not long after she began working at The Oaks, Parrish asked Lewin to pose for the photographs on which he based his paintings. Soon, it is not clear when, they became lovers, and they would remain close until Parrish's death some six decades later.

Their relationship—and Parrish's art—is a dream of stopped time. Looking at his paintings starting in 1905 is to see Lewin appear again and again, a constant muse, in this guise and that, as girl, as boy, as magician, as clown, in Jello ads and Renaissance gardens, on book covers and chocolate boxes. Sometimes Lewin appears multiple times in the same painting, as in Parrish's 1909 picture of the *Pied Piper*, commissioned by the Palace Hotel in San Francisco, where she seems to be all or almost all the children following the man. She is always there, so it seems, and she is often curiously static, conveying a strange effect—I don't know how else to describe it—of prolonged frozenness. Consider one of Parrish's photographic studies (fig. 8) that serves as a contrast to Hine's melting New England muse, Addie.

In the photograph Lewin is overstill, if there is such a thing. She holds her pose in a way that goes curiously beyond the requirements of a photographic source or study aid. Her absolute likeness to the way she appears in the painting based on the photograph provides a clue to her static state (fig. 9). It is as if Parrish wanted to create the sense that finished paintings such as this one were built up, not from photographs, but from careful *drawings* of his model—drawings that would have required that model, naturally, to hold her pose for a long time. But in reality all

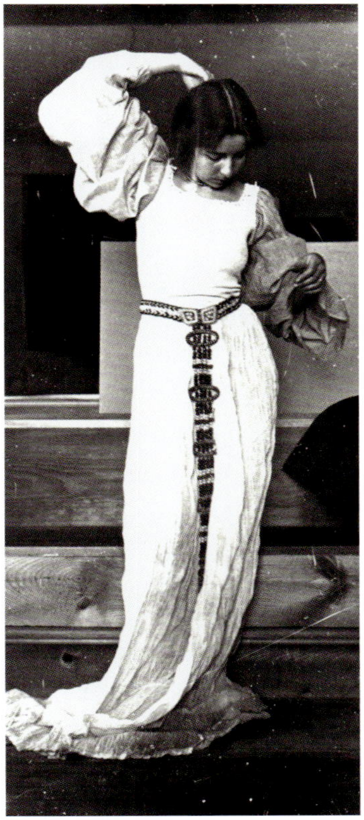

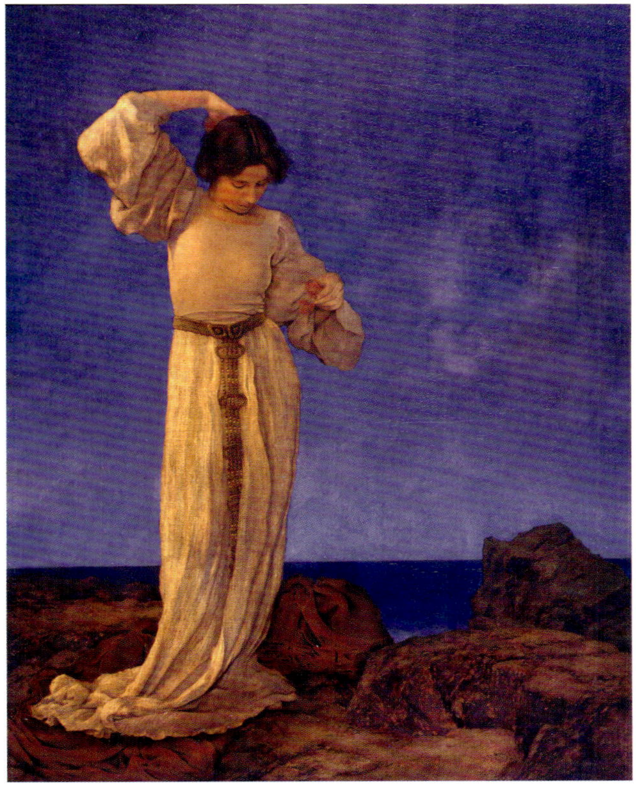

Fig. 8
Maxfield Parrish, *Susan Lewin Posing for Griselda* (*Seven Green Pools at Cintra*), 1910.

Fig. 9
Maxfield Parrish, *Griselda*, 1910.

that long-held stillness was condensed to a moment—just the click of the camera button—in which Lewin had only to impersonate a model posing for an artist over a period of hours.

The static-granite of these eternal poses is a lovers' vow. They are a pact between artist and model, which like the oath of lovers requires a solemn fidelity and a breathless sense that it will outlive time, outlive death. The curiously enameled duration is cold and chillingly statuary, at least as scary as the nook-nosed frazzle-haired clowns and eye-spy goblins that Lewin also posed for. Parrish's art may wish to extract a promise from us that we good-naturedly accept its plain oddities, treating them as a fey winsomeness of some inscrutably original kind, but it is difficult to get beyond their lacquered dreams of immortality, their lovers' concords as of paralyzing poisons. The princess is imprisoned in the castle, not because she is waiting for her prince to come but rather just because he *is* there.

Just in those same years that Lewin was starting out as Parrish's muse, a hundred miles down the road Addie appeared before Hine. The difference is that Addie, another New England working girl, is not meant to last. Hine knew her for a few minutes instead of sixty years. In Hine's photograph there is no blood oath of perpetuity, and this momentariness changes everything. It is not just that Addie is not as statue-like. She too, after all, strikes a pose. And it is not as though she cannot be appropriated to fit anyone's ready definition of an image frozen for all time. Hine's camera doubles her stillness into the *in memoriam* of what's become her postage-stamp likeness, her calcified portrayal of "work" in such a way that in the frigid genealogy of these things Addie has become a presteroidal Rosie the Riveter, sleeves ever at the roll. The difference instead is the humility of a feeling Hine and Addie might have shared—I doubt they could articulate it—that theirs is a moment that does not last, cannot last, that is so far outside thinking of perpetuity that the two of them hardly deign to consider the eternity that waxed Parrish to his cold ecstasies. There is a thought of promotion, of calling attention to wrong, yes, but beyond that immediate documentary use there is a feeling of inconsequence, of falling away, of subsiding, of drawing down into the bedraggled spindrift of some immense futurity before which the photograph bows with a sense of its own unimportance. If there is kindness and tenderness here, as there is in Parrish's photographs of Lewin, it is of a different type: the sense that we two are together just for this moment, and that the fairy tale of our humanity consists in the mutual recognition not of our lives but of this momentariness we share. That is what remains as Hine walks away.

Could there be love in these moments? The socialist attitude to love—love floating around like the fluff in the mills—was the air Hine and other reformers breathed. "Debs has given love for love," John Spargo told audiences in 1908, stumping for the socialist presidential candidate Eugene Debs. "How much the outpourings of his love upon the hearts of his comrades has meant to the socialist movement will never be measured." That love comes from deep down: "Debs draws love from a million hearts as a well draws from showers and springs; and like a well he gives it back to all who thirst for love as they cross the desert of life." And love is a reason to endorse: "Our love for Eugene V. Debs, the greatest lover of us all, entered into our choice of him as the bearer of our standard, the scarlet banner of the sacred cause, the symbol of a world-brotherhood to be." A month after Debs lost the election, Hine loved the Whitnel spinner girl, as he would love Addie Card.

Beware, though. Not all socialist love was like Debs's. "I once knew a revolutionist who thought he loved Humanity but for whom Humanity was merely a club with which to break the shins of the people he hated," wrote the progressive econo-

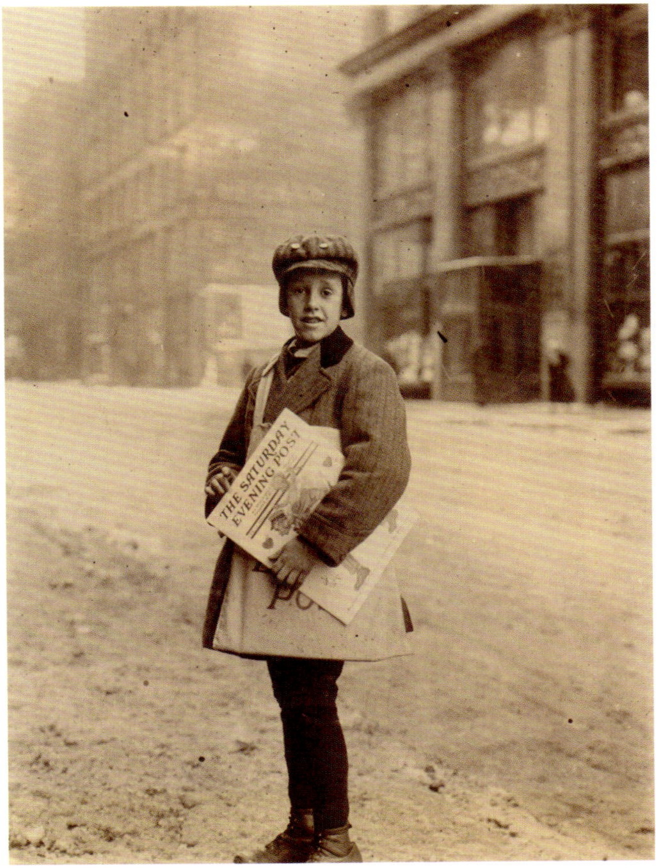

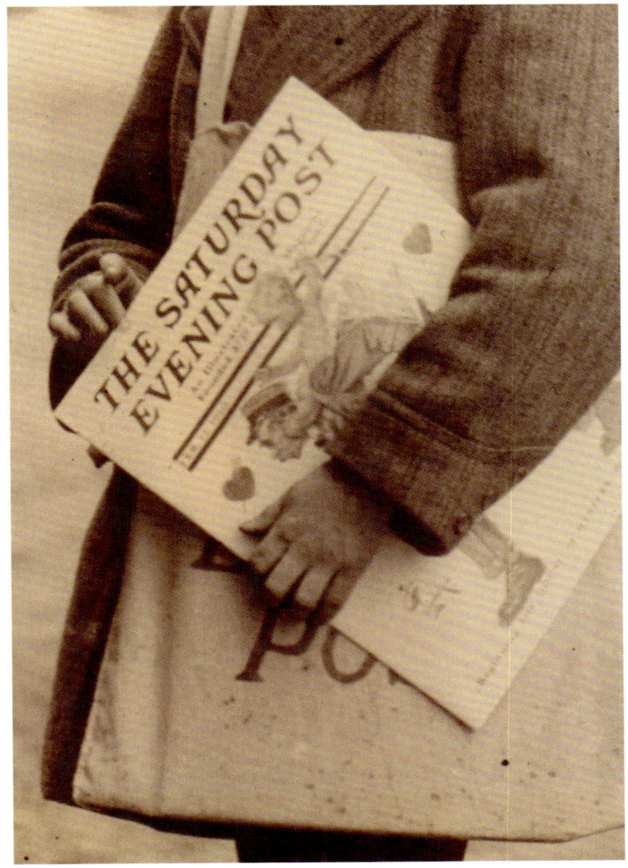

mist Walter Weyl, whose most important book, *The New Democracy*, was published in 1912. "Really he was in love with hate and not with any cause." In 1906 H. G. Wells envisioned a time fifty years in the future, when the tenderhearted citizens of a newborn world could recall the selfishness of the early twentieth century with serene remove: "In the old days love was a cruel proprietary thing."

Hine was not in love with hate, but what kind of love is present in his photographs? Consider one he took in Rochester, New York, in February 1910, the same year he photographed Addie Card. It shows a ten-year-old newsboy named Marshall Knox selling copies of the February 12, 1910, issue of the *Saturday Evening Post*, the one for Valentine's Day, featuring J. C. Leyendecker's cover illustration (fig. 10).

Leyendecker's postman, more visible in a detail of Hine's photograph, sets out to deliver love (fig. 11). Although no inclement weather impedes his way, he is bent down, not just by the sheer volume of Valentine's Day cards overflowing his mailbag, but by a soused Cupid riding him like a horse, bow extended back

Fig. 10
Newsie on Main St. at 2 P.M. Said "our class did not have any school this afternoon." Marshall Knox, 10 years old, 23 Hamilton Street. Rochester, New York. February 1910.

Fig. 11
Newsie on Main St. (detail).

as if to beat him over the head, fat feet clamped to the mailman's head, using his ears as stirrups. It is not rain or snow or dead of night that burdens the mailman but the sheer volume of insincere and obligatory protestations of love that his duty requires him to carry. And so he slogs on, downhearted, not in love with love, through the invisible atmosphere that gives so many of Leyendecker's figures their sluggish velocity: the portly men mowing their lawns, the chiseled football players struggling to cross the goal line.

But in Rochester there was another kind of love than the commercial kind. The city's most well-known pastor was Walter Rauschenbusch, who had achieved national recognition in 1907 for his widely read book *Christianity and the Social Crisis*, published that year, inspired by his previous experience as pastor of a church in Hell's Kitchen.

In *Christianity and the Social Crisis* Rauschenbusch spelled out the problem of love in commercial America. "Christianity bases all human relations on love, which is the equalizing and society-making impulse," he wrote. "But in urging the social duty of love, Christianity encounters the natural selfishness of human nature." More direly, it encounters modern commercial society, where the ethos is about self-preservation and vanquishing competitors. "The social value of business," Rauschenbusch notes with scorn, "is reserved for ornamental purposes in after-dinner speeches. There all professions claim to exist for the good of society." But in America now "the law of the cross is superseded by the law of tooth and nail."

Rauschenbusch might have been suspicious of Hine's photograph of Marshall Knox. It looks like just another boy trying to get ahead. Hawking copies of the *Saturday Evening Post*, Knox already appears on the path to being his own man. His splendid autonomy and kempt appearance (the hat with ear flaps, the neat and warm collared jacket) show that he is ready for the demands of business. Sure, it's not easy. You've got to start somewhere, and if the road is not necessarily glittering with promise at least the snow has been plowed. The rest is up to you.

But Hine brought a sense of love to his work equal to that of the Rochester pastor—equal but different. Hine's love was not Christian; it was instead a devotion to a moment without higher significance, whose beauty was its way of expanding as it elapsed. Hine's mission, unlike Rauschenbusch's, was only to the ephemerality of the encounter. Knox is not a native awaiting conversion, struck down in his daily round, but rather Hine's collaborator in the look of the street that day, the numbingly periodical nature of time, the fast and slick pages not only

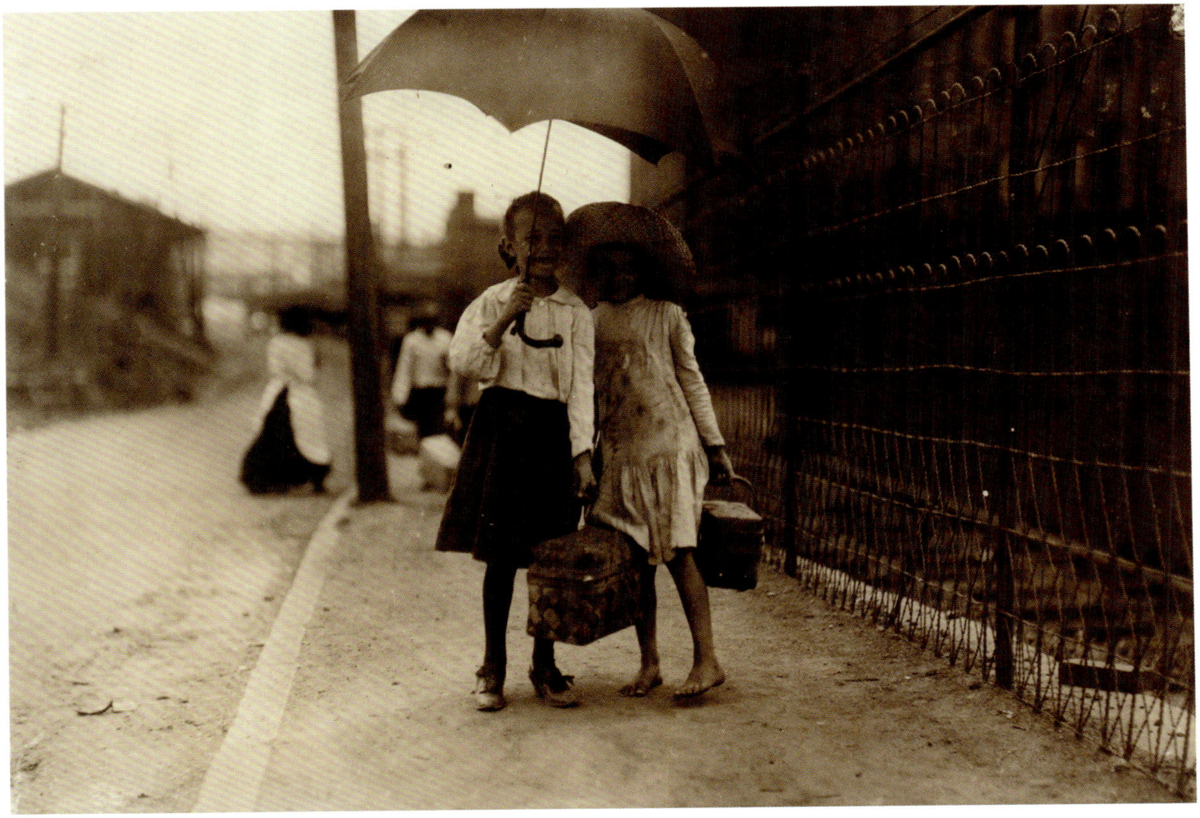

of the *Post* but also of the blank-sheeted road, graded and paved, that's the big emptiness a person walks in. And in that void what connects us can only be felt in passing. An intuitive feeling for brevity makes the deepest pathos of Hine's pictures.

Fig. 12
A couple of dinner-toters at Riverside Cotton Mills, Danville, Va. Myriads of these little ones carry dinners to the mill workers. The Supt. of Schools and teachers in Danville said that many children toted dinners and did nothing else not even attending school. Danville, Virginia. June 1911.

The power of this man with the camera must have been awesome, even terrifying. Hine's failed pictures, his duds, give a sense of how fearsome this power could be. In June 1911 he photographed two "dinner-toters" outside the Riverside Cotton Mills in Danville, Virginia (fig. 12). The girls with their baskets bring lunch to brothers or fathers in the mills—Hine considered dinner toting a form of child labor and photographed the girls accordingly. And he gets most of the picture right.

The two girls, front and center in direct relation to the photographer; the funnel of space, here on the street instead of between the sides inside a mill, but still forceful, dizzying—the iron grid of the fence closing off one side, the street flaring in a dirty blur on the other. Meanwhile, the background characters strike their notes, the woman crossing the street, the white-shirted man carrying a basket along the sidewalk, the arm of another man carrying a basket a little closer to us. The man whose face we can see is black, deputized like the little girls to carry lunches.

The photograph gets the jagged gleam of day. One of the dinner-toters wears a big straw hat, the other holds that enormous umbrella, gripping it high on the fish-hook handle because otherwise her thin arm could not support it. The telephone pole leans one way, the umbrella the other, the two little girls tilt left and right, a contrapuntal array held in suspension, a fragility of forces whose leitmotif is the left foot of the barefoot girl, slightly lifted off the ground, the gap between that foot and its shadow calibrating the picture's overall balance of weights: the laden baskets, the little girls, the iron fence latticed into a heavy thinness, the umbrella canopy on its stalk—the feeling of air trapped in its dome—the sky between the umbrella and the girls' heads, the sidewalk between the girls' shins and below the hanging baskets: levity and weight, the skewed equilibrium of a moment.

But the little girls' faces are obscure. They recede into a murk in which their features subside, grainy, the taller girl's teeth a bright gray. The woven harlequin pattern of the nearer lunch basket is good and clear, like the tips of the taller girl's shoes and the fine highlights on the big toenails of her companion, but that far basket is as smudged as their faces. Perhaps the daylight and the local shadow of the umbrella proved too difficult for Hine to reconcile. Whatever the reason for the picture's failure, the feeling it gives is of Hine's power—a power of holding (or not holding) a person-in-time in his hands. Then and there in that moment it will be decided if they exist for all time or do not.

Imagine that you are a child bringing lunch to your father on that day in Danville, Virginia, in June 1911—that you are one of these nameless dinner-toters on that afternoon. The chances are almost astronomically against any record being preserved of you on that day, or on almost any day. There is only one person in the entire United States who is going around to the mills to photograph children such as you. He operates by no predictable system, and indeed he is obscure—you do not know of him any more than anyone else does except for a handful of socialist reformers.

But you are in luck. In fact, your luck is extraordinary. Because on this day of all days, when you have been asked to take lunch to the mills—who knows but that you do not do this all the time—the very man, the only man, who could take your picture and make it stick for all time is in town. And not only that, but he has stopped in front of you and your friend and asked to take your picture. The stage is set for an event that is improbable to say the least. You are about to be immortalized, not just in the simple sense in which someone, anyone, might take your picture. And not just in the more complex sense in which Hine, via his special gift, might intuit you as a fellow-being-in-time, barefoot a-skate in the gritty ambit of life's ceaselessly forgotten moments. But in the most extravagant sense—because Hine's intuition of time is one in which, all in a moment, *only* in a moment, he might invent a person's soul.

Not that you do not have a soul already. Or that people have not told you that you have one. Your religious life is independent of what happens before the man with the camera. If anything, this incident on the street is a carefree escape from the daily round not only of work but of piety itself. The practice of your faith and the security of your soul, who knows, might even beggar this event, making it barely register in the tolling of your days. It is you who are rich and he who is poor.

But he brings with him something that you do not have. The moment that you consent to—the image he will make—might set loose something so volatile you scarcely knew it was a part of you. Indeed, it was not, until he came along. Whatever it is, it may contradict your whole life. The rituals that you have been told daily build your soul now vanish, spread to the winds as inconsequential, replaced by a sensation like a breeze passing across your face.

For Hine, who we are is our momentariness, alight in the scatter of our circumstances. That sensation, peaceful and disturbing, is not a bourgeois mysticism. Allan Sekula was right when he said that Hine's work is different from the paeans to indefinable feeling found in those years in Alfred Stieglitz's *Camera Work*. Something else appears in the moment. Sifted through the mesh of that scarcely recognized gradation of time is a feeling so fine that not all the deep trawling of moral explanation and pious beauty could ever lift it to the surface. The photographer throws away the hourglass and contents himself with a few grains of sand. Seeking the way life is tossed and forgotten, he looks for the precious grit of what will never be seen again. So at Danville the one little girl might have said to the other: here is this man to give each one of us, you and me, a soul. Here is the soulmaker.

But he misses the photograph. He does not get it right. He has not been making photographs for that long, after all, and in any case the two of you beneath the umbrella are a difficult technical challenge. The result is that the photograph does not immortalize you and your friend but instead gets your two faces *just on the other side* of having been ensouled. From behind blurs the apparitional girls peer in as at foggy windows, always—and this is the terror of it—within an eyelash of having been created. This is no romantic struggle of *nonfinito*, Michelangelo's writhing slaves still in combat with the marble block, but rather the wan-ness of waifs consigned to a lasting unrealization. The barefoot girl's left foot crosses over from the lifeless zone, fully realized, a first step of creation, but her face has yet to shed the mucus of photographic process, the embryonic sac of chemicals and light that will deliver her and her friend into being. Like a botched operation—it was no one's fault—the miracle does not happen. The girls remain nearly as faceless as the black man trudging up the sidewalk behind them, asleep and not awakened.

Denied their souls, they are denied a future. The two dinner-toters pause in the long funneled space of the road and sidewalk, a vista that feels temporal as well as spatial, as if the road implies a long futurity. The future was *the* mystic tense of socialist thought in those years, more so than even the present, and Hine understood that futurities are a part of any moment. In *The Future in America*, his socialist travel book of 1906, H. G. Wells wrote of a "forecast," a "horoscope" for the nation's 1,700,000 child workers. At Danville the little girls' faces do not completely come into view, but the abortion does not prevent us from seeing the nearly full development of their skeletal structure, the armature of bridge and hut, chimney and sky, the entablature of blood vessels and intricate muscles that was to have been the future that these girls unborn will never see.

But when the Soulmaker on his rounds did his work well, the clarity of the faces activates the vista. Soul and future then emerge eerily together. In a photograph Hine took in Kosciusko, Mississippi, in November 1913, three young mill workers stare back at the photographer (fig. 13). Stopped, arrayed before him, black stockings rooting them to the ground, they have come from down the road where the mill is. That road behind them is their past. But in a curious way the road also seems like their future. Pluming away from them, the path marks their life as it has been but also as it will be.

If that is so, the visionary futures differ for the three girls. The central girl, lifting her left hand to her face in a pose of pretty poverty like a Bouguereau peasant, is framed against the workers' house behind her. The same is true of the girl on the left, the one in the smudged gray smock, hands behind her back, sister-like to the central girl, the two of them framed by that same house. Their future—if you like—is foretold in this domestic relation to one of the row of workers' houses, mill

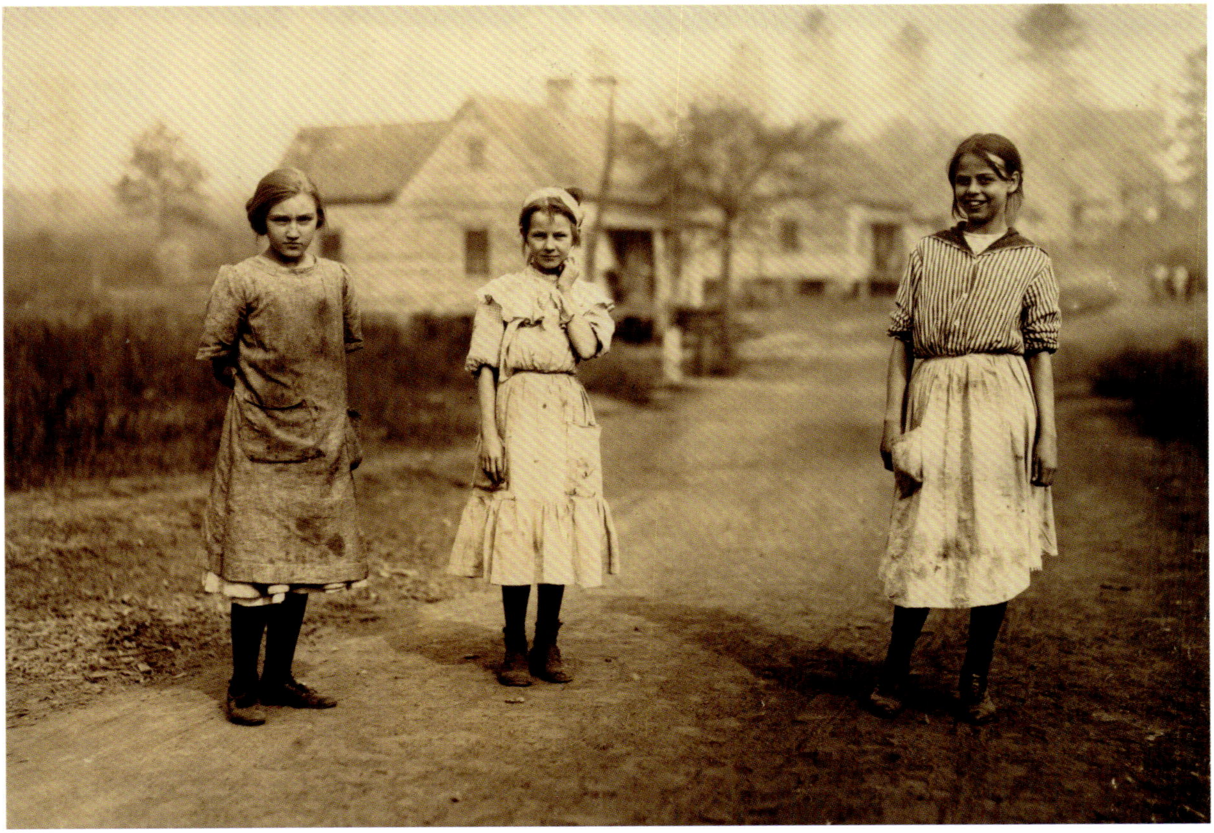

properties, that potentially mark a beleaguered and perpetually weathered stasis in this one spot. This is of course to say nothing of who these girls *actually* were—at this point not even Joe Manning knows the answer—but rather how the photographer, using his Wells-like horoscope, imagines them to be.

Fig. 13
Some of the young workers (not the youngest) in the Kosciusko Cotton Mills. Superintendent objected to my taking photographs. Kosciusko, Mississippi. November 1913.

Then there is the girl on the right. Her relation to the road is different. Unframed by the near house, she appears against the more mirage-like structures in the distance. Set off from the other girls by a wider space, more relaxed than they are with her hipshot pose and slight lean to the right, she smiles charismatically at the photographer, her hair loose around her ears and forehead, her relation to the moment of being photographed less guarded and structured than that of the two other girls. Against the road, as tall as the trees blurring the sky above her, she appears as the person the photograph most "creates," which is to say, most conjures in the moment, as if her substance were as apparitional as the nowhere she has

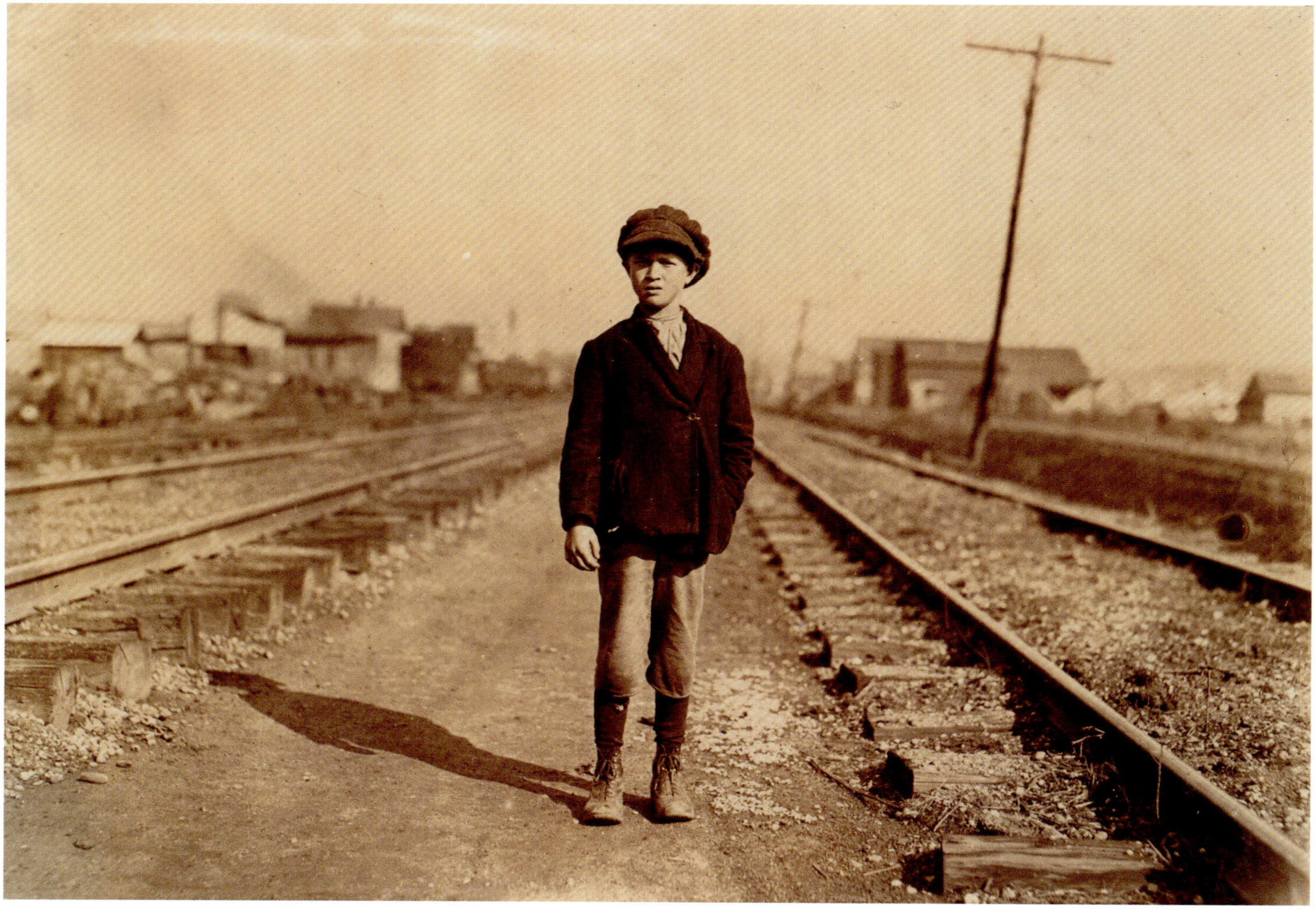

Fig. 14
Maple Mills, Dillon, S.C. John Roberts, Been in mill 2 years. Runs 4 and 5 sides. December 1908.

emerged from and that, just as surely, she will forever disappear into. The terror of the soulmaker is all here, because his gift of bestowing a life upon this girl is the same as his power to make her vanish. She is sped into oblivion at the moment she is created.

When Hine puts the children on roads and alongside railroad tracks, the futurity-effect is almost too vivid, too obvious (fig. 14). His photograph of John Roberts, taken in Dillon, South Carolina, in December 1908, places the little boy before a zooming pair of rail lines. Roberts occupies the vanishing point, as if the uncertain look on his face were a pondering of his prospects, and not just the circumstance of being photographed by this decent stranger. These are the grooves of his fated tracks, laid down, who knows, long before he was born. Hine called it “the Road They will Travel” in one of the posters he made for the National Child Labor Committee in 1913, a road more serpentine than Roberts’s, but no less finite in its outcome. The ailments and other misfortunes awaiting the child worker—accidents, illiteracy, moral dangers, premature old age, and early death, says the poster—might as well be Roberts’s hardscrabble environment. The rails stretch back so far and zoom forward, too, controlling all routes. Like the folded wings of a great industrial bird fanning its steel skeleton, resting in its power to traverse space, the rails clutch the boy Ganymede-like in the flat omniscience that structures all fates, laying out the quickened velocity of his whole life. Here maybe the socialist message becomes almost too formal, too clear.

But when the background blurs more ambiguously, the effect is unknowable. Hine’s picture of Eugene Bell, taken in Gastonia, North Carolina, in November 1908, shows the boy stiffly posing, his fingers nervously twiddling in batwing shapes, the right hand maybe holding a cigarette (fig. 15). Back behind him the wooden worker housing and young trees blur hauntingly. Yes, this is where he lives. Yes, he is going to work. So much is information. But Hine’s focus on Bell makes the background dissolve to an evocative mist he can hardly have minded as a mysterious effect in pictures of this kind.

It is a question of thick and thin. Bell is so vividly present that his thin waif’s body becomes thick. His lips are thick and everything else about him is substantial, even the most delicate detail—the buttons on his coat, the wrinkles in his pants, the sliver of shadow beneath his collar, the dark ovals of his cuffs. Meanwhile the background thins out, draining like smoke from a genie’s bottle. The slender leafless tree behind him is the boy in effigy. The other trees sprout in vagueness—echoes or premonitions of his person. The tree and shack to the left, closer to him, are some intermediate zone of thickness—substantial like the boy but softer, the shack’s roof lacking the depth of his chapeau.

Bell and the thin world around him are both slightly off-kilter. His face, shoulders, and torso square up to the photographer, but his feet point to the right. He twists slightly. His shoulders are uneven, sloping at the horizon. The world around him seems to shift accordingly. Together, the boy and the place conspire to shove the photograph’s symmetry around, as if the plan to center Bell—to put him halfway between the shack and the slender tree, centered ceremonially as a typical case of child labor—should have shifted by its own energy, becoming something stranger and more “off” in the actual execution. The result is that his future—all

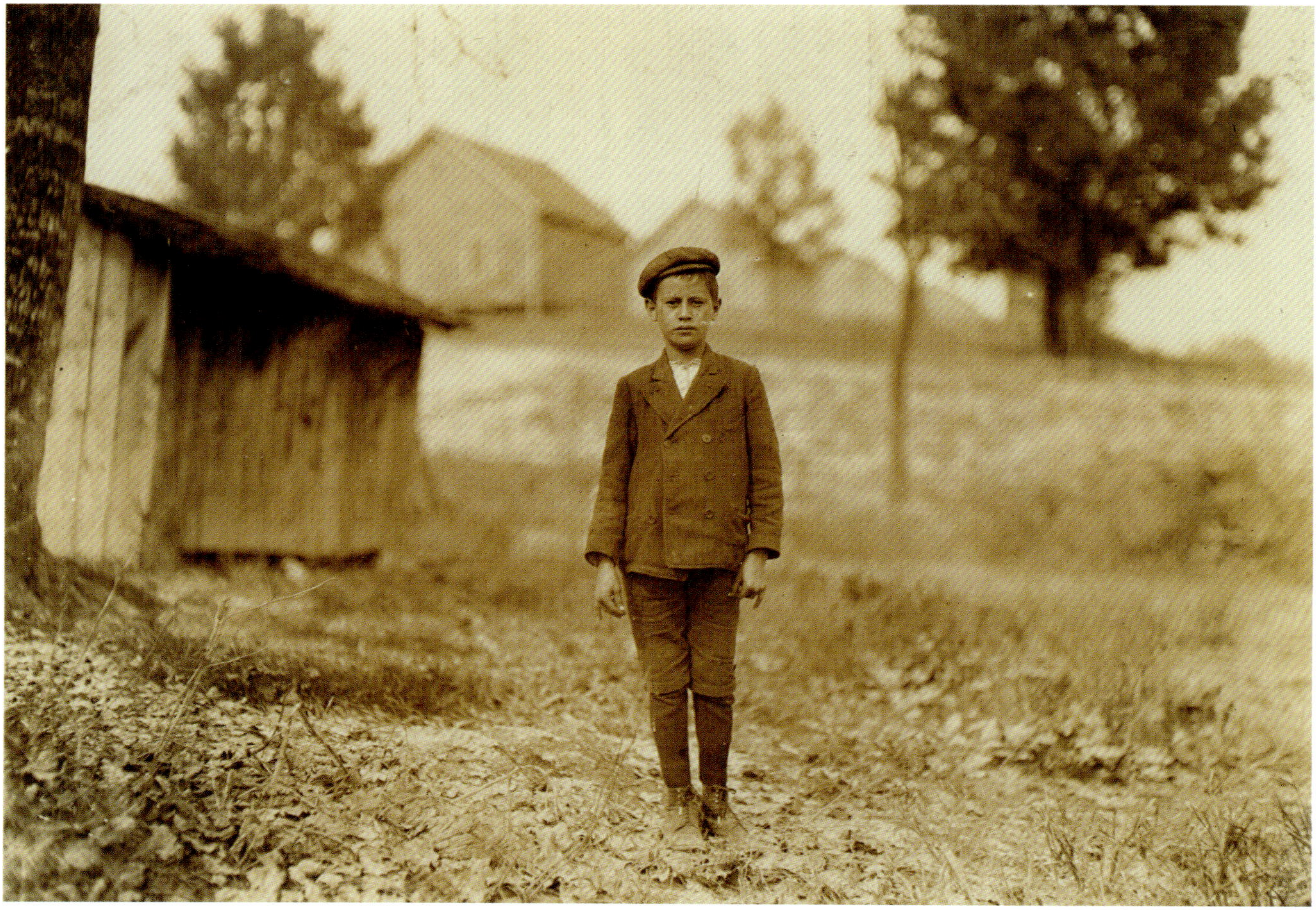

Fig. 15
Eugene Bell, House 48 Loray Mill. Said he was 12 years old. Gastonia, North Carolina. November 1908.

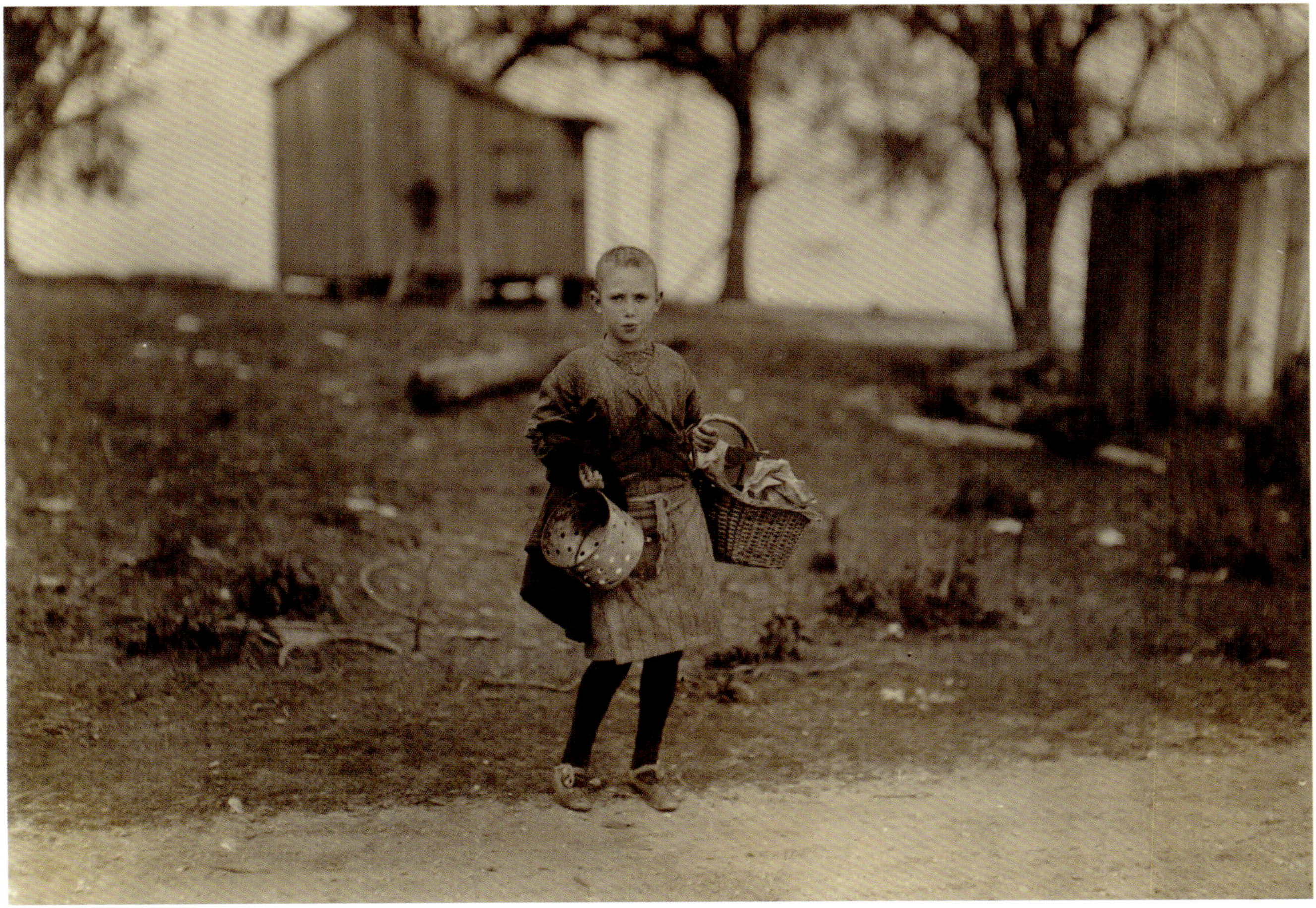

Fig. 16
Sadie Kelly, 11 years old, Picks shrimp for the Peerless Oyster Co. March 1911.

the wan world of the smoky distance—becomes a seismic intrigue spread to the place where he stands: the chattering flutter of leaves in the foreground, the belts of grainy flatness in the midground, seem to move around him in a kind of autumn lava of becoming. What will become of this boy? The photograph is an unnerving horoscope.

Hine's temporal power is alarming. His photograph of the eleven-year-old shrimp-picker Sadie Kelly, taken in March 1911, shows Kelly on her way to work in Port St. Louis, Mississippi (fig. 16). Face composed, head shaved (lice, most likely), she transits, legs bent, poised on the edge of the road, shrimp can and basket in hand, coat folded over her right forearm, on the go. That momentariness imparts a fleeting quality to the background, the raised shack of vertical boards behind her, the spectral trees. The scrub grass and sticks and small plants behind her start to blur as our eye moves up the hill. The log behind Sadie Kelly's right shoulder is hardly more than an amorphous shape, like it has been soaked in water long enough to make it pulp. The horizon line and the trees, the stained wash of the shack, make the picture look like a Photo-Secessionist masterpiece, a triumphant clouding of squalor into pretty effects, save for the little girl's face, which grounds it all as her environment.

That environment is not so much a place as a time, a voyage like her own. Temporary structures and urgent routines combine in rhythms daily and lifelong. Slow rot and speed seem so woven together in this photograph that it is anyone's guess how the one might be separated from the other. The girl has places to go, but she moves through a world that seems to have slumbered to the state of an almost comatose dereliction of duty. Instead of the bracing quick zip of socialist propaganda, wherein the roads might bend or they might be straight but the end of the line always looms, the photograph implores us with a more mysterious sense of fate. Almost weightlessly poised on the dirt, Sadie Kelly feels part of a world reduced to the speed of organic decay and generation, as if Hine's task were truly (no time-lapse photography allowed) to watch the grass grow. Like a Bruegel villager on some inscrutable allegorical round, Sadie Kelly is the mistress of a time so warped that we do not so much see her future in that pervasive haze as behold an existential nomadism—the end of time—in the apocalyptic bleakness through which she walks.

In Hine's intuitive temporal imagination, the little girl is the heroine of a future Armageddon in which no one else has survived. In Wells's *In the Days of the*

Comet (1906), a meteor approaches the earth, casting an expansive green-white pall that makes night into eerie day. Destruction seems imminent. But the Change turns out to be utopian—the blast releases chemicals that spread an opiate kindness and generous love among the populace, creating some incalculable effect of endless tolerance and benignity upon their reborn minds, so that all over the world the lion lays down with the lamb. But Hine's apocalyptic scene is no utopia. Scrounging amid the pots and baskets, feral in her hairless way, Sadie Kelly gives the effect of a marooned survivor surprised, like some exotic derelict, as she sets forth from her cave on a daily round of scavenging.

That apocalyptic future is however not any real future, sociologically imagined, but the moment of the photograph as Hine imagines it. The future in this picture is the moment it is made. Sadie Kelly walks through the landscape of her own death. The funereal orchestration beggars the sense in which any photograph, in its generic congress with mortality, might do the same thing. The elaborate drumbeat of decay is the hollow tapping of this photograph's heart. What makes this a killer picture is that it is, in Diane Arbus's phrase, "a disaster in slow motion."

Wells, in keeping with socialist faith, calls the hours after the comet has struck "The Awakening." But Hine's awakening is of another kind.

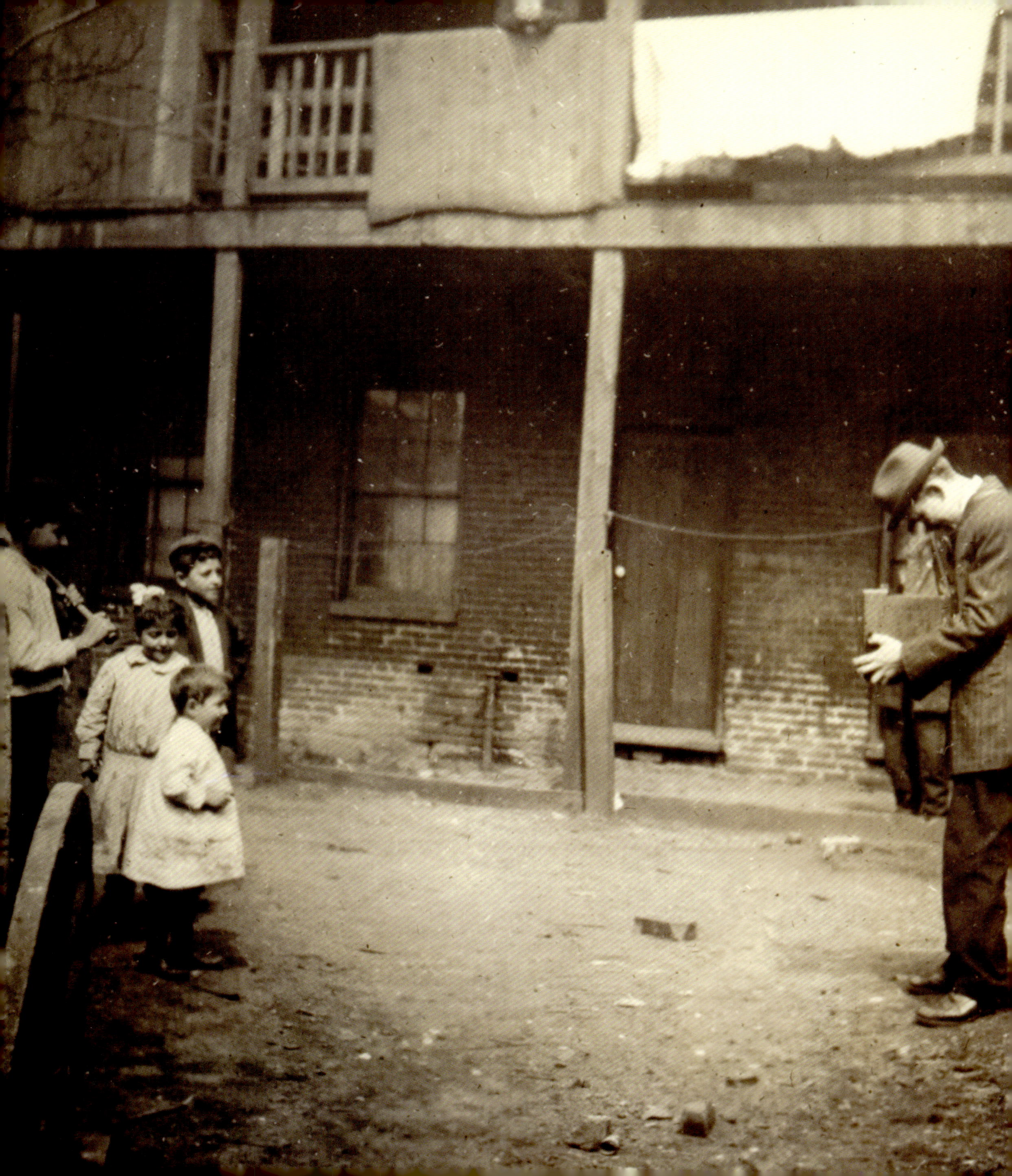

2 THE MAN FROM OSHKOSH

The man who wielded this disastrous power was small. A photograph of Hine taken about 1912 shows him looking down into his Graflex, steadying the camera to depict the white-frocked child in front of him (fig. 17). Three other children look on, the largest resting a baseball bat on his left shoulder. Hine, not much taller than his subjects, holds the camera low, getting on the level of the kids. On a slatted second-floor balcony above, a person takes in the scene, but Hine and his subjects do not notice. In their own world, the charmed zone of bright dirt between them, they attract one another, a small world.

Hine liked to be called by the diminutive "Lew," but he lived and worked in a big era, a time of outsized reformers and gargantuan powers-that-be. Photographs of Albert Beveridge, the progressive Indiana senator who had made the three-day speech decrying child labor on the Senate floor in January 1907, make him look every bit the outsized progressive politician he was (fig. 18). In Hine's home state of Wisconsin, the famous progressive Robert La Follette, himself a noted orator, perfected a fiery uncompromising style, a flamboyant plainspokenness, his lion's mane of hair the heraldic emblem of a fierce refusal to be sold and swindled (fig. 19). Jack London was dashing and charismatic and drunk, a socialist of the sun, plotting out his stories in lightning flashes glinting on muscles and gutters, the better to seduce and exhort, a celebrity of rage. And in Hine's immediate socialist circle, the personalities were equally ready to fill all available space. John Spargo, Hine wrote in 1921, made himself feel big by making others feel small.

Hine's lack of status gave him an advantage portraying children, but his effect on adults was underwhelming. He "seemed a rather unlikely person to do an assignment of any kind," noted a *Fortune* magazine employee who met him in the 1930s. Elizabeth McCausland and Berenice Abbott, who befriended Hine in the late 1930s and championed his then nearly forgotten work, were charmed and even

Fig. 17
Photographer unknown, Lewis Hine taking a photograph, ca. 1912.

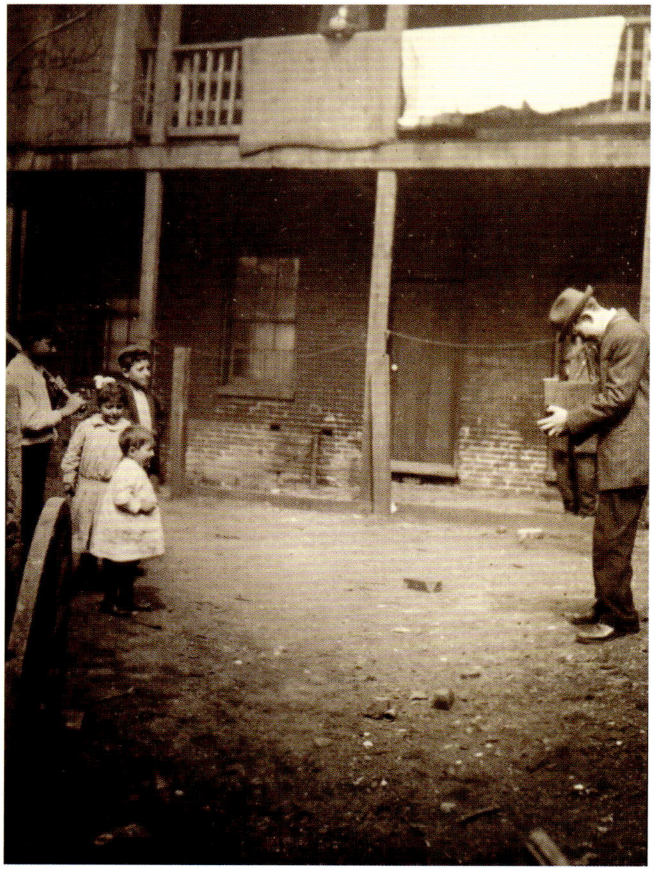

Fig. 18
Photographer unknown, Albert Jeremiah Beveridge, ca. 1914.

Fig. 19
Photographer unknown, Robert La Follette, ca. 1911.

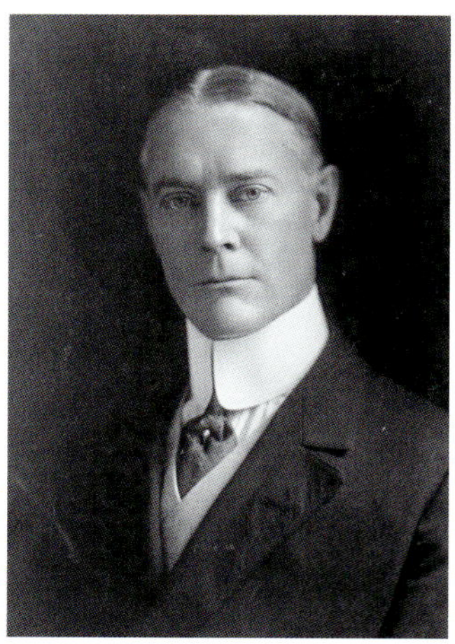

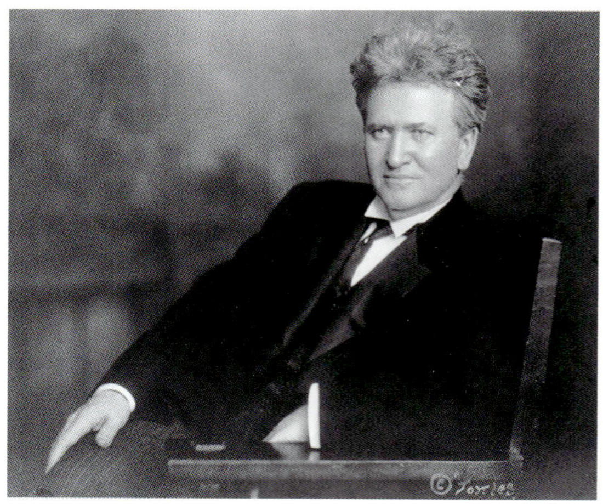

saddened by his modesty. He looked and talked like a wheat farmer, McCausland wrote in 1938. "Try to get him to pose for a photograph," she went on. "'Oh gosh,' he says, 'what shall I do with my hurrah?'"—that is, his hat. "Even today, at sixty-four, he will say with a naïveté both lovable and sad, 'How is it that you make so much better prints than I do? Is it because your enlarger is better than mine?'" She goes on: "Disarming is the trustfulness with which he accepts advice. 'Oh, Mr. Hine, I wouldn't crop that picture that way. Leave in more of the street. It tells more, the more you have in it.' 'Yes,' he will answer, 'I guess you're right. So-and-so said the same thing.'" Hine was a far cry from the La Follettes and Londons and Spargos of the world.

H. G. Wells had a name for the kind of man Hine was—Smallways. Bert Smallways is the protagonist of Wells's science-fiction novel *The War in the Air* (1907), the story of an unassuming little man who saves the world. A village bicycle repairman, Smallways has no special ambition until one day on a seaside jaunt he accidentally falls into the basket of a hot-air balloon as the aviator sweeps his craft upon the sands. The aviator falls out as Smallways falls in. In that basket are complete plans for the innovative hot-air balloon design the aviator is preparing to sell to the German army. When the man falls out and Smallways falls in, the rest is history—Smallways ends up a hero. It is only by chance that Hine became the one to say that the sky is falling.

In Oshkosh, Wisconsin, where he grew up, Hine did, however, entertain his fantasies of rescue. Somehow he would save people. A careful drawing he made in 1898, when he was twenty-four years old, a few years before he took up photography, shows a young woman seated in a leafy carriage drawn by a team of butterflies (fig. 20). Called *The Solution of the Aerial Problem* (a title Hine wrote out on the back of the sheet), the drawing resolves human flight in the years prior to Kitty Hawk, using the idiom of Victorian fairy art. A tiny charioteer holds a tether attached to the butterflies in his left hand while with his right he cracks a curlicue tendril whip. His beautiful passenger, shaded by the bell of a flower, sits in the cup of a leaf as the butterflies pull the chariot clear from a spiderweb at left. The picture is part of a portfolio of drawings Hine made that year and the most intricate among them. Executed delicately in ink, Hine's drawing is about saving a young woman from a spun trap. The web is the original Hine spinning mill. The little chariot driver, having alighted from nowhere and already on his way elsewhere, sees her clear.

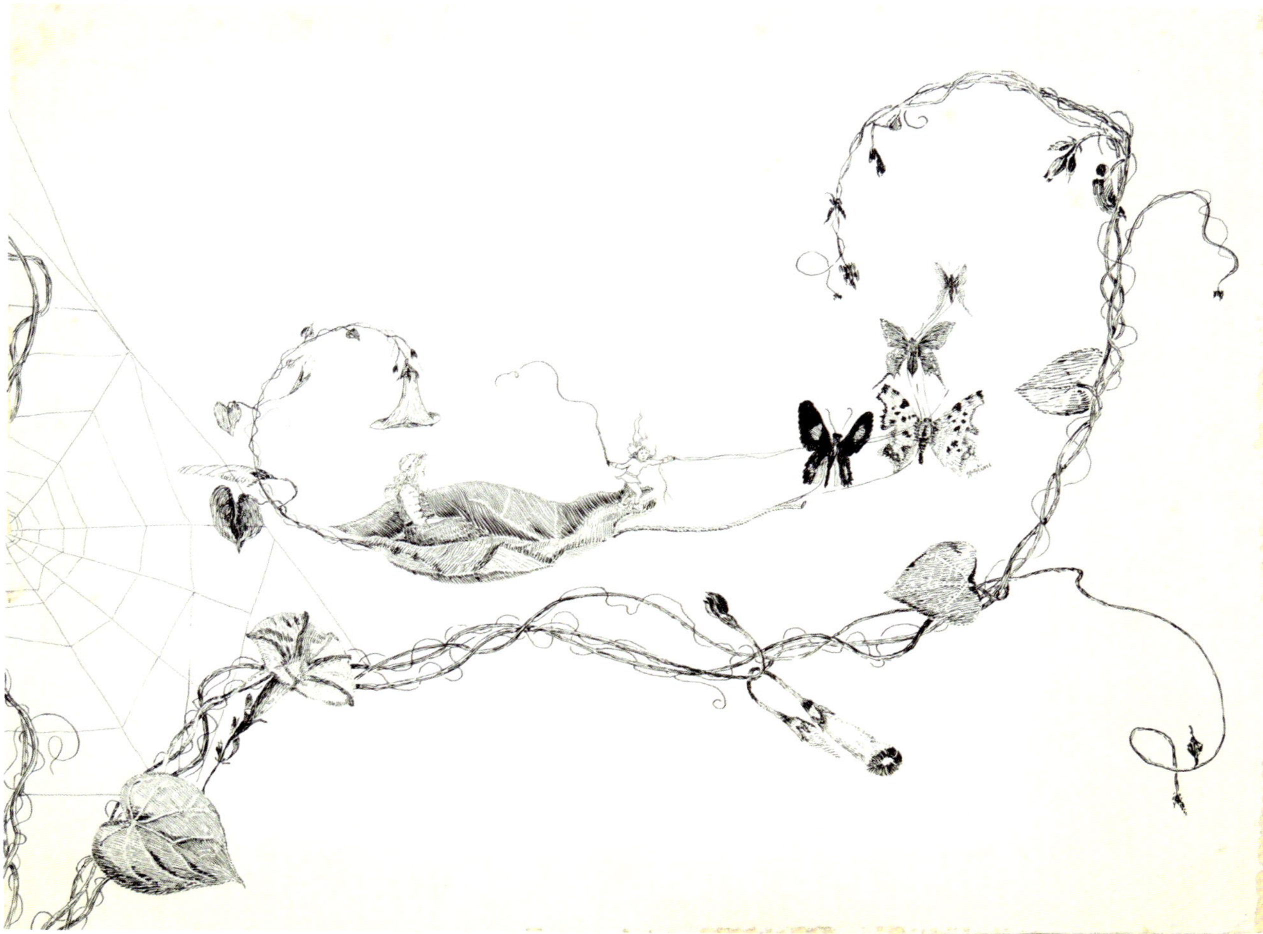

Fig. 20
The Solution of the Aerial Problem, 1898. Ink on paper, 13¼ × 10¼ in.

In those days there were more celebrated ways of escaping from traps. Harry Houdini (real name Erik Weisz) grew up near Oshkosh, in Appleton, Wisconsin, twenty miles or so away, where his father had moved the family after they had emigrated from Hungary. Hine's contemporary (they were both born in 1874), Houdini soon became an escape artist of international celebrity, the hard-muscled opposite of the man from Oshkosh. The two could not have been further apart. If Hine ever sought the miraculous escape of his imprisoned figures, liberated from their banks of spindles, his stage name could hardly have been less inspiring. The Great Hine. The Inimitable Smallways.

Yet there is a curious likeness between Houdini and Hine, a likeness manifest when they both were at the height of their powers. A photograph of Houdini taken in New York on July 7, 1912, shows him pausing as he climbs into a packing crate that will then be nailed shut and lowered into the East River (fig. 21). In February of that same year, also in New York, Hine took a photograph of a girl entering a factory door at 526 West Broadway with a box of artificial flowers she had made at home (fig. 22). The girl and Houdini are both photographed prior to disappearing—proof that they really are entering into their perilous situations. When the crate descends into the water, Houdini's fate will appear no less sealed than when the door closes upon the girl. The one fate might be a quick suffocation, the other might be a smothering that will take a lifetime. But the grim outcome will be the same. Their kinship is all the more striking because the girl willingly enters into that dark disclosure, of her own free will and mind disappearing behind the door, just as the magician does. She too is an escape artist, albeit of a more anonymous kind, just as Houdini is a laborer, submerging in the danger of his workday. The trick for both is to survive.

Hine is, however, even more the magician than the flower girl. His death-defying feat is the singular art of poising someone on the threshold of oblivion in order to draw her back from the trap she steps into. The girl steps into the doorway as if stepping off a dock, a convincing portrayal of someone likely never to be seen again once the wooden container is shut tight. The photograph, itself a container, will also be an airtight seal—no one escapes from being fixed in time like that. It looks impossible. But Hine extracts the girl from this fate. At the last second he stops the whirring saw blade. In an inscrutable process, he somehow brings her back to life, raising her from the photographic murk—not by making her retreat from her fate (quite clearly she enters it) but by some other sleight of hand that might be called, not Before, and not After—nothing so dichotomous—but the slivered shutter of shade when something has neither happened nor not happened: when the girl is between states, poised between the categories of life and death. In his best photographs Hine's subjects somehow elude the trap of being photographed. Some part of them escapes. And to make the trick properly unaccountable, the element that escapes simply *is* what Hine photographs.

How did he do it? Hine's naive faith and fantasy, never far from the fairy drawing, allowed his subjects to escape time, going free. That faith was there for

Fig. 21
Carl Dietz, Harry Houdini stepping into a crate that will be lowered into New York Harbor as part of an escape stunt on July 7, 1912.

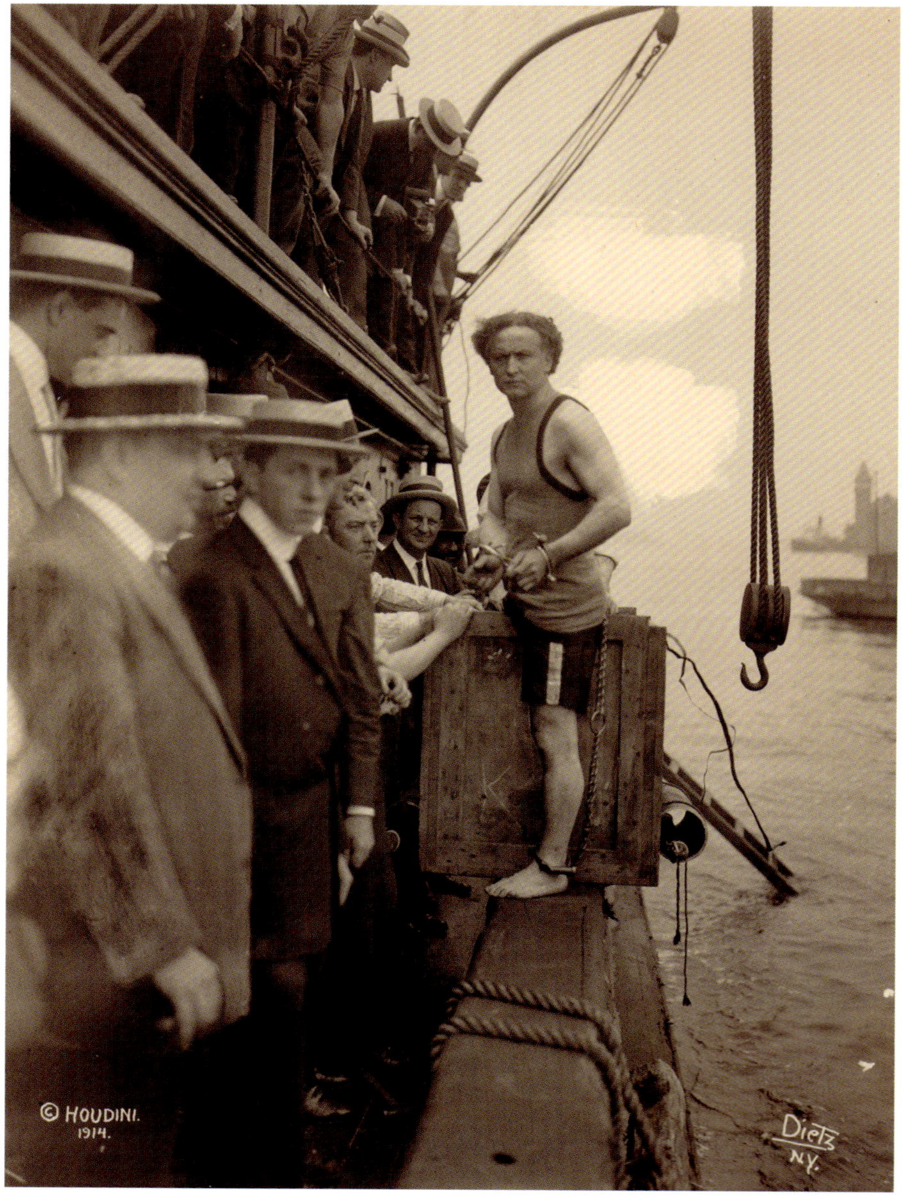

Hine even when he stood at epicenters of swiftly passing eras. In 1903 he wrote to his hometown newspaper from the Catskills, where he had gone on a travel jaunt to visit the land of Rip Van Winkle, the man who ages twenty years in a night. At Sleepy Hollow Hine noted the place thought to be Rip's house and went out back

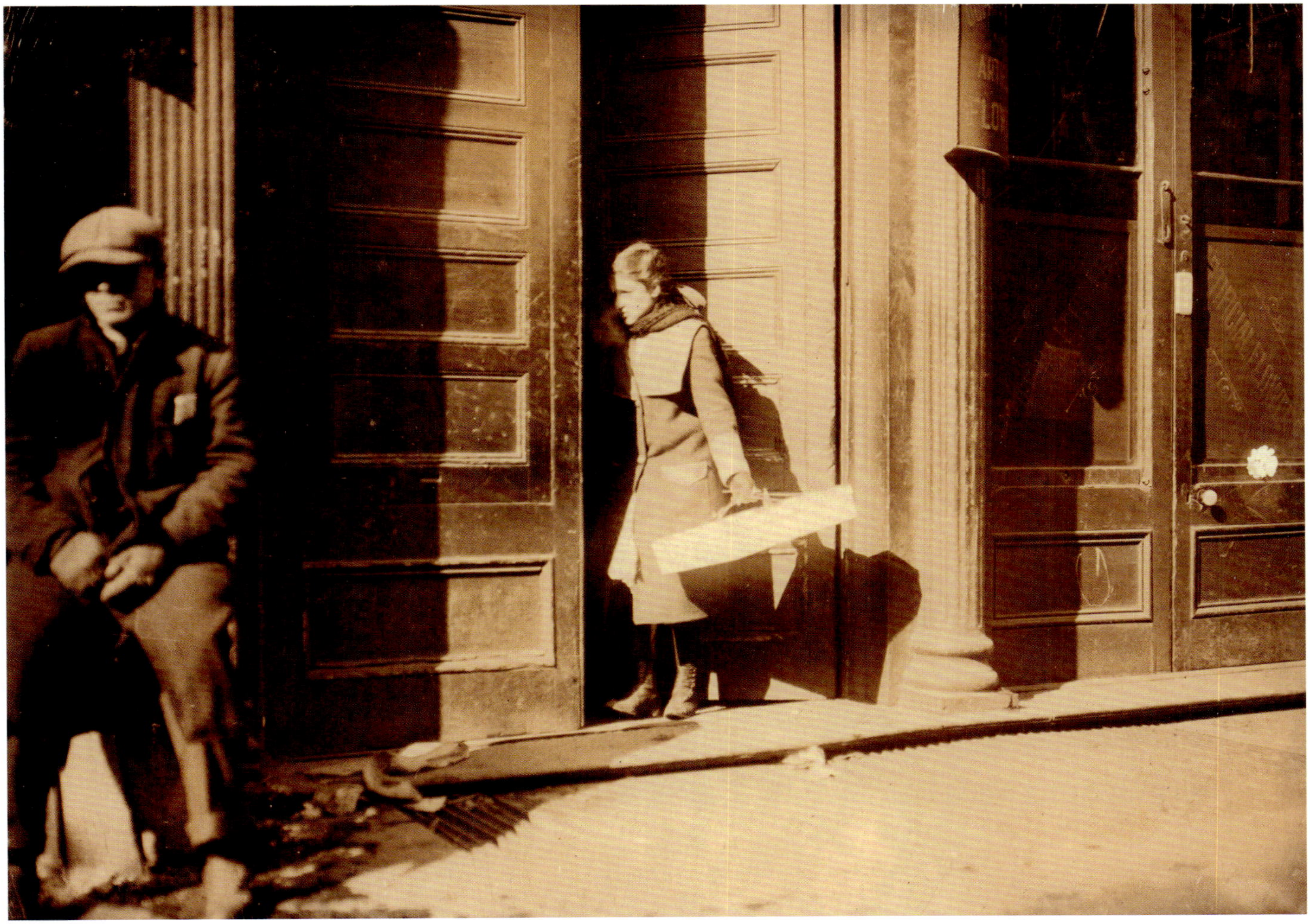

to drink "long and deep at the little spring" behind it. A few steps up the mountain, he sat on the rock where Rip sat, fancying that he could hear "among the distant mountains, the booming of the games of nine-pins" that once drew Rip's attention. If a bush crackles, Hine said he "turns, half expecting to see the old, bent form with his white hair, tangled beard, and rusty fire-lock, looking anxiously for his lost dog and his amiable helpmeet." It is all make-believe, but Hine has faith. "If asked, 'Do you really believe he ever existed,'" Hine writes about Rip, "you reply, 'Of course he did. If you doubt me, I'll show you where he lived.'" Epochs change—the hair grows white—but belief is always in the present tense.

Fig. 22
Noon. Girl entering the factory door, 526 W. Broadway, with artificial flowers made at home. New York, New York (State). February 1912.

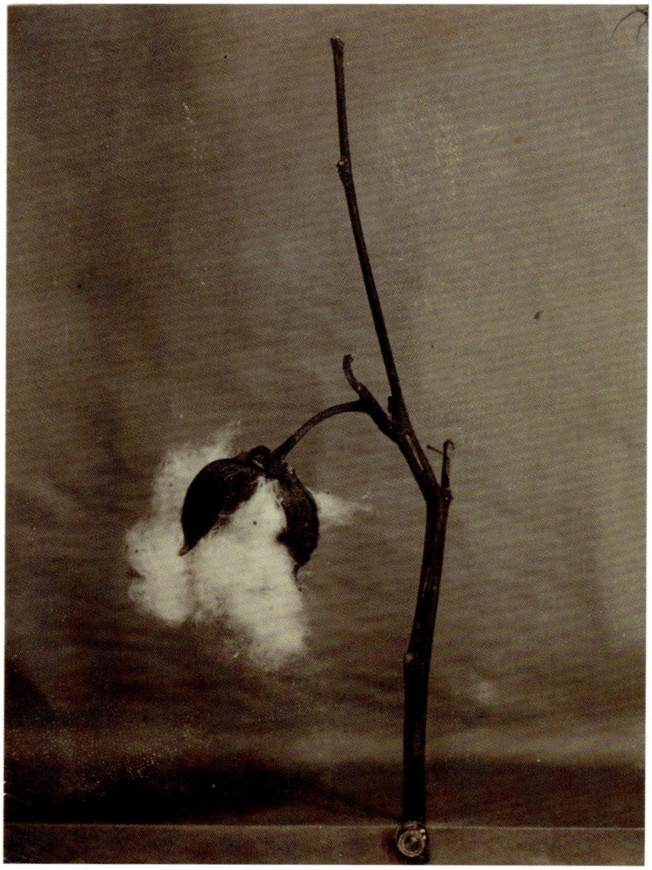

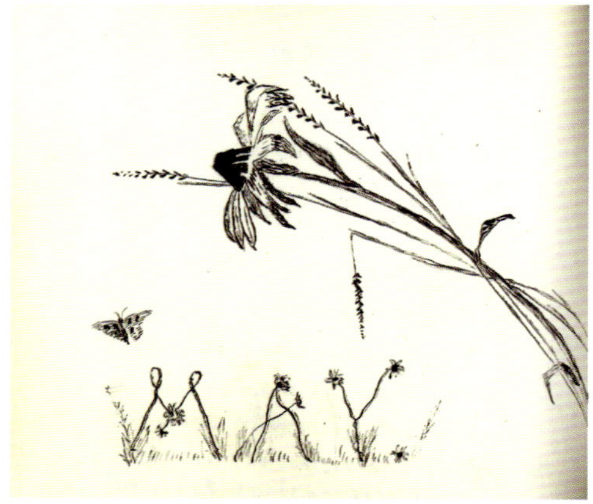

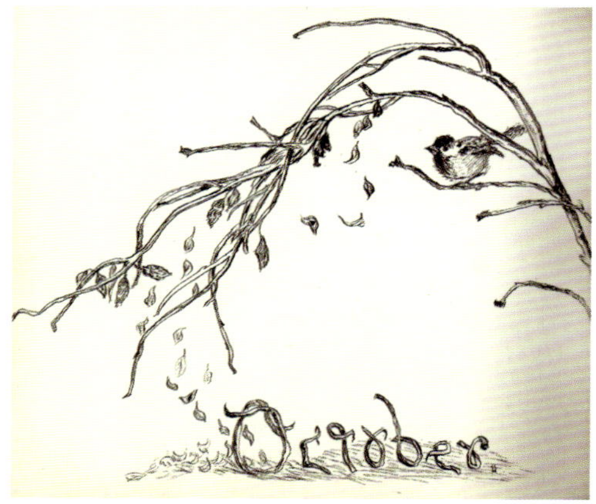

Fig. 23
Cotton as it is when growing. Ca. 1912.

Fig. 24
May. Lewis Hine Poem Book. Ink on paper, 3⅝ × 4⅝ in. 1898.

Fig. 25
October. Lewis Hine Poem Book. 1898.

It is this fantastic dreaming, not the medium of photography itself, that suspends time in Hine's photographs. There is something more delicate in the air of his pictures, a dandelion-burr atmosphere finer than clouds of lint, that bestows his children with their eternal youthfulness. What is documentable and dated—what is really there, the labor and the conditions—contains this second element, imperceptible at first, then manifest as a kind of silvery thinness. The fine detail of wooden floorboards and beveled stone windowsills—in the artificial flowers photograph, of pockmarked doorways in the winter sun—is a rendering of the camera, yes, but it also feels strangely like the linear touch of Hine's drawings. It is not just that his photograph of a cotton plant, taken around 1912, resembles the delicate drawings of the months Hine made back in Oshkosh in 1898 (figs. 23–25). It is that the air of fantasy in the drawings carries over to the photographs, where

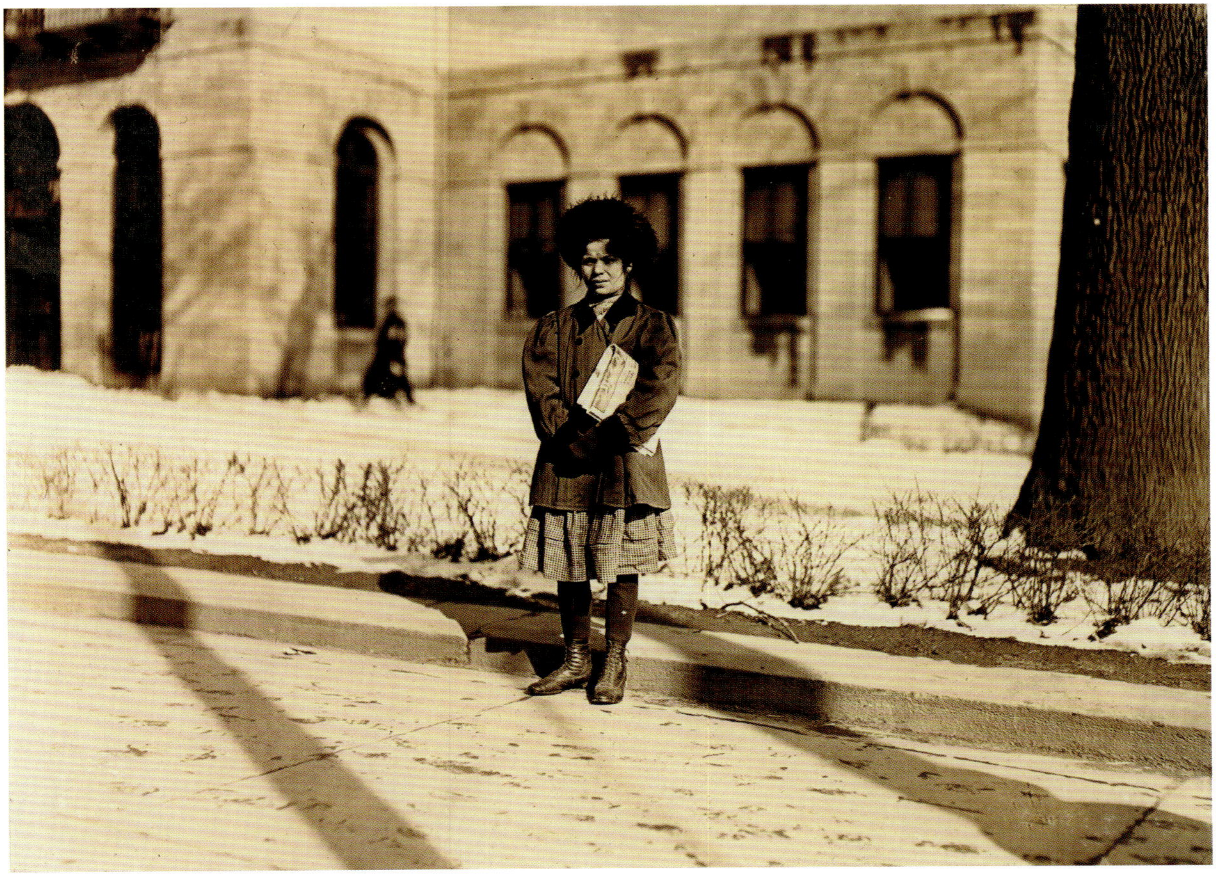

a light touch traces the stones and shrubs, the seams of overcoats, the bark and the buttons (fig. 26). Everything is dusted in an animating minuteness, the thick curbs and slabs and strong severe edges of the coarse world undergoing a subtle transformation into filigreed lines. The effect, not always present in Hine's work, is a treatment of photographic focus as if it were a form of drawing. And for Hine, whenever there was the feeling of drawing (for of course it is only a feeling), the photograph becomes folkloric, fantastical, Cinderella-like, taking on an enchanted temporality that dazes the days.

Fig. 26
Mary Dunn 11 years old. Been selling 1 year. Sells until 7 P.M., Hartford, Conn. March 1909.

One of the mysteries of Hine's photographs is that his methods were so dry while the photographs themselves often are not. Hine got a good education in the school of dryness back in Oshkosh, where he studied under Frank Manny, head of the city's Normal School. Manny's heart was in the right place—he was a progressive commonsense educational reformer—but he was an arid writer. "Our hope for a deeper enjoyment of the meaning of activities on the part of adults lies in making use of the fact that some value is attached by the adults to this phase for children in the plastic period," runs one of Manny's typical sentences, written in 1907 at the Ethical Culture School, where he had gone to be an administrator and where he had hired Hine to teach in 1901.

But Manny's good-hearted dryness was next to nothing compared to that of *his* mentor, the great pragmatist John Dewey, from whom Hine took classes at the University of Chicago after leaving Oshkosh and before coming to New York. Noting the "gracelessness" of Dewey's plodding writing style, Alfred Kazin pointed out how Dewey's prose "always seemed curiously abstract, despite his profound capacity for realism." Kazin cited the opinion of the philosopher George Santayana: "Dewey's theory of experience ... told a story rather than contained one." In this pragmatic sociological school of thought, Hine was given a righteous but fatefully mild set of materials, like a magician allotted a powder whose chief feature is that it truly is dry as dust. Oshkosh was called "Sawdust City," after the huge lumber industry there, and Hine seems to have taken that powdery waste as his working material.

So if Hine stepped out of the pragmatic classroom and made photographs that do not illustrate progressive doctrine, the mystery is how he did it. One of the Houdini tricks of his work is that he entered into places as a socialist photographer of child labor, squarely within a pragmatic tradition that taught him everything he knew and believed in, and yet ended up making photographs that go beyond chalk and blackboards.

How did he do it? Hine's work does not come from a "source," a liquid point of origin. When I think of the place his photographs emerge from, I am not reminded of paintings of lounging river gods, their beards flecked with shoreline flowers, muscles strongly reposeful, hands fingering the reeds in a surfeit of languorous power, while great earthen jugs tip from gullies deep in the earth to bubble up founts of an artist's basic material. Consider the photographs Hine made in Knoxville, Tennessee, in 1910 against the very wet writing of two authors born in that city.

One of these authors is James Agee. In "Knoxville: Summer 1915," the prelude to his autobiographical novel *A Death in the Family*, Agee recalls summer evenings when he was a child. What he chiefly remembers are the neighborhood fathers watering their lawns with hoses at dusk:

> *The nozzles were variously set but usually so there was a long sweet stream of spray, the nozzle wet in the hand, the water trickling the right forearm and the peeled-back cuff, and the water whishing out a long loose and low-curved cone, and so gentle a sound. First an insane noise of violence in the nozzle, then the still irregular sound of adjustment, then the smoothing into steadiness and a pitch as accurately tuned to the size and style of stream as any violin. So many qualities of sound out of one hose: so many choral differences out of those several hoses that were in earshot.*

Agee continues, recalling the fathers "*gentle and silent and each snail-like withdrawn into the quietude of what he singly is doing, the urination of huge children stood loosely militarily against an invisible wall, and gentle happy and peaceful, tasting the mean goodness of their living like the last of their suppers in their mouths.*" The evening sound of locusts is "*rasped and vibrated,*" but on the lawn at night, "*on the rough wet grass of the back yard,*" Agee and his mother and father and uncle and aunt spread quilts, lie on their backs, and look at the heavens. The memory is an elegy for Agee's father, killed in 1916 in a car crash when Agee was six years old, and the tone of the memory, italicized, sibilant, is as wet and silver as the stars.

In his most famous book, *Let Us Now Praise Famous Men*, an account of Alabama sharecroppers accompanied by Walker Evans's photographs, Agee's prose likewise emerges from a secret place, a source like the spring of a sharecropper family, a spring with its

> delicate yet powerful odor of wetness in constant shade, a broad windless standing-forth of a new coolness as from a refrigerator door, and a diminutive wrinkling noise of water.

Agee goes on, describing

> the spring, the dirt all round dark and strong-rooted and fragrant, tamped smooth as soap with bare feet, and a mottled piece of plank to kneel to water on. The water stands forward from between rounded strata of submerged dark stone as from between lips.... So, at the end of a slim liana of dry path running out of the heart of the house, a small wet flower suspended: the spring.

The wet ground, fertile, labile, virginal, is some slaking font back at the primitive concealment of things, center of ritual and of life, cranked out of the earth in Agee's mythology of words.

Cormac McCarthy, the second Knoxville author, draws on another kind of wetness, water only one of the pigments on his palette. McCarthy's novel *Suttree* (1979), set in Knoxville and on the Tennessee River running through it, opens with its own italicized look down at the city's grounds, only here there are no lawns but just a kind of viscid mud and ooze and even worse:

> *Here at the creek mouth the fields run on to the river, the mud deltaed and baring out of its rich alluvial harbored bones and dread waste, a wrack of cratewood and condoms and fruitrinds. Old tins and jars and ruined household artifacts that rear from the fecal mire of the flats like landmarks in the trackless vales of dementia praecox.*

No less Catholic than Agee, McCarthy writes of the rain falling on this river of waste, making "*a grail of quietude*" amid the muck, here in this opening where the author is just flexing his muscles, a pianist playing a few scales, ranging up and down the raw and stinking materials from which he will compose the novel's plague-stricken Job-like beauty: rivers of shit creeping from exploded sewer pipes beneath Knoxville, biblical deluges and disasters. Amid the sweep he places the small fonts of private sacrament: "At the far end of the warehouse was a brass spigot. Beneath it the cracked red clay lay shaped in a basin centered by a dark ocherous eye where the water dripped. Suttree knelt and laid out his things."

The photographs Hine took in Knoxville in December 1910 may be just as sacramental, but they are not wet. Consider one he made of two girls in plaid dresses looking out at him from the loading dock of the Knoxville Knitting Works, one of twenty-one he made at two Knoxville mills that month (fig. 27). Since many of the other photographs show the children more or less mugging for the camera, happily posing on and around the same loading dock, it appears that this picture of the two girls striding out alone—eyeing him as if initially—is the first. The girls look at him tentatively, as if coming out to investigate his presence, maybe encouraged by his greeting and apparent trustworthiness but still not certain who he is or what he wants. Descending the wooden gangplank they arrive at the flat loading area where, still superior, higher than the man with the camera, stuck up on their platform, they take a better look. Meanwhile, a woman in white, to the

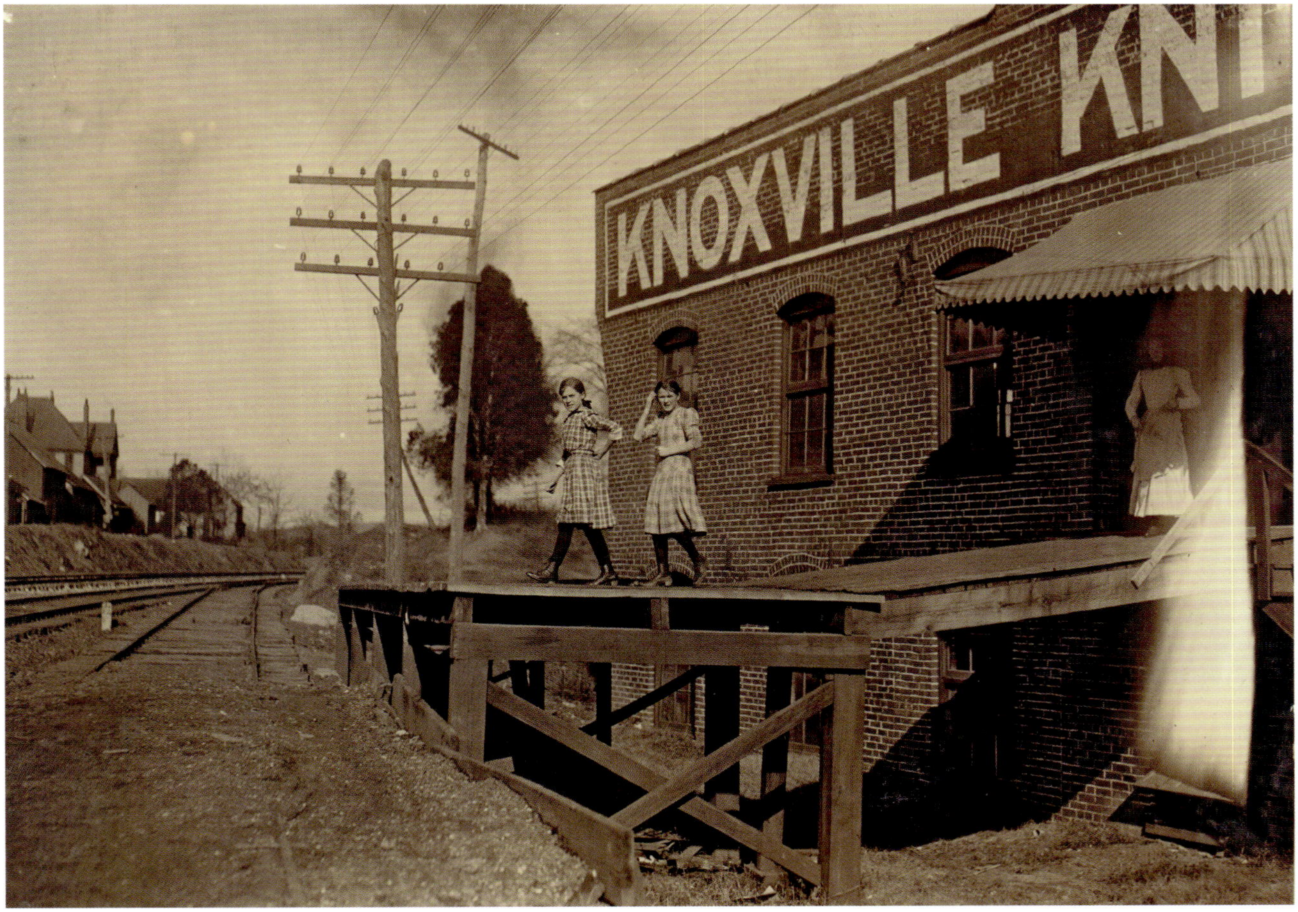

Fig. 27
Knoxville Knitting Works.
Knoxville, Tennessee.
December 1910.

right beneath the awning, faces toward Hine from near the ghostly blank spot caused by a light leak in his camera. Still in the shade, the woman has not come out into the winter sunlight like the girls, their cautious tread into the day one of Hine's social revelations.

The girls are on a break, a magical interruption of their daily round. Amid the many hours six days a week they stand at their machines—"thirty-six thousan' moves a day . . . twelve million moves a year," calculates the boy-worker in London's "The Apostate"—they venture forth to behold a stranger whose presence stops the work he would portray. Something about their position against the sky portrays the specialness—the once-in-a-lifetime feeling—of encountering the stranger-photographer. And if there is daylight in floods, the light belongs to another kind than the illumination of a labor the photograph does not show. Instead we see the girls, one with her hand at her belt as if adjusting it, the other with a hand to her hair for the same purpose of adjustment, the bells of their plaid dresses swishing and delicately drawn. Out by the trellis yardsticks of the telephone poles, they are two tilted caryatids that usually help keep the building standing but that here momentarily release their load of bricks. They and the sky are light.

The special moment is fairy-like, strewn with the magic talcum of Victorian fantasy. The girls recall the girl in her leaf chariot, which would make Hine the little stage driver with his team of butterflies, unspinning the spinners from their spinning. The Knoxville telegraph wires might be the electrical tendrils among which the girls levitate, rescued from their problem. A sighting, we might even call the apparition of them, these Peter Pans of the railroad siding. Hine could not have drawn it any better. Where then does the poignancy of the image come from? What is Hine's wellspring if his source is not the fungus beneath the timber, the stains on the ground, and all the other wet well weather that Agee and McCarthy would draw their social visions from? Is it solely a matter of Victorian fantasies of precious children awaiting their salvation? I do not think so.

In the Knoxville photograph there is the feeling that "every hour and season yields its tribute of delight." The words are Ralph Waldo Emerson's, as copied down by Hine in his poem book of 1898, when he recorded a different poetic maxim for each day of the year, perhaps as a present for his future wife, Sarah Rich. Among the 365 entries, Emerson makes the most appearances—fifteen—including Hine's entry for January 15 (fig. 28):

> Not the sun or the summer
> alone, but every hour and
> season yields its tribute of
> delight; for every hour and change
> corresponds to and authorizes a
> different state of the mind,
> from breathless noon to grimmest
> midnight.

As the girls gaze at Hine, and he at them, the world is not what it had been a moment before, or would be a moment afterward. The girls stride into a space

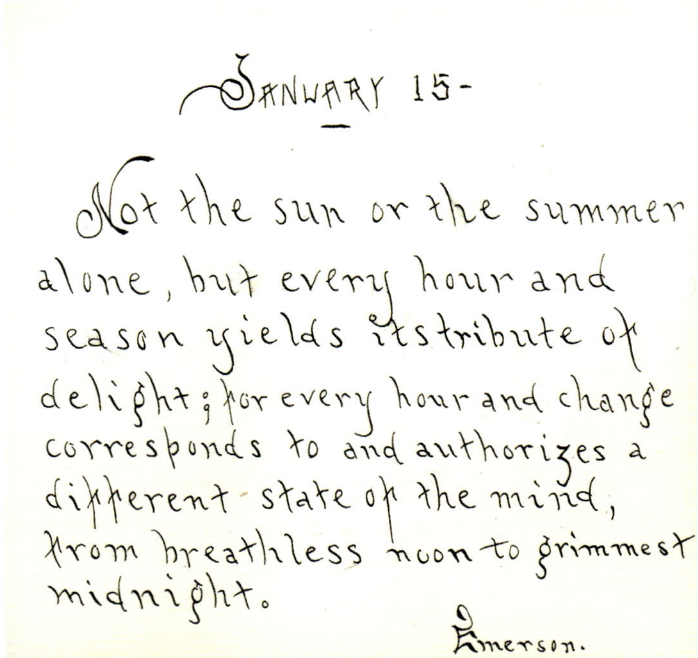
January 15-

Not the sun or the summer alone, but every hour and season yields its tribute of delight; for every hour and change corresponds to and authorizes a different state of the mind, from breathless noon to grimmest midnight.

Emerson.

Fig. 28
January 15. "Not the sun or the summer." Lewis Hine Poem Book. 1898.

that with Hine they make at that moment, as though the planks down which they walk, the handiwork of a carpenter genie, had not existed prior to then but had been created for the occasion. The princesses preside over a domain as new-made as if it had been struck into being by the camera's eye. The forlorn details of their bent world, the strident letters on the brick, the unpromising wooden tenements on the other side of the tracks, the pocket of cold shadow beneath the platform's crossed beams, not to mention what cannot be seen of their surroundings (the trolley line at Hine's back that probably transported him there; the baseball field a few hundred yards beyond the mill to the right)—all of this scrabbles into a winter lucidity as fresh as the December air. His lines as crisply drawn as the tracks and wires, strung in suspension by the sun, Hine's inspiration is the moment he takes the photograph. In Emersonian fashion, he and the girls make the time. Without this collaboration, the world would not appear.

Hine's newness is not progressive. It is different from the novelty then in Knoxville, where the New South was much on people's minds. In September and October of that year the city hosted the Appalachian Exposition, a World's Fair promoting a vision of the New South as a place of entrepreneurial and cultural promise. The cover of the Exposition prospectus shows a genteel woman gesturing to a mountain vista—promise of all that's to come—while a rustic man not nearly as visionary as his companion nonetheless takes a good look, ready to be uplifted by

Fig. 29
Appalachian Exposition Guidebook, 1910.

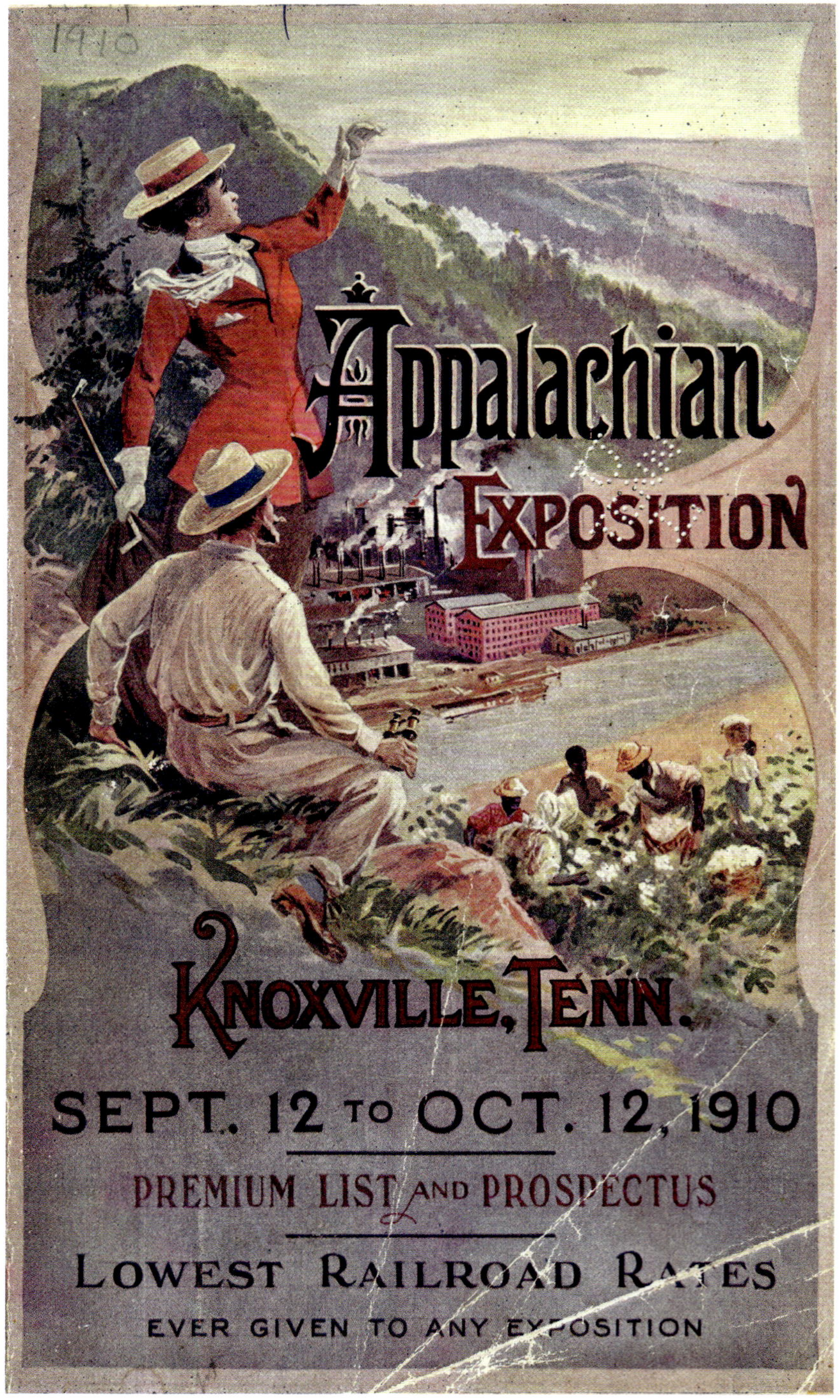

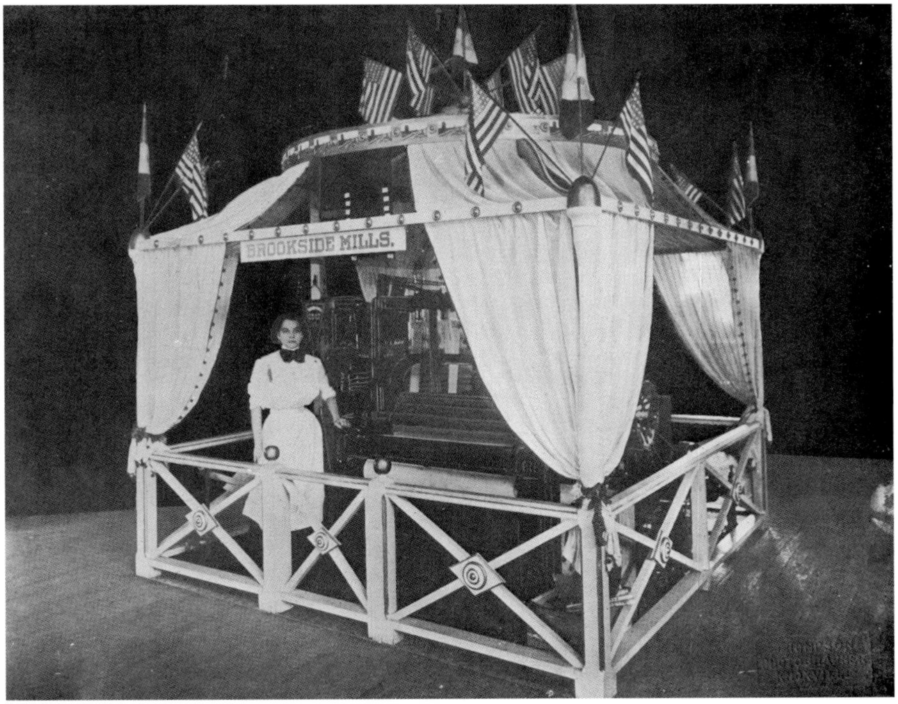

Fig. 30
Anonymous photographer, *1910 Appalachian Exposition, Textile Exhibit.*

the future (fig. 29). On the near slope black people pick crops as nearly like slaves as the artist can make them, while industry smokes and hums on the far bank. The fairgrounds were only a few miles from the Knoxville Knitting Works, and maybe the girls in Hine's photograph even saw the "textile exhibit," a hygienic simulation of their own industry (fig. 30).

Certainly they saw the Exposition's primary sign of newness—airplane, airship, and air battle. On every day of the Appalachian Exposition—from September 12 to October 12—an aeronaut named George F. Strobel flew his dirigible in the afternoons and evenings, "migrating through narrow by-ways, around mountain heights, over valleys and hills" (fig. 31). Strobel's balloon would have been seen all over the city, in and outside the fairground. From September 22 to 29 the biplane of Wilbur and Orville Wright flew over the city, too (fig. 32)—the first appearance of an airplane above eastern Tennessee. Then there was "the ordinary parachute leap, which itself is the most dangerous feat in aerial flights"—a daily spectacle at the Exposition—as well as "the most daring feat of aerial wire walking ever seen" (fig. 33). But the most spectacular event in the sky—besides the

Fig. 31
C. A. Wayland, *Strobel's Mammoth Air Ship*, 1910.

Fig. 32
C. A. Wayland, *Wright Bros. Airplane*, 1910.

Fig. 33
C. A. Wayland, *Watson's Bicycle Act*, 1910.

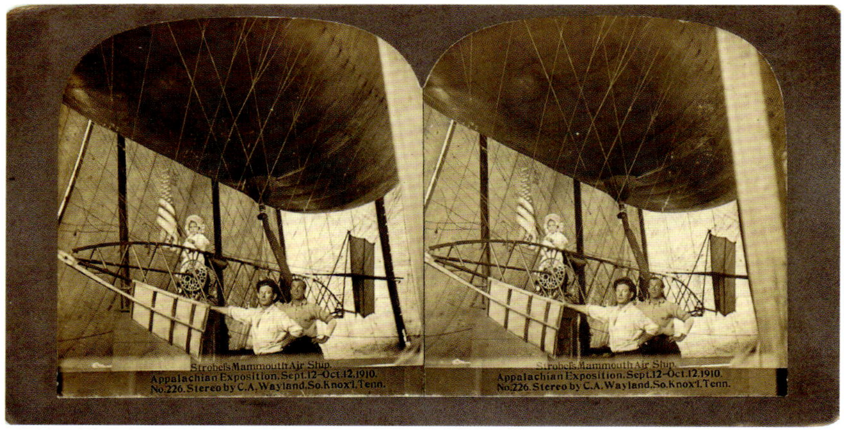

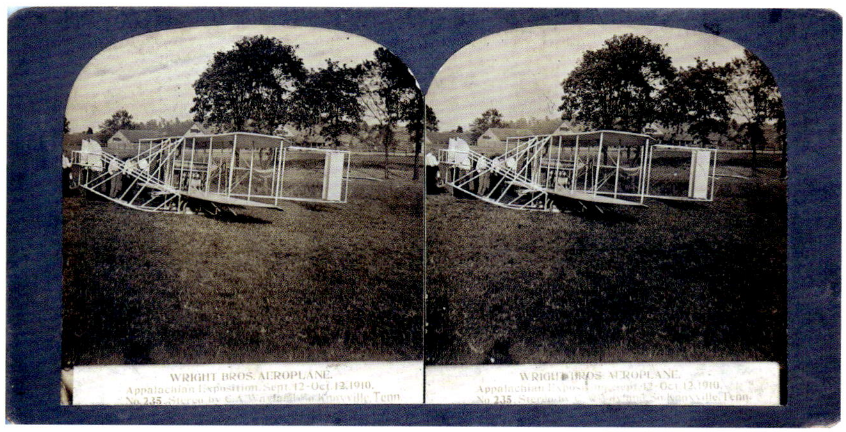

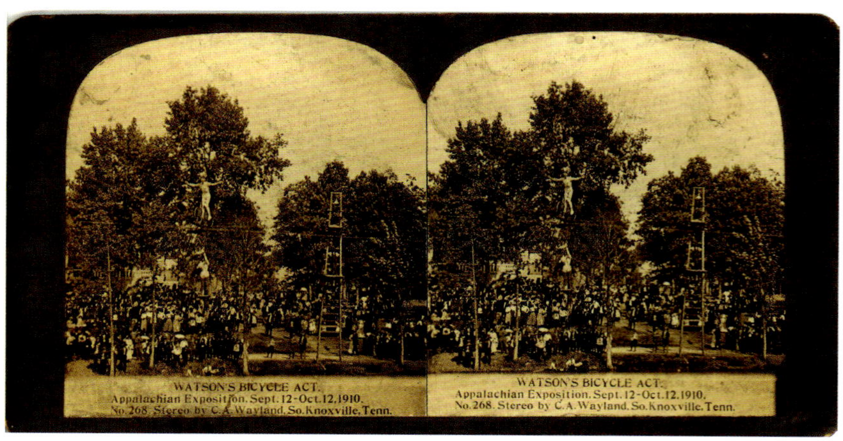

Fig. 34
Anonymous, *Strobel's mammoth air ship over Knoxville*, 1910.

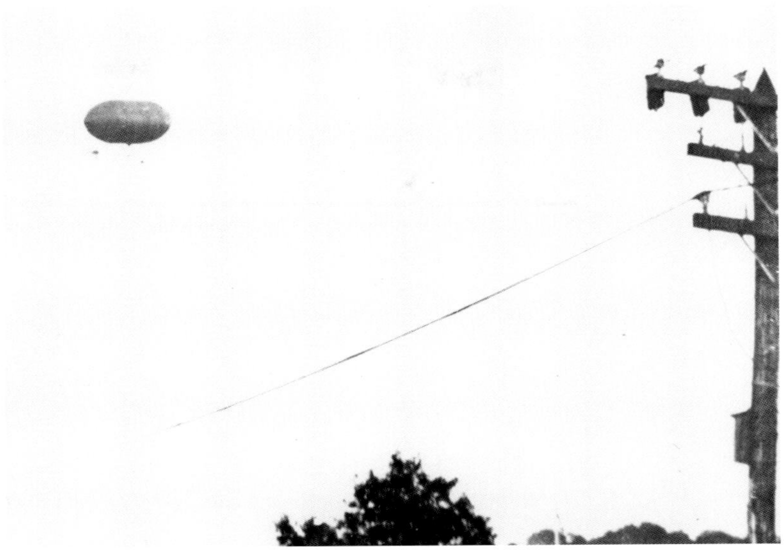

fireworks that took place every evening of the fair—was the H. G. Wells–like "Battle of the Clouds," a staged combat between Earth and Mars, each side represented by dirigibles "equipped with deadly fighting apparatus," shot at from the ground by automobiles with "fire-belching guns of great power." The spectacle took place for an hour or more every night from September 19 to 24. This "allegory of the future," as one Exposition official called it, was as free and available as the skies above the mill.

But that December the two girls at the Knoxville Knitting Works portray a sky vision of another kind. They walk along the tightrope of the instant the photograph was taken, a balancing act between Hine and his subject. Delicately on the slapping wooden boards the girls traipse as if walking on the wires above them, filaments of some almost weightless communication between distant and unseen points. "The most daring feat of aerial wire walking ever seen" would be the gait of these two girls traveling who knows where, transported by the photograph. The empty sky around them, if magnified *Blow Up*-style, might even contain the trace of Strobel's dirigible as an anonymous photographer portrayed it that year above another of the city's telephone poles (fig. 34)—as if this anonymous photographer's picture were actually a detail of Hine's own. But Hine's miracle is of another kind, without blimp auguries and other inflated predictions. The mill enshrining the vision is the place of some holy rite amid the creosote and dirt, an alternative and more mystical Exposition, the making of a single moment, the levitation of ordinary persons.

The miracle knows its own fragility. The failure of the light seal allows a vapor of blankness to wave across the picture (a not uncommon error in Hine's photographs). It suggests a spirit of eradication, ghostly in its shroud, that floats near or at the scene of any realization of the world. As if a banshee of nonrepresentation, jealously presiding, should never be far from where its nullity has until then ruled the day. The weird way that the spirit echoes the white shape and place of the possibly reproving older woman beneath the awning—the one who would chaperone the girls' independent excursion—suggests a resentful flare-up, nigh on to ugliness, that cannot quite consent to the winter light of the sky.

Hine's praise of the delicate moment, the fragile newness of perception, went back to his hometown. Emerson spoke in Oshkosh in 1867, seven years before Hine was born, and the famous philosopher's visit endured there long afterward. "The most precious beauty, that of the moment, the indicator of sudden nobility—she put in our own keeping," Emerson told his audience in his Oshkosh lecture, a version of a speech called "A Man of the World" that he gave many times between 1866 and 1868. A person who attended the lecture wrote a story in the Oshkosh *Daily Northwestern* in 1903, on the occasion of the centenary of Emerson's birth, recalling that when he was young he had walked nine miles into town on a cold winter night to hear Emerson's talk, that he gave it plenty of thought on the nine-mile walk back that night, and that it stayed with him many years later. Emerson spoke to his Oshkosh audience about the rarefied beauty that a specially attuned person can perceive. The full sentiment went like this: "Nature distributed vulgar beauty unequally, as if not valuing it; but the most precious beauty, that of the moment, the indicator of sudden nobility, the expression—she put in our own keeping."

One such moment was the winter night Emerson gave his lecture in Oshkosh, when following the talk he took a sleigh ride to the small town of Ripon, some twenty miles away, where he was to give another speech the following night. Five days later, from a small town in Iowa, Emerson recounted the sleigh ride in his diary, thankful for the grace and power of the horses that got him through. "In riding in an open sleigh, from Oshkosh to Ripon, in a fiercely cold snowstorm driving in my face, I blessed the speed and power of the horses."

The snow blows on Emerson's face, and the speed and power of the horses is sacred. Experience is direct, bracing—an exhilarating transport. Inestimably strong and enduring, speeding and powerful, the horses are what Emerson blesses and others ignore. The horses in these towns, he laments,

> seem left out of doors in the snow and wind all day. Around this square before the house, I counted just now twenty horses tied. Some of them seem to stand tied all day. Last night, just before going to bed, I looked out;—there stood two or three at that hour,—the farmers perhaps listening to the railroad men in the court-house, or sitting round the bar-room fire.

What no one else sees, the horses around the square in the middle of the night, are the bedtime prayers of a man who sees what everyone else is too busy or bored to notice. The personal vision partakes of a special kinship with these animals, a rebuke of how indifferently their owners regard them. As the magnificent horses race through the landscape without fanfare, so the moments pass without anyone's special notice. That is because the only time these practical citizens know is that of Progress. "As soon as these people have got a shanty built to cover them, and have raised one crop of wheat, they want a railroad, as the breath of life; and, after one railroad, then a competing railroad." But what gets the poet through is what saves any poet, the lasting effect of a blessed beauty of transport, animal sleek and strong in the waste: "Their endurance makes them inestimable in this rough country."

It gets the photographer through, too, on his own lengthy trips to rough places. In Hine's Knoxville photograph what the two girls are unaware of (even as they live it) is the moment in which they are alive. And for Hine that moment is bound to the power of another pace, not that of speed, not that of locomotion, and not that of leisurely clip-clop village lore either, but of some urgent race of unappreciated and enduring beauty. This is what lights up the children's faces, causing them to be seen.

But disaster portends in these places. Hine knew this better than Emerson. It was not just that Hine came later, that he was chastened by the brutality of a vast industrial America Emerson never saw. If the novelist William Dean Howells "united the world of Emerson and the world of Zola," writing books including one of the mills called *Annie Kilburn* (1888) with a blend of realist sharpness and Emersonian reverie, social dislocation mingling with "a perception of the unity of all things under the sun," that combination does not fully account for the look of Hine's photographs. Something more personal stirs in them.

Fig. 35
Unknown photographer, *Court House after the Fire, Oshkosh, Wisconsin*, 1875.

Fig. 36
Cigar Box Lid, ca. 1880.

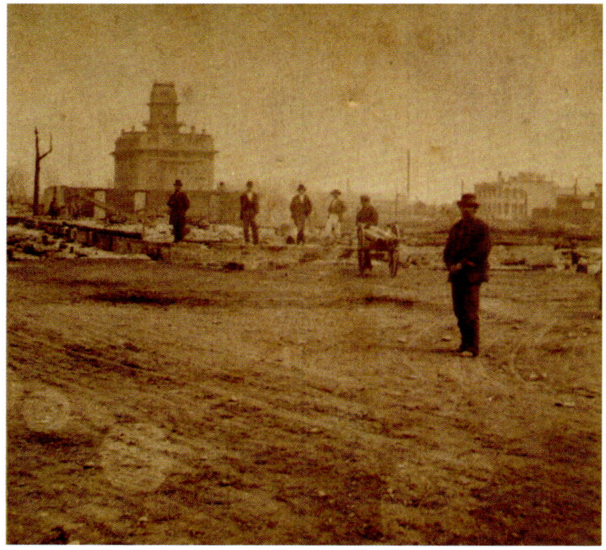

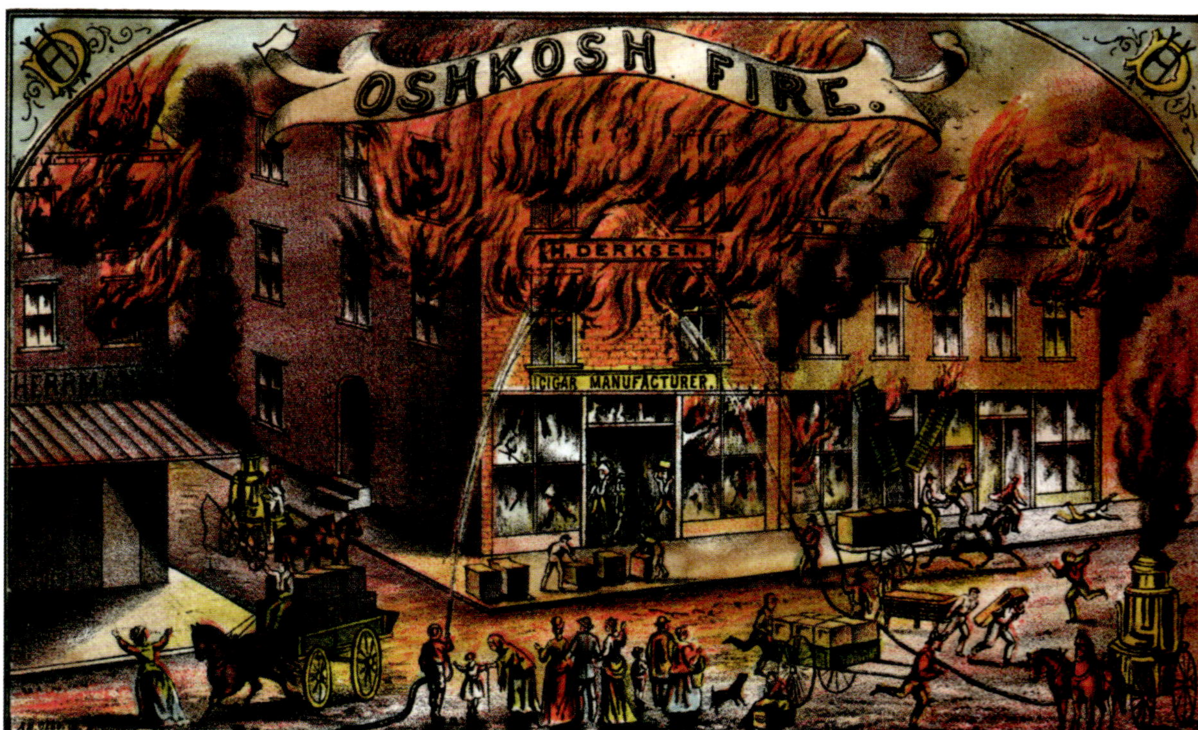

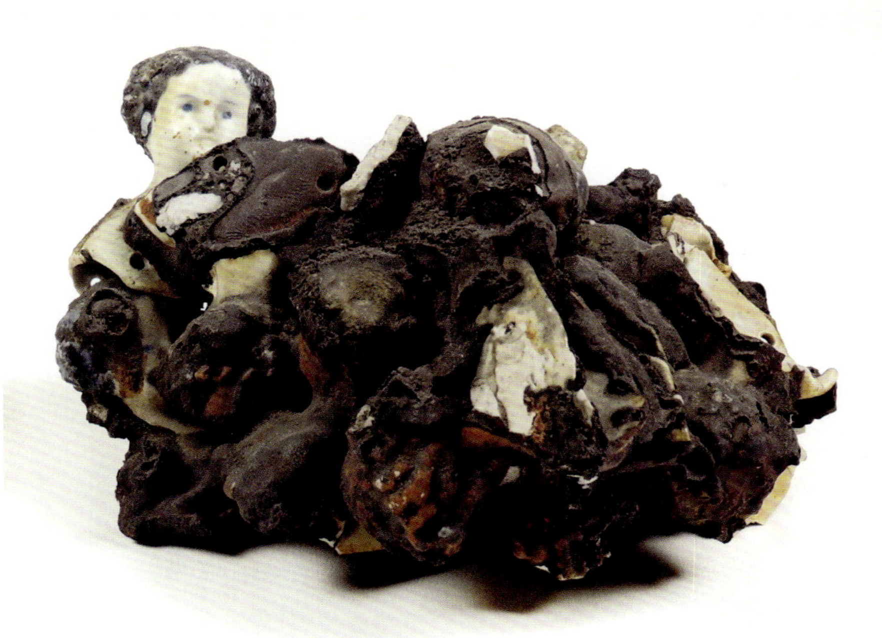

Fig. 37
Dolls' Heads, ca. 1875.

Oshkosh burned down in 1874, seven years after Emerson's visit and two months before Hine was born. It burned down again the following year before Hine's first birthday (fig. 35). The kindling enormity of Wisconsin's lumber industry made the state so vulnerable. Not far from Oshkosh, the great Peshtigo Fire took place on October 8, 1871, the same night that Chicago went up in flames several hundred miles to the south. An artist well versed in the conventions of disaster designed a cigar box lid depicting one of the Oshkosh fires (fig. 36). The flames emerge like harlot hair from the upper windows of brick city blocks, a destructive passion, while below on the street, their shadows cast by the flames, the town's proper citizens stand in orderly array to watch the firemen douse the blaze. The commemorative legend—*Oshkosh Fire.*—bannered inflammably above the flames—floats as the legend surviving the conflagration.

A fused mass of china doll heads is another memento of the Oshkosh fires, this time of the 1875 blaze (fig. 37). Melted together like a congregation of angels tumbled into an incinerator, some of the doll heads retain their pinkness while others have been baked black and brown. Likely the warehoused contents of a stockroom yet to make their way to the homes of individual children, the dolls die as a delegation, uncovered in their mass grave, drowned in a shipwreck of fire, a coral reef of scorched mermaids.

Anyone living in Sawdust City would have been deeply aware of sparks, struck matches, and other potential ignitions of acres and acres of planed boards and new-made furniture. The man lighting his cigar from his box of exciting flames might well have paused amid the pleasures of smoke inhalation to chuckle grimly at the oddity of playing with fire in so tindery a place, careful that his private excitement not become too much a public one. The constant threat of fire would also take a more chronic form, call it living with disaster, a perpetual intimation or recollection of fear. It stayed with people who grew up there, remaining with them their whole lives. Hamlin Garland, a writer born in Wisconsin in 1860 who grew up in the state, recalled many years later how when he was a boy the fires all over Wisconsin in the dry fall of 1871 gave him "a growing uneasiness which became terror when the news came to us that Chicago was on fire. It seemed to me then that the earth was about to go up in a flaming cloud just as my granddad had so often prophesied." Garland's terror increased when his uncle David's stable burned down with all his horses and the man trapped inside, the uncle escaping only by burrowing into the earth and emerging on the other side of the blazing barn wall. "This incident combined with others so filled my childish mind that I lived in apprehension of similar disaster."

Garland recalled these scenes in his memoir of 1917, and Hine, too, might never have forgotten the perilous conditions of his home. A sense of disaster lurks somehow in photographs such as the ones Hine took in Knoxville, including a picture of mill boys innocent in their moment, each looking self-possessed and personable before the camera (fig. 38). The disaster is not literally a fire or other industrial calamity that might await them. And it is only nominally the fate of becoming "human junk," as Hine's National Child Labor Committee posters proclaimed. It is instead some other catastrophe, a horror of long-fusing time that gathers over any photograph, yes, but something also that is burning in Hine's conception of what he sees.

In 1892 Hine's father accidentally shot himself while cleaning an old revolver at a downtown Oshkosh business. The bullet entered his chest and penetrated his lungs. According to a man who was there, Douglas Hine was talking pleasantly at around nine thirty in the morning, working at a bench, when all of a sudden there was a noise. "Have I shot myself?" Hine asked. "Mr. Hine seemed to be so

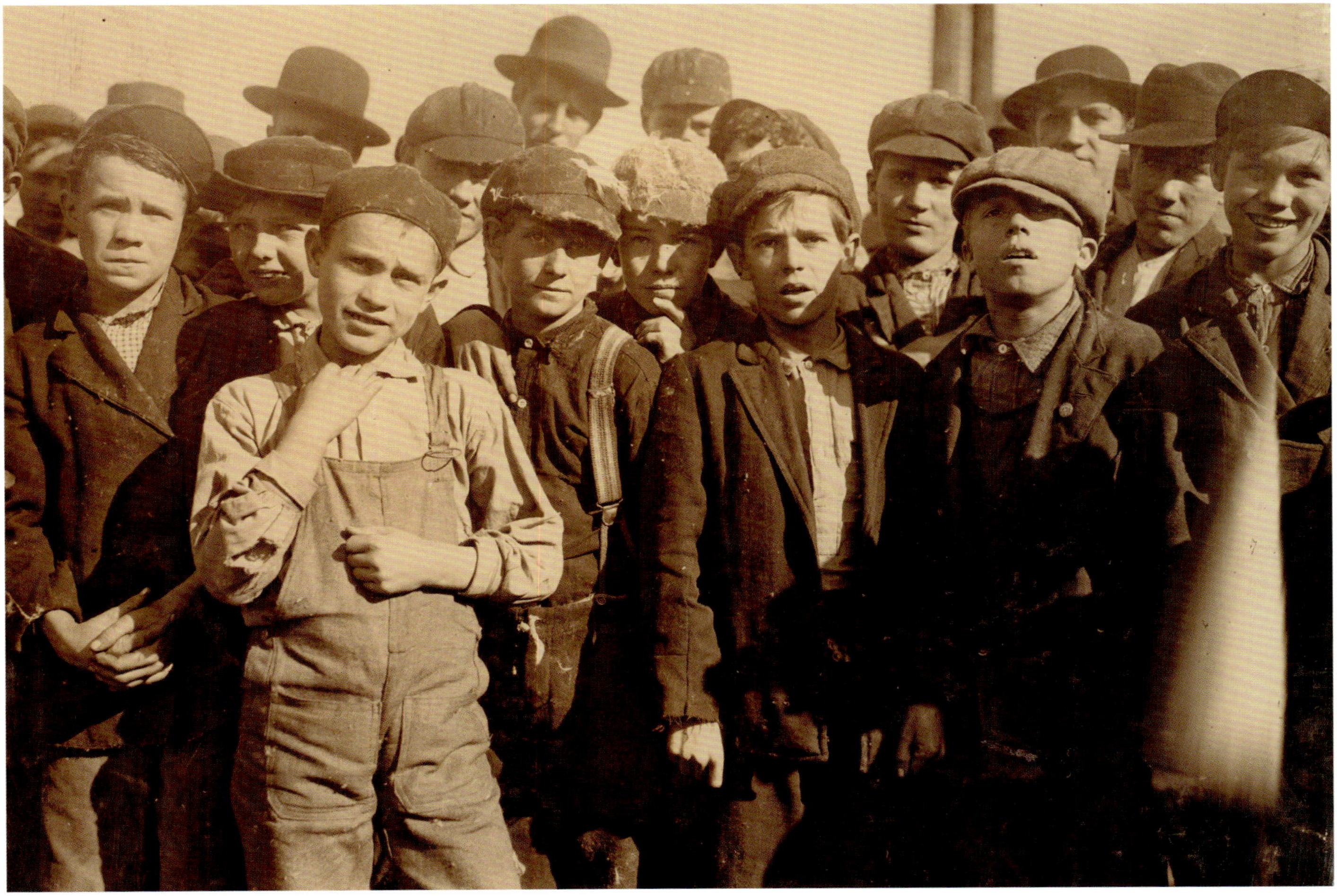

Fig. 38
Doffer boys in Knoxville Cotton Mills. Knoxville, Tennessee. December 1910.

astonished at the explosion that he did not realize he was shot," a reporter wrote the same day. At first it appeared he did not suffer and it was hoped the wound was not serious, but having been taken home Hine died at noon, surrounded by his wife, two daughters, and his son, eighteen-year-old Lewis.

Are the children in Hine's photographs all orphans? Are they all bereft? All liberated? The girl floating on her ivy-leaf carriage drawn by its team of butterflies is the soul taking flight, the ghost given up. The specter of Douglas Hine, coffee-shop owner, born in New York State in 1829, resident with his wife in Guatemala for five years in the 1850s, proprietor of a restaurant on Oshkosh's Main Street, is a flitting genius one could almost too easily make glide across the scenes of his son's

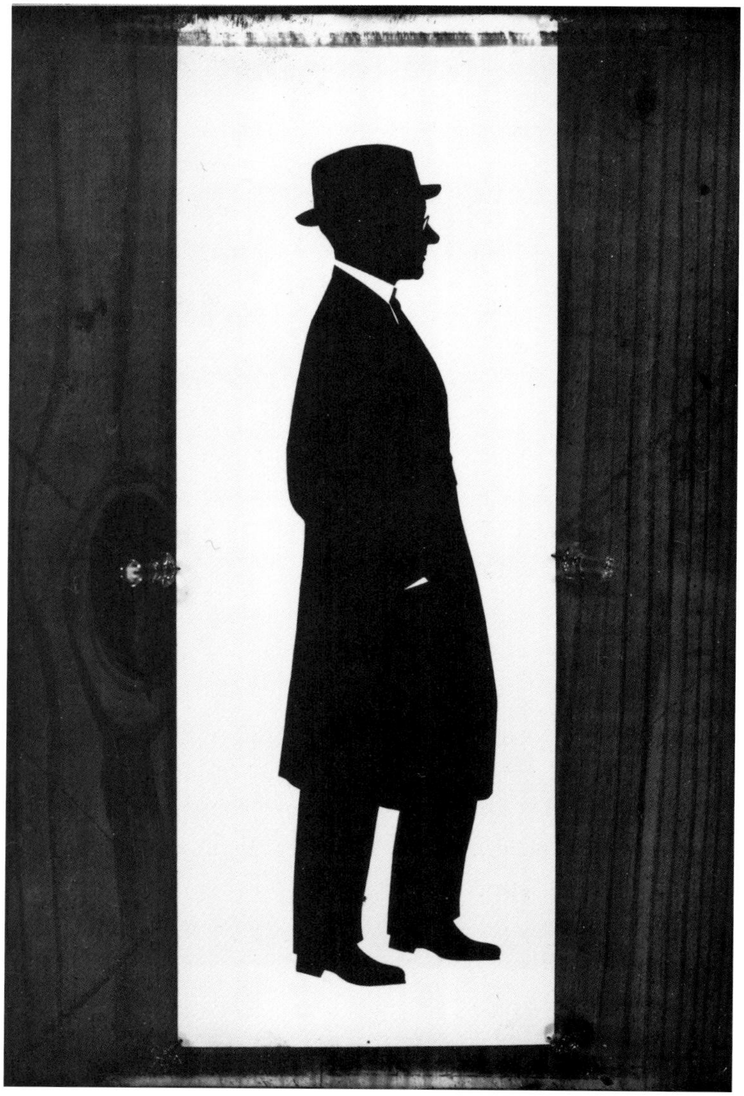

Fig. 39
L.W.H. Silhouette, ca. 1920.

pictures. Every Knoxville boy is without a father, just like Agee in that same city six years later would be without a father. The hoses drain on the lawns, or they do not. The joy of the moment is bound up with loss.

Hine gathered the children he photographed into a private feeling, ecstatic and dangerous. At his camera he was a pied piper. Children like the Knoxville boys came to him, maybe sometimes flocked to him, eager and curious and often trusting. A silhouette made of Hine around 1920 suggests this pied piper quality, the expressionless calm of the decent and unknowable man (fig. 39). The boys crowd close to him. He leads these trusting children into the beauty of the moment, a realization of life. But more sinisterly he led them into time itself. And that time was multiply eerie. It was the melancholic time of photography. It was also the backwash of the photographer's own spectral Peter Pan-ism, a potion of forever-youthfulness that must have been like the elixir a witch wants you to drink. And it was something the children possessed—so needful to the photographer that without it his dram of time would not cast its spell. What he needed was their youthfulness that makes the boys not of this world. Scrabbled and would-be wise-guy tough in their dungarees and overalls, their workingman's caps cocked and slouched, they nonetheless appear like a whole gallery of Victorian angels squeezed into a lint-flecked choir, pretty perfections not of this world. It is that element they do not even know they possess that Hine needs, that he must make sure to hook his thread upon. The boys having given him just this drop, the man at the camera may now vampirically take his liters. The sweet faces appear and appear and appear as if multiplying by some rabbit-fecundity implicit in the lens. The pied piper has no limits to his followers, and if he could stand back to include more space, then more children would appear.

Not that he is a bad man. Not that he is an unkind man. He is good and his intentions are good. But he wields a power that grows vast at the boys' consent. Not knowing what they possess, they do not know what they have given. Inducted into one of Hine's moments, the boys beam in splendid contentment at their good fortune. Lo and behold, out of nowhere, as in a magic act, a man has appeared and now they are not only shown but also invested with the souls they did not know they had. The fact that many of them, if not all of them, will never behold the soulmaker again contributes to the wonder of the occasion. Who was he?

But a cloud passes across the soulfulness: a sense, Hine's sense, that there are more times here than just the one then. Backstories and sepia futurities flutter across the scene, the mystery of who and how a person comes to be, the nameless voids on either side of life. The children whose faces shine with pleasure have agreed to something that is eternal.

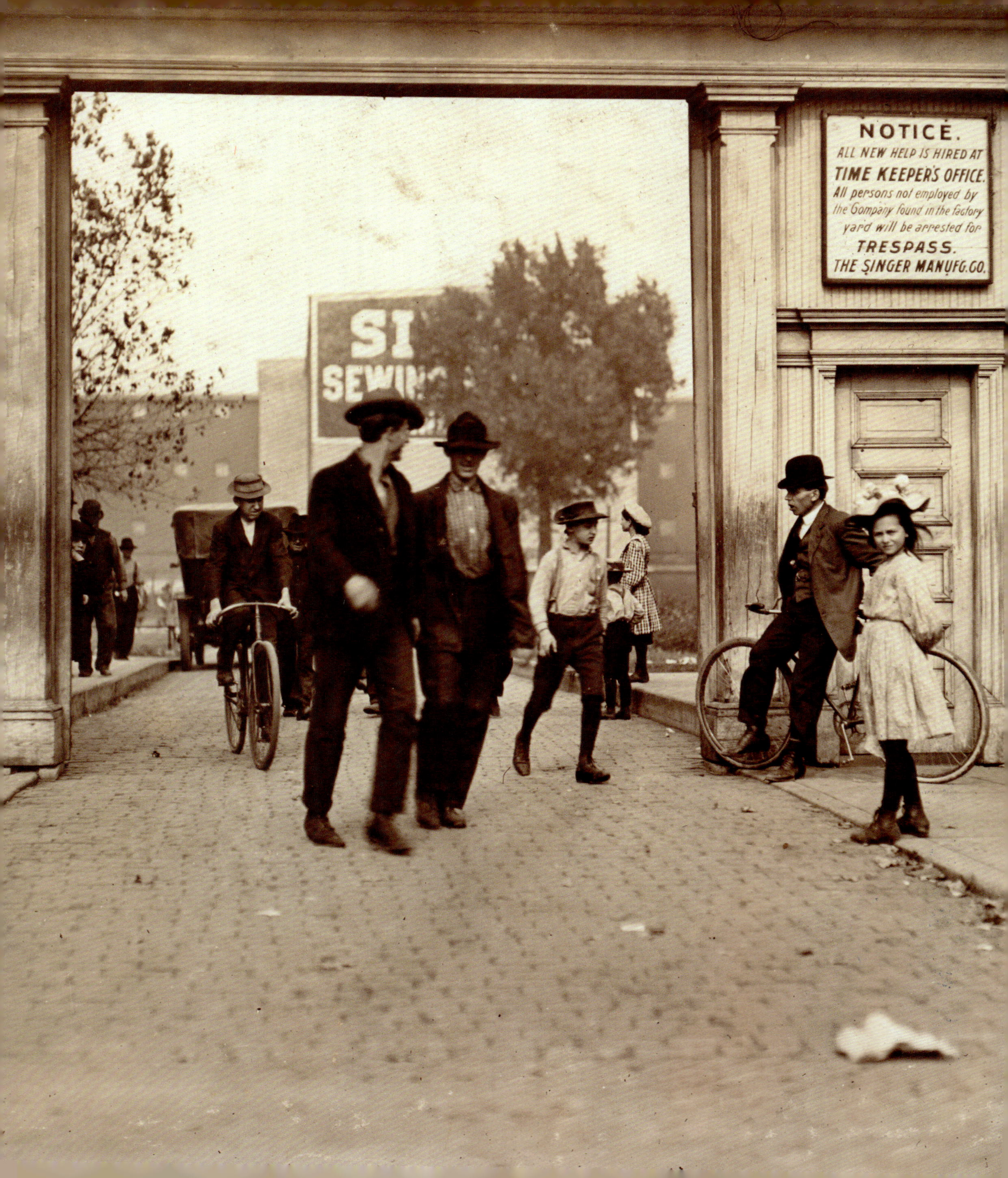
NOTICE.
ALL NEW HELP IS HIRED AT
TIME KEEPER'S OFFICE.
All persons not employed by
the Company found in the factory
yard will be arrested for
TRESPASS.
THE SINGER MANUFG. CO.
SI
SEWIN

3 THE CEREMONIAL ARCHITECTURE OF TIME

In Hine's photograph of a gateway at the Singer Manufacturing Company in South Bend, Indiana, the workers come out at lunch (fig. 40). Two men in hats emerge talking and laughing while behind them another man rides a bicycle. A boy strides to the right, passing a man leaning on his bicycle beneath a trespass sign. Nearest to us—or at about the same distance as the two men striding out of the gate—a girl in a white dress and white hat looks back at Hine. She is not a Singer worker but a dinner-toter bringing lunch to a brother or father. As the near man looks back to speak to his companion—perhaps making a joke about the little photographer standing in the middle of the cobbled road—she stares at Hine quizzically.

In second, third, and fourth photographs made that day the girl is still there. In the second (fig. 41) a new set of boys and men walks through and past the gate, among them two young men dispersing to the left and the right, each with a hostile glance at Hine. The girl has turned to look inside the factory grounds, holding her left hand to her head as if perplexed, the lunch pail now visible. In the third photograph, showing more male workers walking quickly to make the most of their lunch break (fig. 42), she has turned back away from the gate, hands bashfully at her back, lunch pail dangling down, looking to see if this new group contains the person she knows. In the fourth photograph (fig. 43) she again faces the gate as still other workers file out. This time she turns her head as if asking a question of the man in workman's cap and overalls who passes swiftly to the right. Looking back over his shoulder, his left foot a blur, the man appears to smile.

Then the sequence ends. There are no other photographs at the gateway. Perhaps the girl's father or brother emerged in the next moment. Perhaps Hine witnessed it. We will never know. The photographs strand the little girl in time, marooning her there. For all we know, she is still at that gate, faithfully awaiting a person who never comes.

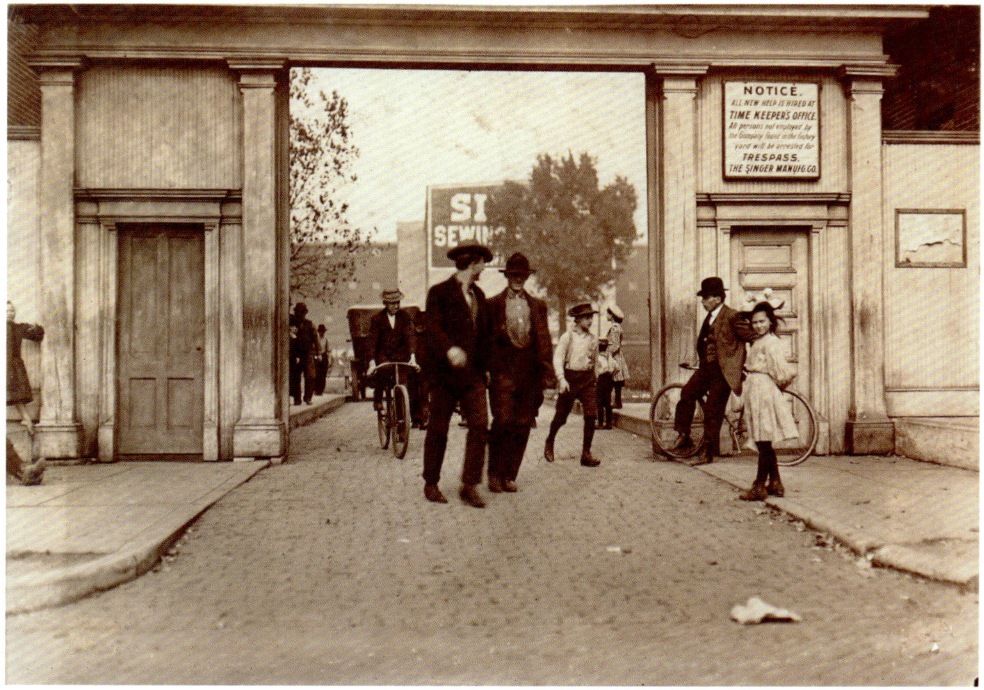

Fig. 40
Noon hour, Singer Mfg. Co. Boys work there: girls carry lunch. South Bend, Indiana. October 1908.

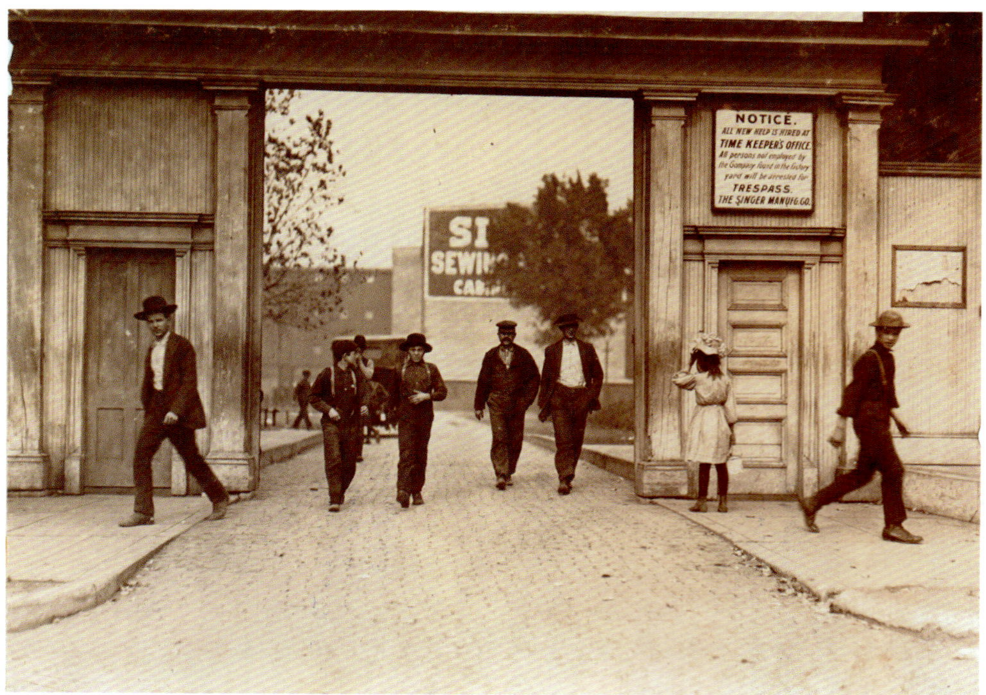

Fig. 41
Noon hour, Singer Mfg. Co., The Boys work there. South Bend, Indiana. October 1908.

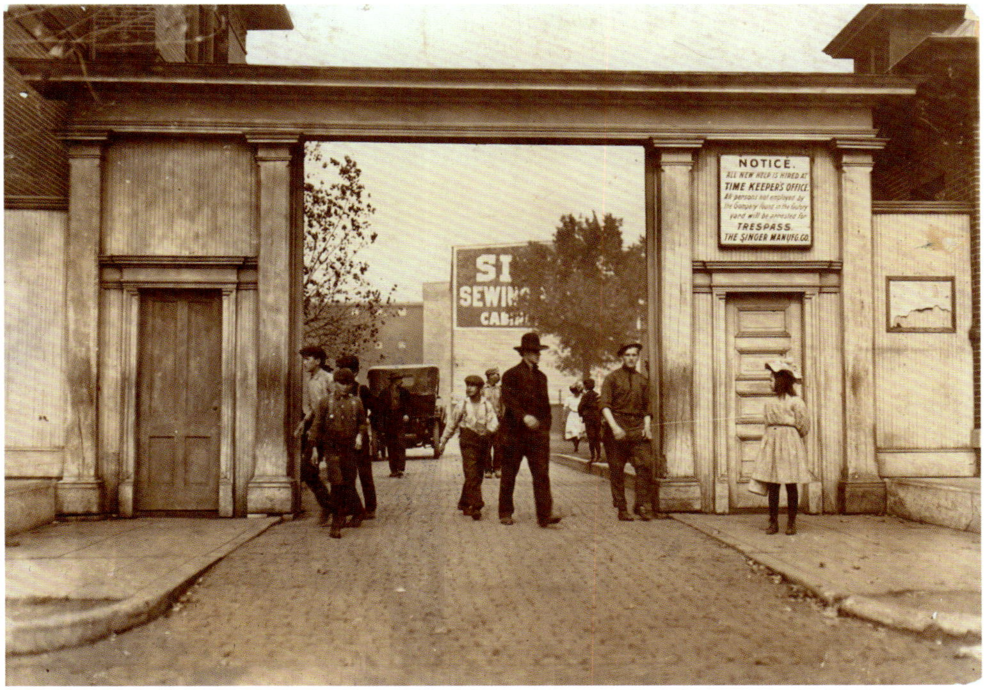

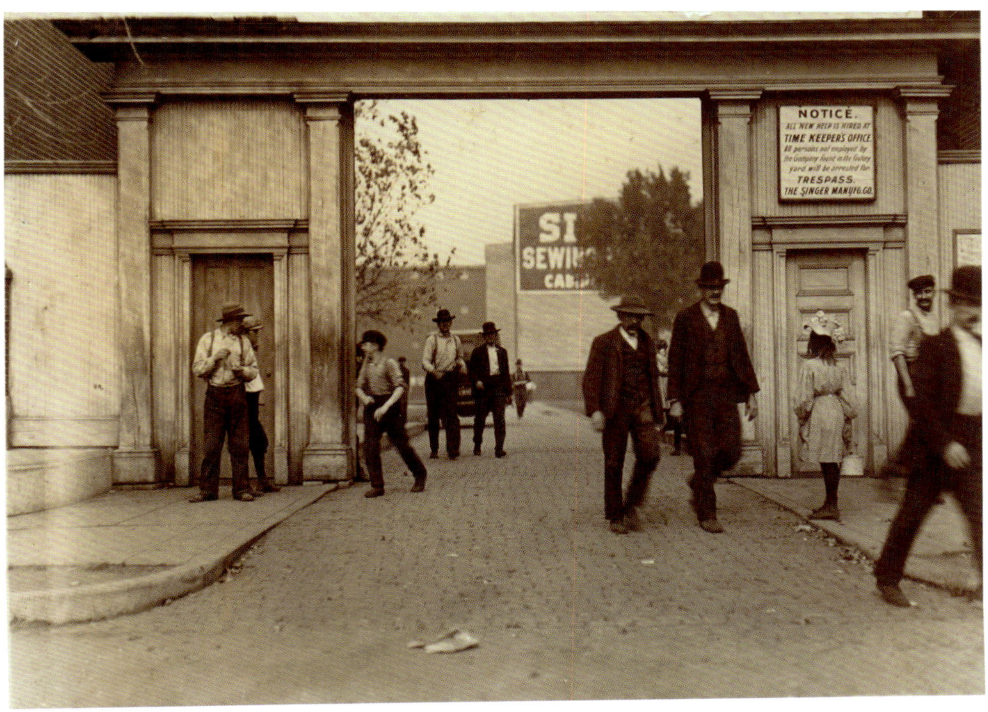

Fig. 42
Noon hour, Singer Mfg Co., Boys work there: girls carry lunch. South Bend, Indiana. October 1908.

Fig. 43
Lunch hour. Singer Mfg. Co., The boys work there: girl carries lunch. South Bend, Indiana. October 1908.

She stood there in the month before the presidential election of 1908. Then the forlorn little child was a topic of concern to all parties. Samuel Ehrhart's cartoon in *Puck* from September 1908 shows policeman-politicians leaning over a tearful lost boy who wipes his eyes and sobs, "I'm a-all turned round. Boo-hoo!" (fig. 44). Fat William Howard Taft and coaxing William Jennings Bryan, lean Eugene Debs stroking his chin—no law-upholding politician could afford to ignore the sorry waif on the street. The boy here is just the childish pampered American voter—Fauntleroy, not Ragged Dick—but he aptly shows the centrality of the child in American affairs that year. Indiana was the home state of Albert Beveridge, the progressive senator who in January 1907 had called for an amendment prohibiting interstate transportation of the products of child labor. Indiana was also the home state of Debs, the Terre Haute native and socialist candidate for president, who had spoken in South Bend in September 1908 on a stop of his "Red Special" campaign train. Maybe some of the workingmen and boys tramping out of the Singer gate had heard him. In South Bend in October, Hine was in only his third month working full-time for the National Child Labor Committee: *The Bitter Cry of the Children*—Boo-hoo or not—was in the air, and so there is Hine's little girl in white at the South Bend gate.

She is punctual, like Hine. He too must have arrived at the factory to the minute, waiting like the man leaning on his bicycle behind the girl in the first photograph, just as surely as the girl herself. Maybe a few minutes before that first photograph was taken it was just the three of them there—them and perhaps the barefooted waif and seated person partly visible on the far left. The first picture is the scene of a former emptiness previously observed by only these few sentinels, but now populated by exiting workers who a minute before had yet to exist.

Now they stream out and Hine shows them in the fluid zone where factory time becomes a quasi-personal time. As of 1908 Singer's South Bend factory had not started the regime of scientific management invented by temporal-efficiency expert Frederick Winslow Taylor, but Taylorized time—based on a precise efficiency of worker movements—would soon govern Singer's huge industrial plant at Clydebank, Scotland, leading to the great strike there in 1911. In South Bend in 1908, even without Taylor time, the workers operated under strict managerial supervision. At lunch their time was their own, but not so much that they do not move quickly, mindful that there is little of it to spare. The sign for the company's "Time Keeper's Office," at upper right in Hine's photograph, puts them all on

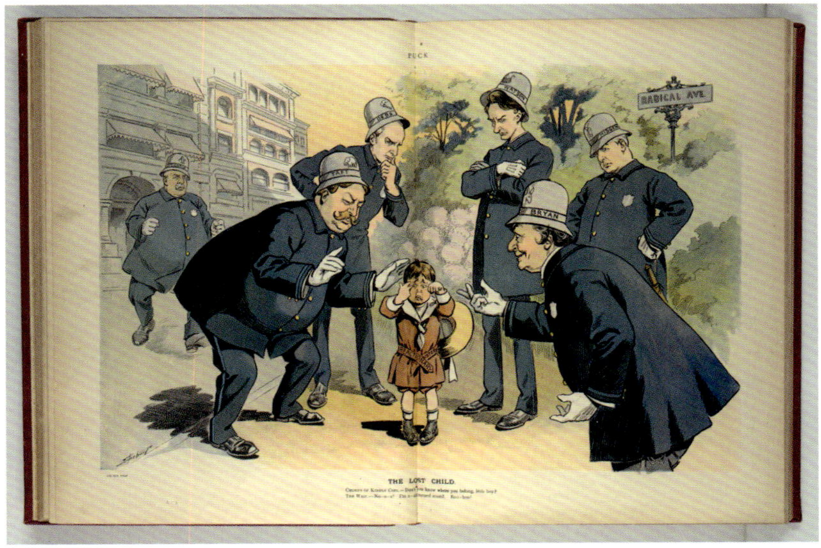

Fig. 44
Samuel Ehrhart, *The lost child.*
Puck (September 23, 1908).

notice. The trees in the background may grow at an imperceptible rate, the trash in the foreground may flutter according to wind-driven whims, but the workers relax with strict efficiency. The camera, no stranger to this disciplinary exactitude, measures the blurred paces of these clothed Muybridge-walkers with a disciplinary mind of its own, an irrepressible temporal back-beat, click-clicking, measuring the cobbles and the footfalls.

The Singer grounds show the company's strength. The company insignia on the distant building, the notice to the right, and the dominance of the shabby gateway all convey a structuring of the workers' lives. The legs and arms of the boys and young men at South Bend may swing freely, bodies casually repossessed during lunchtime, but their ease is only temporary. In May 1893 a boy named Charles Schmalzreid lost a hand in one of the machines at the South Bend plant, received some support from the company (payment of medical bills, schooling, and renewed chances at employment), but not enough to prevent him from harboring a lasting resentment and rage that led him to file suit for $8,000 nearly eight years later, in April 1901—an action the company vigorously fought. In December 1900 a worker at one of the Singer buildings in South Bend rode an elevator noted to be in poor repair; when the rope broke, the elevator fell to the ground, severely injuring one of the man's legs. The worker, named Walenty Kloska, sued the company and again the company fought the claim, concerned that a settlement would encourage others to file suit. On the subject of wages and labor dissatisfaction, the company's South Bend manager, Leighton Pine, wrote in 1900 that only those workers who "feel very kindly towards the company" have received raises. "The agitators are silenced," Pine wrote his New York bosses, "prominent merit has been rewarded, and the sluggards have something to work for."

In South Bend they made the cabinets for the sewing machines. Hine, who worked in a furniture factory as a teenager in Oshkosh, knew his way around such places. The great woodworker strike at the Paine Lumber Company in Oshkosh had taken place only ten years before, in 1898, when Hine still lived in the city. The words of Clarence Darrow, who defended the union leaders at Oshkosh, might have rung in his ears the rest of his life: "This case is but an episode in the great battle for human liberty." Hine's South Bend photographs illustrate the raw material of a socialist electorate, those for whom Eugene Debs would voice "the cry of the Disinherited, the curse of the Doomed and Damned," holding up the possibility of better days.

But then there is the little girl. She too belongs to the world of 1908 and the pressing questions of that election year. But her experience of time—as the photograph renders it—is of another kind. Hers is another labor, a Sisyphean task such as demented gods invent, the requirement that she stand there forever. Alone clad in white, a visitor from the outside, she belongs to another world than the workers. That is why among the doomed and damned, the fate of Schmalzreid is mild compared to the little girl's. Among the misfortunes that might befall a person at the factory, hers is the accident of time itself. It is not what she bargained for when she brought lunch that day.

The aged factory gateway formalizes the little girl's fate. In Hine's composition the gateway makes the space ceremonial, giving it a structure and formal clarity that intensify the pathos of the girl's vigil. In Hine's photographs of places without architecture—the New Jersey cranberry bogs, for example—the horizontal formlessness of the bogs does little to shape, aggrandize, and comment upon the children's situation. But Hine knew how to take advantage of factory buildings to shape the emotional power of his scenes. In the empty moments before the Singer lunch time, thinking about where to stand and position his camera, he likely studied the effect of the architecture, what it looked like without the people, so he could frame the workers' exit and the little girl's wait with the right ceremonial force. The shabby white gateway rises up behind the girl, declaring the pathetic austerity of her task. Dirty discolored abrasions stain the pilasters to either side—as if made by a thousand sweaty backs rubbed on the temporary temple, the slow accretion of years, the accrued smudge of loiterers and sentinels. Time takes on the alarmingly depressing appearance of this paltry shrine, scrabbled and nailed and

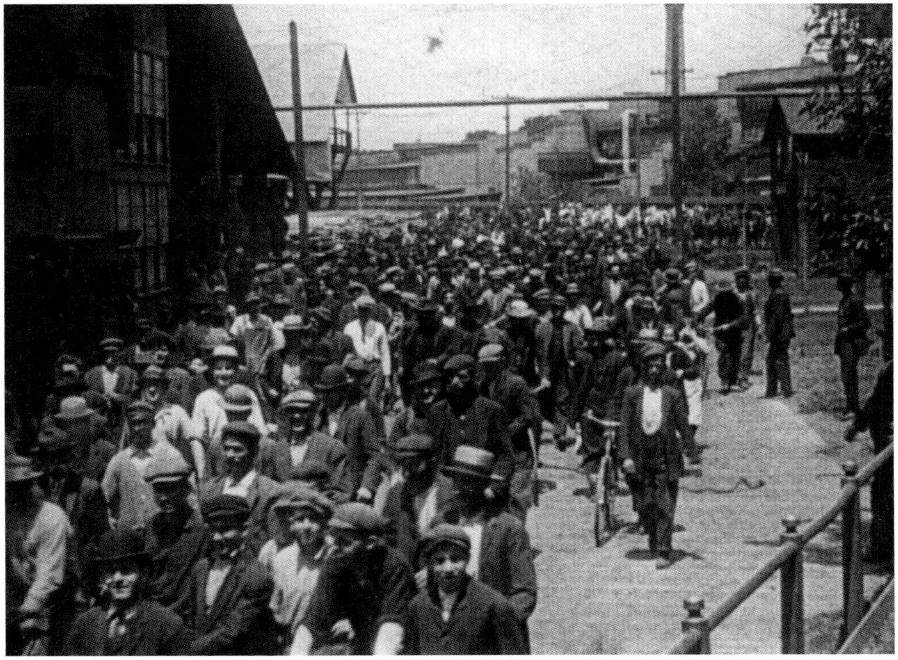

Fig. 45
Carl Laemmle, *Oshkosh in Motion, Paine Workers*, 1912.

cheaply painted, yet not without its disheveled dignity. This is a pitiful degraded solemnity that Walker Evans would have loved.

The sequence of four images is a fairy tale movie of the little girl's fate. One of Hine's fellow Oshkosh residents for several years was the future founder of Universal Studios, Carl Laemmle, who operated a men's clothing store in the city before opening a chain of nickelodeons in Chicago in 1906. Laemmle then founded a nationwide film distribution service before creating Universal Pictures in 1912. That year he returned to Oshkosh to film the city's landmarks and daily life, including a prolonged shot of thousands of workers streaming from the city's Paine Lumber Company at the end of a work day (fig. 45). The employees flow as if in concert with the reeling of the film—cinematic and factory time merge. Before a similar gateway several years earlier, Hine made his own type of movie at South Bend. The little girl in white, could she move about, would stutter and skip in a blur of frippery not unlike the heroine of Edwin S. Porter's 1907 movie *The 'Teddy' Bears*—tasting the bowls of porridge, trying out the beds. Only Hine's girl is orphaned by time itself. The sequence of the frames—one, then another, then a third and fourth—is a loop that plays her wait perpetually, without end. At South Bend Hine made a Zapruder film of time itself.

The timekeeper's notice above the little girl says it all. Hine, there with the camera, turns out to be not an ordinary clock-puncher, holding a stopwatch to the elections and issues of the day. He introduces some other element, some more perpetual and suspended time. To do so, he must place his heroine in her day, but this fixation is a precondition to the escape Hine allows for all along. As if the little girl should have been required to take a double draft of poisonous time as an *antidote* to being only "of her moment." So are Hine's captures a kind of freedom. The freedom he grants, however—liberating the delicate thing from the net—is no customary immortality but rather a floating grace of waywardness, the girl unmoored from all secure positions, left to wander in a dream of who she will be, of who she was.

Another of Hine's factory-gate photographs is called *6 P.M., May 24, 1909. Coming out of Amoskeag Mfg. Co.* (fig. 46). Hine took it and others like it at the great industrial complex—thirty mills in all—in Manchester, New Hampshire, during several days in May that year. In that place of work the gleeful boy at the center running toward Hine is isolated almost as if the weary adults around him were giving him the space to be something other than who they are. They seem to steer clear of his exuberance, treating his pleasure as a contagion they know enough to avoid. It is only a Monday night, after all—the boy, if he only knew better, would conserve his energy.

Everyone including the boy has changed into respectable street clothes before leaving the mills—"We were proud we were weavers and dressed well," an Amoskeag employee remembered years later—but the boy's happiness is more than self-respect, more than just boyish enthusiasm too. It is the cadence of an ecstatic time different from what else was in the air. According to a piece in the *Manchester Mirror* in 1907, during the twenty-three minutes it took for the city's textile factories to empty at six o'clock, each of the city's thirty mills rang its own bell, the chimes ringing from towers designed to be visible in all directions. The stunning noise of the textile rooms still rings in the workers' ears as they emerge into this other ringing coming from everywhere, the pealing of the industrial church, the spirit of capitalism radiating from battlement towers, their lord and master, even at the blessed relief of quitting time.

Those bells set the tune to what we see. A row of hatted men in dark clothes trudging slump-shouldered some feet back of the boy, filing forward in the scattered formation of their decency, each alone. The wiry boy to the left looking back;

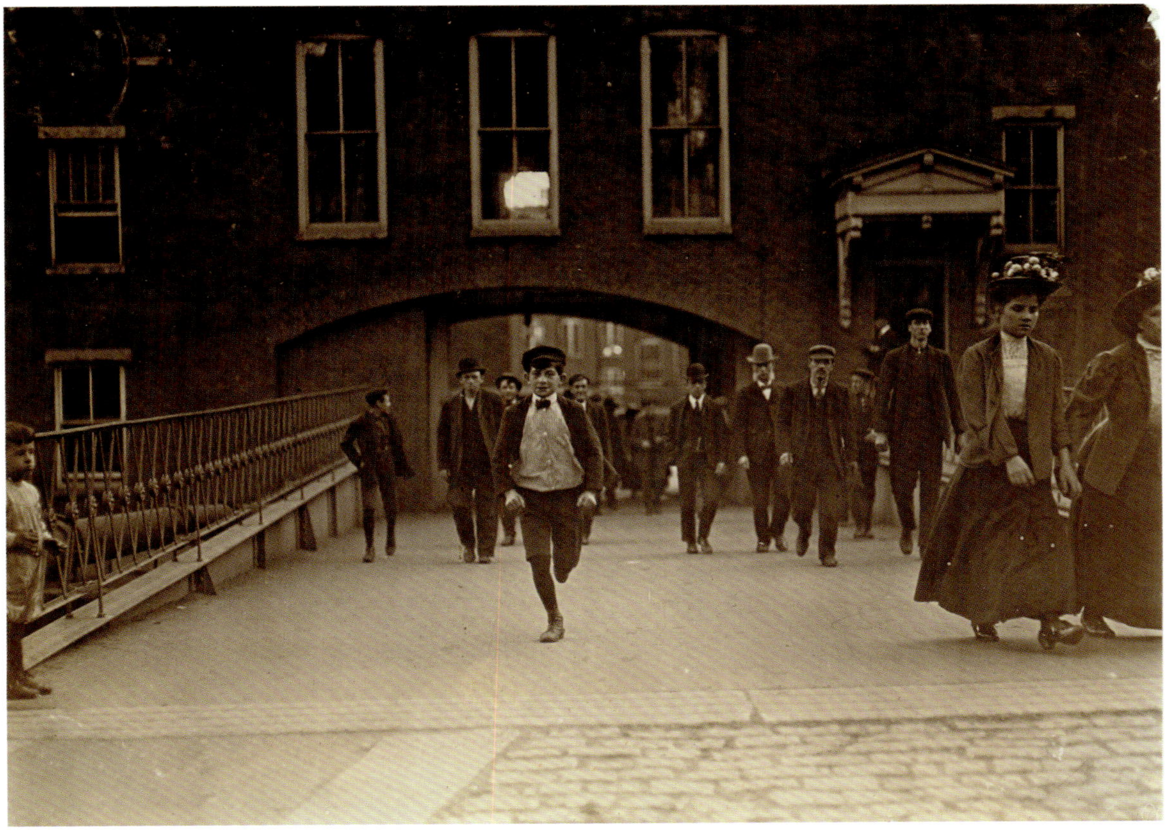

Fig. 46
6 P.M., May 24, 1909. Coming out of Amoskeag Mfg. Co., Manchester, N.H.

the very tall man loping erectly to the right. The small child in the left foreground standing to one side of the running boy, paying him no notice. The younger and older woman striding out of the picture at near right, maybe holding hands, a flurry of heavy skirts. But Hine and the boy create a moment that is different from the heavy time of the bells.

The gateway above the boy frames his run. Above the arch three windows give a subtle glow to his sprint. In the central window directly above the boy a box of light appears. It is a chance occurrence, the double-framing of the setting sun on a New England spring evening. The view into the window and then through another window at the far side of the brick archway, fuzzed and indeterminate, a blank squared above the boy like white ether, is like some floating patch of the youth that so far has kept him from becoming one of the drones around him.

Not that the architecture does not comment on the adults, too. The two other windows above the arch are dark, and the hollow weariness of the adults' faces begins to look as glassy. The man immediately to the left of the running boy stares absently, without much light, from beneath his tilted derby hat. Tall like the adults, stretched like the exceptionally tall man to the right, the windows repeat the workers' formation and even their push forward—the longer one looks at it, the more the photograph gives the impression not just of a field of people but of shapes and objects, including the windows, all coming *toward* us. Meanwhile, the small wooden cornice to the right feels as heavy and slumped as the young woman striding out of the picture nearly beneath it, as if it were a bonnet or bracket, the ornamental sign of her heaviness squared and framed. So complete is the picture's forward exodus that it gathers even this heavy background element into the advancing tide. Yet this same cornice also pulls the young woman back, as if signifying the heavy shape of another day. And beneath that cornice, almost hidden in the darkened doorway, stands a man who is perhaps a manager or detective or one of the watchmen the Amoskeag employed at every gate. Studying the outflow of workers, he appears like a Renaissance cardinal at a religious rite, a prayerful Yankee sanctifying the ritual of darkened souls. But the boy is bright.

Joe Manning, the Hine sleuth, has found out that the boy's name was Napoleon Camire and that, small for his age, he was fourteen when the photograph was taken. Down through later life Manning tracked Camire, finding photographs of him with his wife and children, of him alone, a jowly man in late middle-age, light glinting off wire spectacles, standing before a gray tropical backdrop in some photo studio of the 1940s. Manning found that Camire came from Quebec (many of the workers at Amoskeag came to New Hampshire from French Canada), and that he died at age seventy-two of a heart attack in Maine. That trackless future is all part of Hine's photograph, no less so than the deaths of Camire's dirge-marching fellow workers, the photographer's peculiar art having been to portray them all as pallbearers at their own funerals.

But the sacramental tone of the picture—the wet font of light above the French Canadian boy's head—is the rite of just that moment. The picture swarms to a standstill, the surge of congregants at our Lady of the Blessed and the Damned. The little boy at the left edge might as well swing a censer, like some dwarf or infant made to stand at a ceremonial daubing and ministering of kings. As if he wore on his chest some imaginary version of the stamped-metal boutonnieres that extend

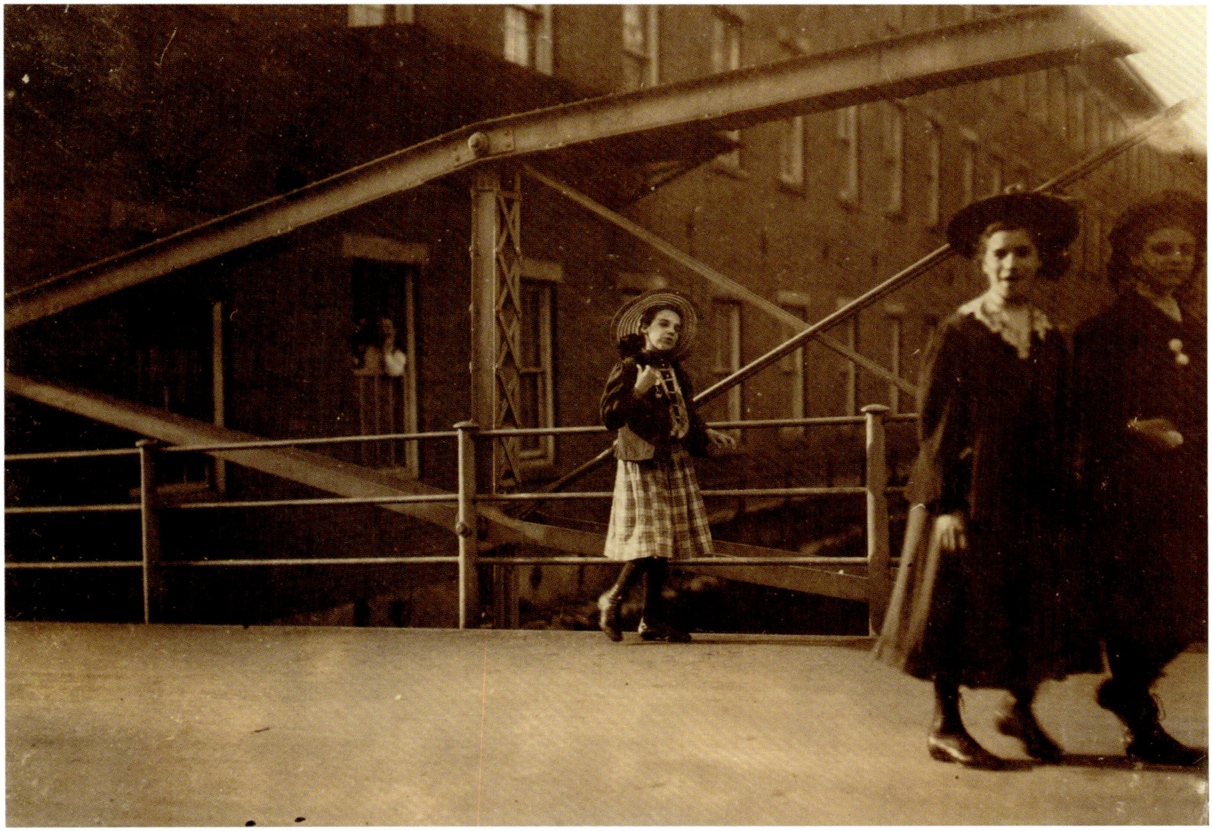

Fig. 47
This girl works in Amoskeag Mfg. Co., Manchester, N.H. May 1909.

down the railing to the brick wall, the little boy looks like a child who has been told where to be, playing his part as formally as anyone else in this rite of spring. And the running boy himself, the only person guileless enough not to fear the camera, runs straight toward Hine, making him his aim as Hine does him. Little does the boy realize that to be so completely in the moment he must be the picture's sacrifice—a virgin of time, immolated in his instant, the chosen one of a village ritual, the spring rite wherein the sweetest and least offensive of them all must expend his soul so the others can continue to plod. He cannot escape the lottery of having been chosen as the one whose relation to time is so exuberant that it cannot be sustained. Like the spring light in the blank window, the moment burns up.

Or it vanishes. In another of Hine's photographs taken at Amoskeag that May, a girl in a plaid dress walks slowly along the railing of a mill bridge (fig. 47). The two older girls to the right, bigger and bolder and nearer to the camera, stare back at Hine, one of them glancing austerely and the other opening her mouth and smiling. It looks like she is saying something to him, or about him. Back in an open window, a man in white shirtsleeves also looks at Hine, chin in hand, joined by a woman in darker clothes who peers at the edge of the same window. But the girl in the plaid dress does not notice the photographer. Her dark eyes and eyebrows emphasize her inward expression. Head tilted, lips pursed, she looks like she is whistling or singing a song. She might move at the same pace as the two nearer girls, but her posture makes her appear more languid. We half expect her left hand to be idly strumming along the railing instead of floating before it. The bridge spans whatever time she takes, but its beams and girders do not structure her thoughts. The empty space around her—the blank of the walkway between her and us—also sets her off in her own world. Hine, focusing on the girl, brings out a kind of reverie-time that is slow and solitary, extensive and odd. The foreground girls move smartly, worldly-wise. The background man, head in hand, oversees events with casual interest. They all know how to spend their time. But the little girl is blank, absent, as if she whistled the tune of a fairy tale concerning a girl such as herself who, out to take a walk one day, never was heard from again.

The next summer Hine was in Bennington, Vermont, photographing another group of workers leaving a mill, this time at lunch (fig. 48). Hine was in Bennington likely at the encouragement of John Spargo, who had moved from New York to Bennington in 1909, at first as a place to die (it had been thought he would live only a few weeks longer from pneumonia) but then as his permanent home when he recovered (he lived until 1966). Spargo may have been there with Hine as the photographer stood outside the town's Holden-Leonard Mill, a large building where textiles had been manufactured since the end of the Civil War.

The noon light outside the mill is bright, glinting off the leaves of the tree and the ivy climbing the wall. A teenage boy, the first worker to leave the building, takes off at a good pace, outracing another boy a few steps behind him to the right who kicks up a bit of dust. Two girls in white blouses stride briskly, hand in hand, with a chipper air, while behind them jogs a stout gent in a derby hat. Farther back a more stately group emerges solemn as a congregation from the ivy-covered entryway, as if yet to loosen up by moving past the bottleneck at the door and getting fully into the bright sunshine and tonic day. Above them all and spreading to one side is the large brick mill, its four stories of windows a constant wall.

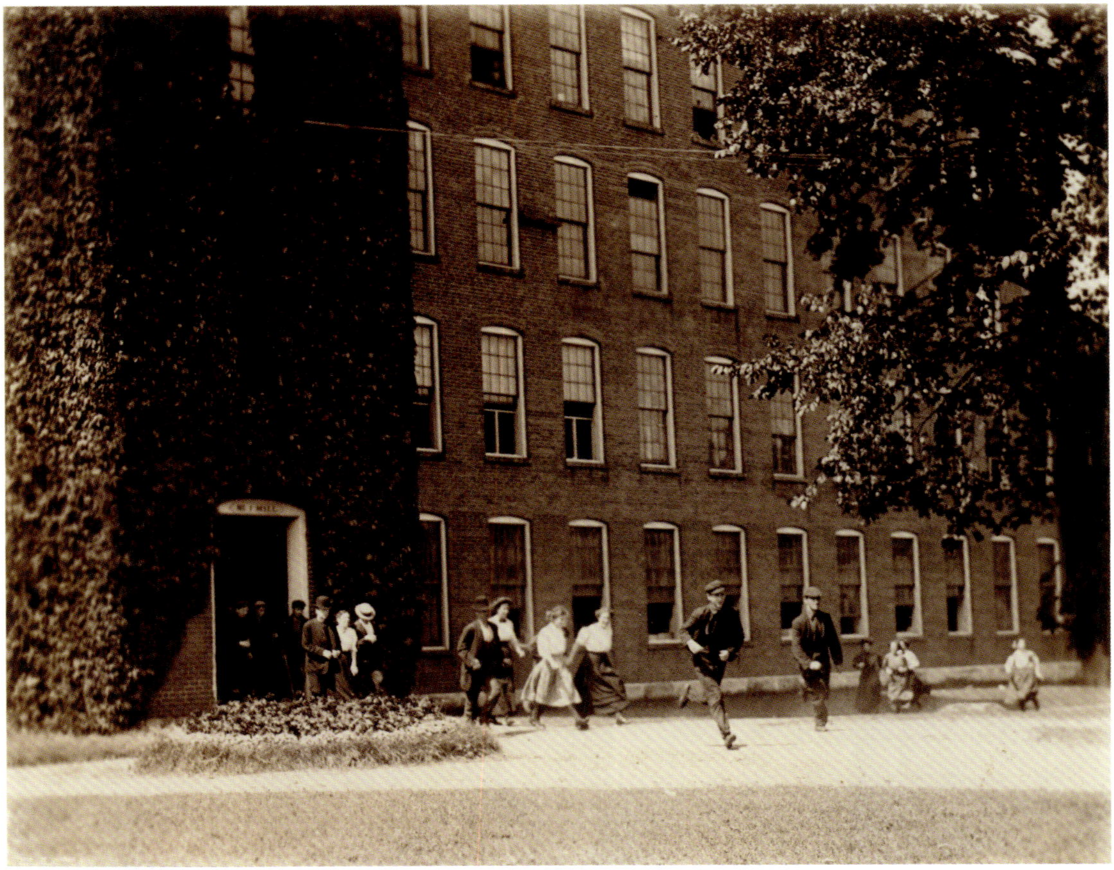

Fig. 48
Noon hour, Holden-Leonard Co., Bennington, Vt. Some of the youngsters working there. Work was slack and force small. August 1910.

That wall of windows above them has its socialist story to tell—the interchange between looming facade and scurrying figures. John Sloan's painting *Dust Storm, Fifth Avenue*, of 1906, shows well-to-do children holding onto their hats and fleeing a sudden whirl of dust caused by the wind-deflecting monolith of the new Flatiron Building above them (fig. 49). For Sloan, a socialist, commercial modernity is an implacable god hovering above even these well-born mortals, redirecting the wind, changing the weather, storming at them as if to proclaim that even souls immune from misfortune should be subject to changes in economic climate brought about by the corporate cloud-splitter. Knock down the little ones and stall the motorcar. Desperately turn the crankshaft of your buggy, master of the universe, because even the ones dressed in white will get dirty. The vengeance is Old Testament–style, the Flatiron Building throwing down unstable weather

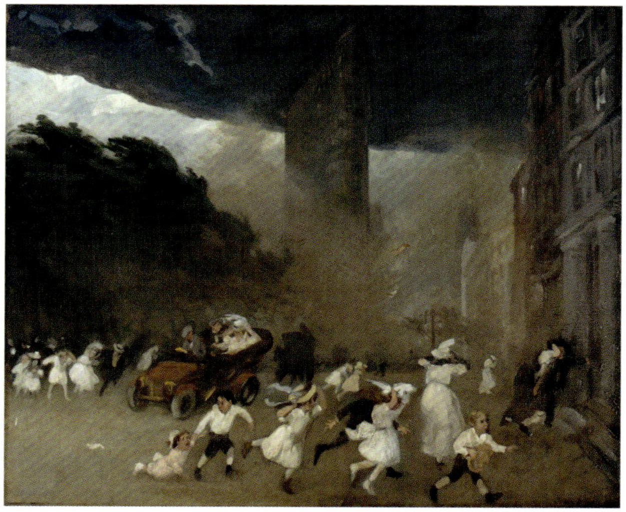

Fig. 49
John Sloan, *Dust Storm, Fifth Avenue*, 1906. Oil on canvas, 22 × 27 in. (55.9 × 68.6 cm).

patterns like snot blown from a nightmarish Semitic nose. In the caricature of the painting, the Hebraic monolith of finance is a Svengali making the little white Americans flee for their lives. It is all satire, of course, Sloan's riffing on pictures of summer picnickers, disrupted in the rococo frippery of their fleeting June pleasures. The monster of the Flatiron Building is a one-liner, a vaudevillian's image of God. But the seriousness of the joke is that no one is free from unpredictable forces that have managed to become both biblical and man-made at the same time.

Hine's sedate Bennington is a far cry from Sloan's Manhattan dust storm. But it too shows a larger force operating from above upon a small populace. What is different is Hine's conception of disaster. His rows of windows do not indicate a sudden safety hazard, the freak storms of economic meteorology. Instead they suggest a slow length of time, a perpetuation of same days and same tasks, one after the other, much like the perspectival rows of spindles in his indoor mill scenes. The rising monotony of the brick, the storm with no wind, is what these employees take their momentary respite from. Unlike the Flatiron Building, the Holden-Leonard Mill must have seemed in 1910 like it had been there forever—it was built in 1865—and that its structuring of the town, of the days and years, was as routine and perpetual as the sound of the thousand-pound bell that rang at the top of its six-story ivory-covered tower, a bell "that ruled the daily lives of hundreds of workers" there, and that rang down on the doorway directly below it as Hine took his photograph.

Beneath that bell the mill workers race time, as if their thirty-minute lunch were an athletic competition. Hine took at least eight photographs at that lunch hour, and this one appears to be the first, made at the workers' first emergence. Two of the remaining lunch photographs seem made moments later, from successively closer vantages, as if he were getting his courage up to walk directly onto the grounds (figs. 50–51). In one of them two boys look at him across the grass, veering nearer to the edge of the path for that purpose—who is this person and why is he taking our picture?—while the adults keep more to the beaten track. The second of these photographs, still closer, shows a gallery of slower figures, the dreg end of the race, a boy striding quickly, matching the pace of the fast-movers about to disappear behind the tree, but also the two girls—basking and almost conjoined—who stroll forth as if the factory grounds were their promenade or park idyll. The workers in all three photographs, no matter their speed, are momentarily as free as these two girls. Small and fragile in the scale of the photograph, time on their hands but with no time to lose, they stride amid the gardened grounds like denizens of a punch-clock fête galante.

The time of the photographs is a strange mixture of quick and slow. The ivy has grown fast on the brick above and around the doorway, but the effect of it is languorous compared to the camera's click. The places on the left edge of the first photograph where the ivy whacks out of focus indicate this temporal incompatibility, camera-time and ivy-time simply unable to get together. The workers run and stride but lunch is only a brief part of their day—as if the ivy will have grown six feet or an inch while they eat, the slow but speeding rhythms of noon having blinded the times. The photographs are attuned to two temporal rhythms of everyday life—the burdensome monotony of identical tasks, and the slow-quick glinting of light on leaves and girls in white blouses striding in the sun.

A veil of forgetting engulfs it all. It is not only that the people are forgotten, though they are. And it is not only that the mill closed in 1938 and that the building remains standing, surviving as a quarried den of karate studios, law offices, and regional college classrooms. It is also that the different times these people work with—the regime of industrial time and the precious brevity of stolen moments—are both insubstantial, evanescent.

Hine with his instinct for fragility, his well-drawn delicacy, renders this being-in-time as a smallness, a tracery of fine lines. The figures shoot forth from the ivy-clad building like the girl sailing on her leaf in *The Solution of the Aerial Problem.*

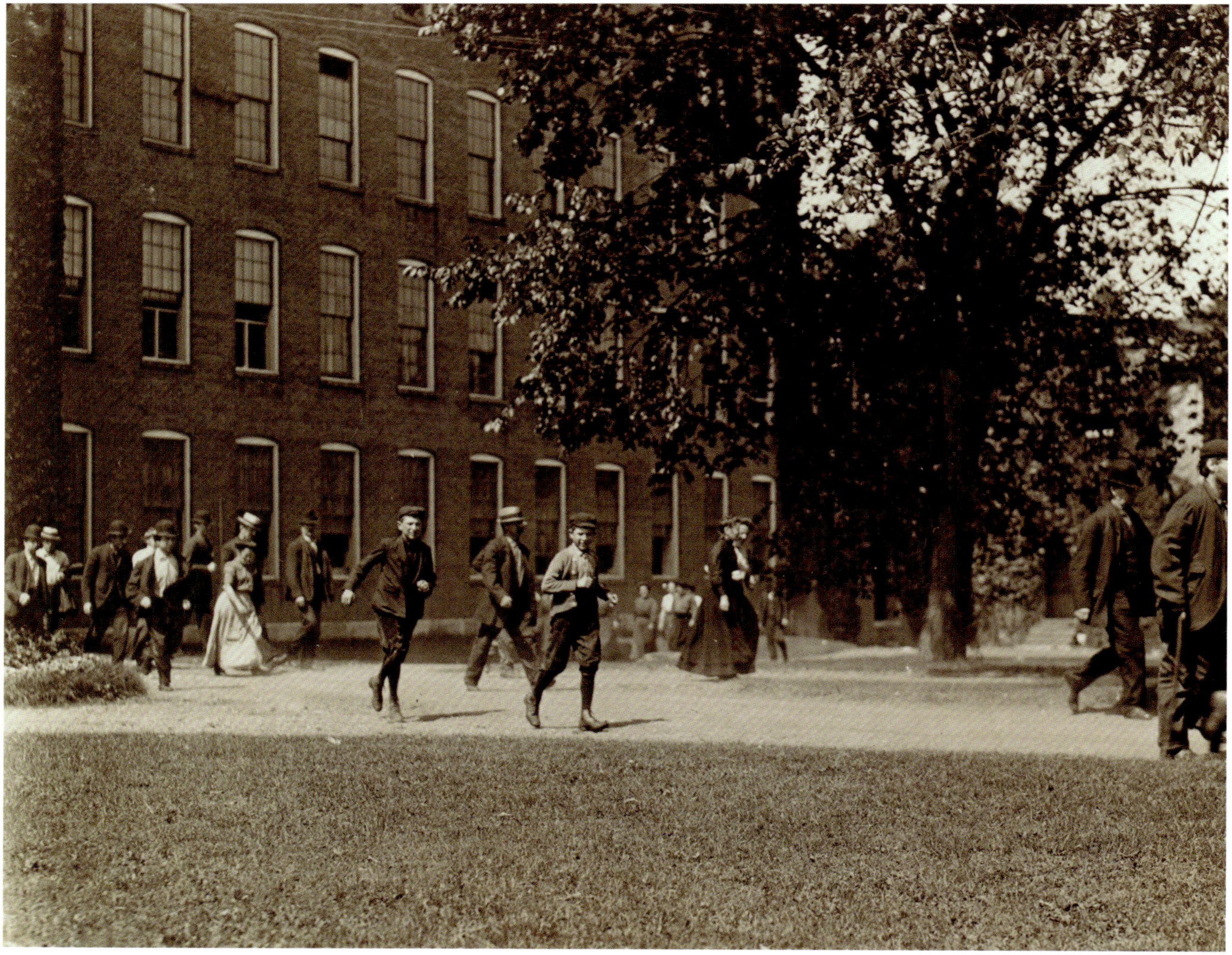

Fig. 50
Noon hour, Holden-Leonard Co., Bennington, Vt. Some of the youngsters working there, work was slack and force small. Bennington, Vermont. August 1910.

But here that same fragility draws the smallness of all that it sees, incapable of finding what is substantial, what will last, though it casts about vainly amid the facade and the windows and the sashes and the habits and dress of the workers for anything at all that will hold and sustain this maddening fleetingness that makes the world run. The boys in their caps appear to be fleeing the very fact that the world flees, trying to escape it in the only way the world permits. It is not that Hine has done that rare thing for a photographer—made a scene to be forgotten rather than remembered. It is that he has made a photograph remembering that what the world does is forget.

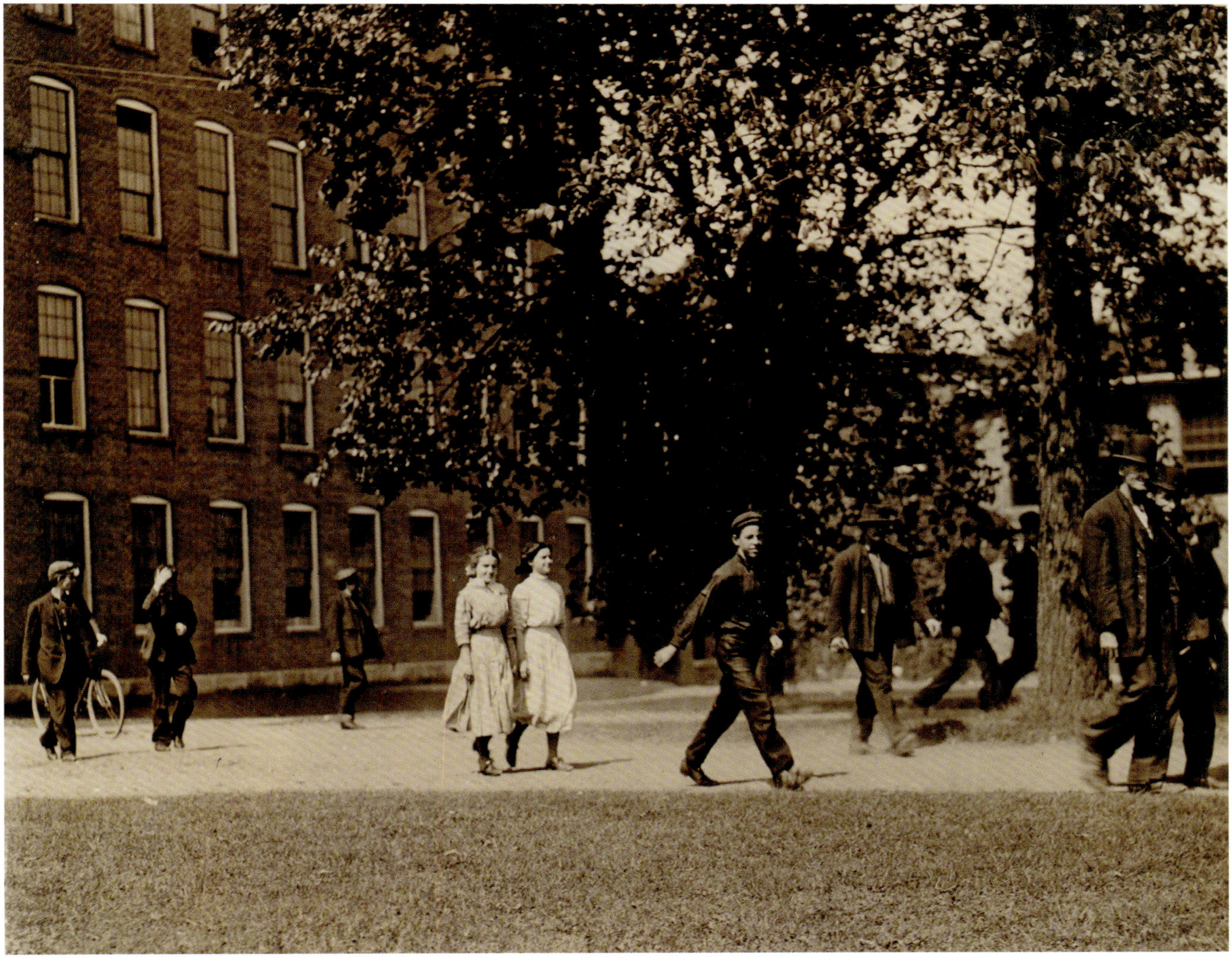

Fig. 51
Noon hour, Holden-Leonard Co., Bennington, Vt. Some of the youngsters working there, work was slack and force small. Bennington, Vermont. August 1910.

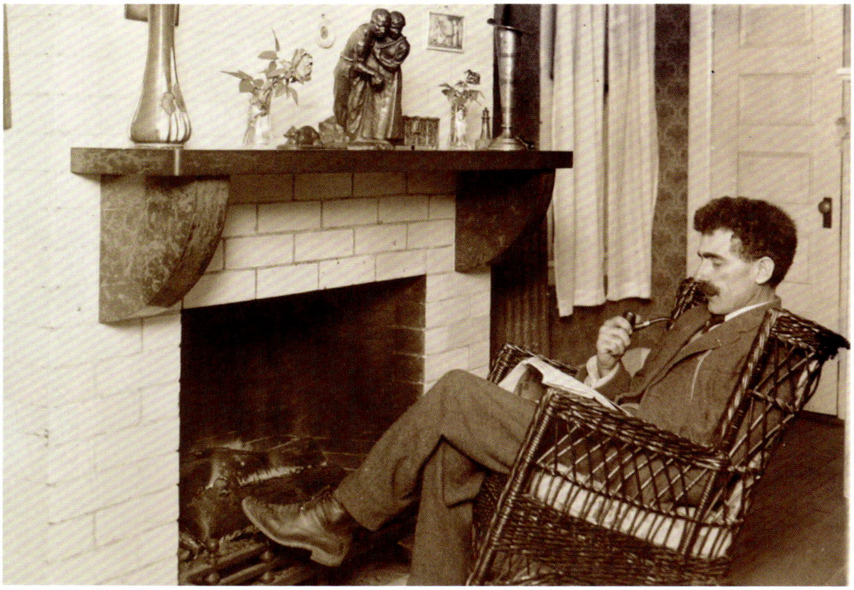

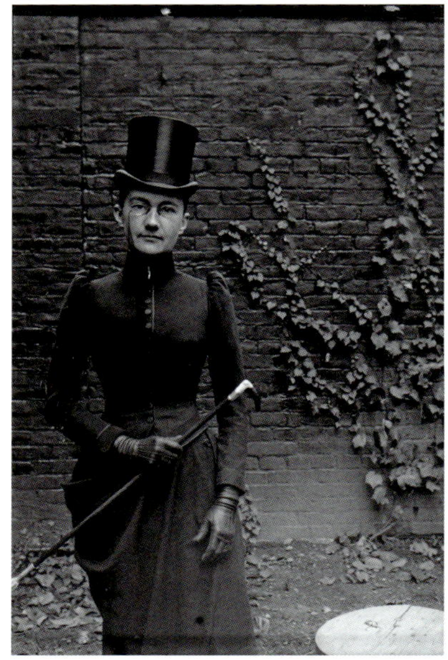

Fig. 52
Unknown photographer, *John Spargo*, ca. 1918.

Fig. 53
Mary Sanford, *Self-Portrait in Riding Costume*, ca. 1895.

How different from the false expectation of memorial, of enduring memory, Hine would have found there. Near the mill the Bennington Monument had gone up in 1888–89, an obelisk rising some 300 feet above the town, commemorating the Revolutionary War battle fought on August 16, 1777. Had Hine stepped back a bit from the mill facade, he could have shown the monument standing on its hill over the right shoulder of the mill about a half mile away. The monument was no less perpetual than Spargo, Hine's likely host in Bennington, who went on to write a book about it (once he had given up socialism) and who considered himself a larger-than-life piece of permanent American history, with an ego to match (fig. 52). Founding the Bennington Museum, Spargo preserved history, not least the history of himself, notably in several portraits of him owned by the museum. He knew perpetuity when he saw it, no less than Hine's likely other host, Bennington's most prominent socialist, the wealthy and powerful Mary Robinson Sanford, an amateur photographer, whose force of personality was equal to Spargo's (fig. 53). Top-hatted, her glasses glinting in a self-portrait taken in the 1890s, Sanford holds a riding crop in one of her black-gloved hands. Ivy climbs the brick wall behind her, an enigmatic counterpoint to her corseted rectitude, but here the ivy is no telltale sign of quickly creeping time but rather a pretty adornment to the brick wall of her poise. Sanford had grown up in nearby Troy, New York, where her father was owner of the United Shirt and Collar Company, one of the nation's leading clothing manufacturers. After graduating from Vassar, she maintained a summer home in Bennington and also spent time in New York, where eventually in middle age she took classes with Spargo and embraced his socialism. It was Sanford who brought Spargo to Bennington in 1909 when it appeared he was dying. Sporting the look of someone whose social prestige is all but a permanent fact, she is not to be trifled with, no more than Spargo himself.

On that day in August 1910 outside the mill perhaps Sanford as well as Spargo stood next to Hine. At least the photographer might have taken a cool drink at Sanford's nearby home or even stayed as a guest. But Hine's Bennington photographs, like his others, feel like a suppression of monumental ego rather than an exaltation of it. And that abatement of self—the willing surrender of it—manifests somehow in the small flight of his figures, the kicked-up dust and gentle blades of grass that stock their summer sun, a swarm of fleeting effects that could only exist—could only be seen—by a person willing to curtail his own presence before what he saw. In her later years Sanford helped establish Bennington College and donated money for a massive 350-pound bell from the Meneely Bell Company in Troy for the cupola of the Commons Building, the same foundry that supplied the great thousand-pound bell that rung at the Holden-Leonard Mill. The new years and the new hours would always strike into being as though forged by her beneficence, a lasting memory to her generosity. But Hine did not think of enduring.

His medium is not what is given but what is taken—the moments stolen and never found. He would have understood when the Holden-Leonard bell, all thousand pounds of it, eventually disappeared. The bell had remained long after the mill closed, staying a part of the building until 1969, but vanished in the 1980s from a warehouse where it had been placed. Likely it was turned into scrap and sold. So the heavy bell ultimately shared the fate of all the moments it ever tolled. Hine would not have been surprised. Long before, back at the scene, he had already portrayed the lost hours, the thievery of time.

How did other photographers portray the architecture of time? In Alvin Langdon Coburn's famous photograph *The Octopus, New York*, made in 1912, the sundial shadow of the brand-new Metropolitan Insurance Building marks the ephemeral hour, a giddy but uneasy premonition of the new century (fig. 54). Like his friend H. G. Wells, who had published his book *The Future in America* in 1906, Coburn was a socialist keenly interested in the present but also trying to imagine what the American nation would be. Wells called his own premonitions "the anticipatory habit," describing his way of thinking as "the other side of the scientific method" because it brings the predictor "into the large temperance, the valiant inconclusiveness, the released creativeness of philosophy." *The Octopus* is a similar speculation. Coburn sees the future as a vertical utopia—"I am satisfied that the architects of the future will do wonderful things in steel and stone, towering to the sky," he said in 1907.

But Coburn also shared his friend Wells's unease. Coburn gave another New York skyscraper picture of 1912 an eerie name—*House of a Thousand Windows*—and *The Octopus* is not the cheeriest title. The paths of Madison Square Park flare beautifully but in a vaguely nauseous way, too. The ground puffs in a bulbous swell, a pregnant distension of space. Height makes you giddy; it also makes you sick. Maybe that is because the big view from on top—the new moneyed view—reveals a predator's grasp. From that vantage the pretty snow-cleared paths turn out to be tentacles grabbing and pressing the round earth, a spider injecting venom into its prey. Coburn said in 1907 that his goal as a photographer was to portray "the ensnaring and illusive vision of things, only half felt and hardly realized." So the view from on top reveals an ensnaring pattern we could hardly see at street level. To the monster will come the spoils, not least to the monster highly sighted, who like his aesthete-accomplice beholds a capital view.

Wells put the violence of height directly at the center of his futuristic novel *The War in the Air* (1907), a book Coburn must have known. Wells envisioned the aerial bombing of New York, the city's giddy altitude turned upon itself, the sky-groping buildings now surmounted by German dirigibles dropping bombs. The German fleet flies over the Atlantic and swings down on Manhattan, turning the patriotic crowds that had assembled in Madison Square Park and other locales into puny and helpless victims. Looking down from one of the airships, we see a bomb drop—"Blinding flames squirted out in all directions from the point of impact." A little man running nearby "became, for an instant, a flash of fire and vanished—vanished absolutely." The elevated view reveals the carnage: "The people running out into the road took preposterous clumsy leaps, then flopped down and lay still, with their torn clothes smoldering into flame." Wells does not say what happened to Madison Square Park itself. But all around the destruction rains down.

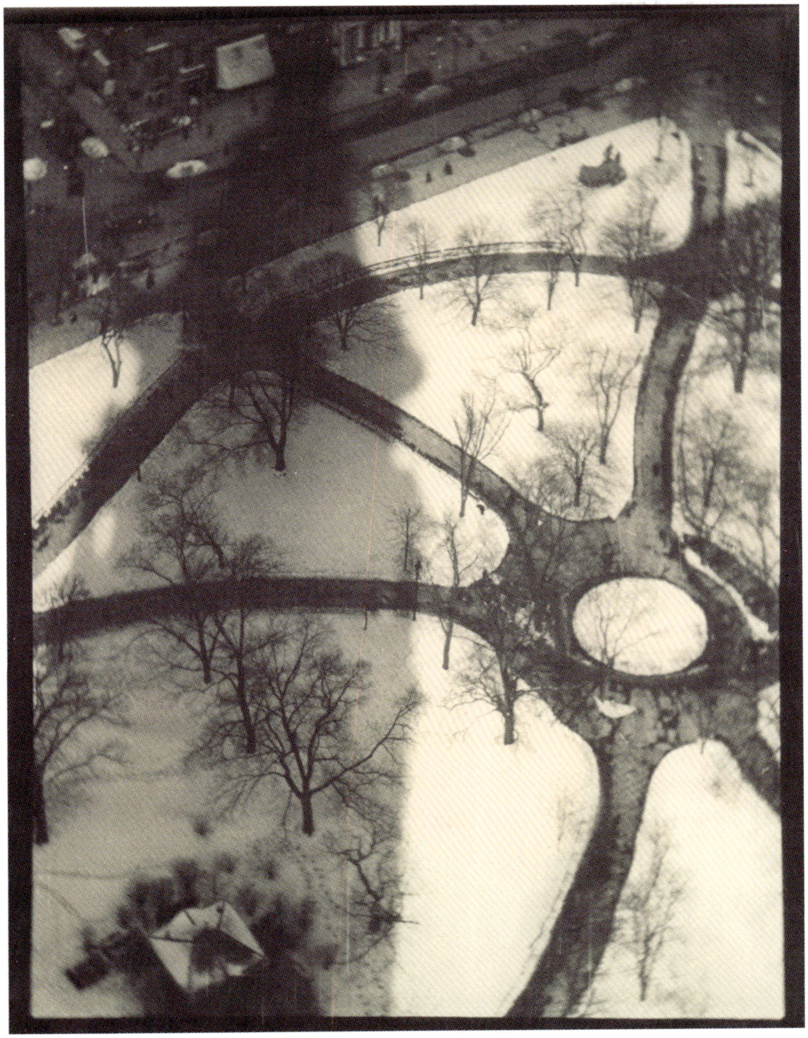

Fig. 54
Alvin Langdon Coburn, *The Octopus*, 1912.

The Octopus is not a bomb-throwing photograph. Its fantasy of dominant altitude takes another form than outright social destruction. That fantasy is the shadow of newness that falls on the scene. That shadow is not a hardened allegory—the Future—but rather an intimation, a subtle passing feeling of the kind that Coburn wanted to portray: "fleeting things like the movement of smoke, the reflections in water, or the ever-changing forms of clouds on a windy day." What these feelings are is not clear, but they are not entirely welcome. For this artist born in Boston, maybe no hedonistic vision of future prosperity could come without a creeping Puritanical revulsion, a sense that the emancipated pleasures of living high and large, reveling in the beauty of new perspectives, will come at a cost. The splendid view bends even as one looks, like an optical curse where glories of angels turn to skulls, all in some despondent neurotic affliction of the eyes. The person who glimpses the future watches pretty paths turn to diabolical designs.

If that was the architecture of the future, what was the architecture of the past? Clarence White's photograph *Croton Reservoir* shows a relatively new structure, the Croton Dam in Croton-on-Hudson, New York, but White makes the dam ultimately a thing of the ancient past (fig. 55). From a hillside vantage amid leafless branches, a waterfall flows in a two-tiered blur. Below, a tower and stone wall divide our vantage from an arabesque of paths winding across the distant grass where a small fountain sprays at the center of a concentric pool. An iron trellis, part of a bridge, appears above it all like a gothic arch.

White's depicts a source—a dream of where it all begins. The new dam holds water for New York City, twenty-two miles to the south, but for White the place goes way back. Partly the dream is of his own origins as a photographer, a kind of ancient history that yet feels mystically close. In one of White's most famous photographs, *Miss Grace*, which he made around 1898 in Newark, Ohio, where he lived then and not far from the town where he was born, a local girl reads a book, her long legs elegantly crossed before her (fig. 56). The wooden pattern of the sofa swirls like the paths in the Croton photograph twenty-seven years later. The white of the girl's dress drops and splays in a triangular mass like the Croton waterfall, and the sofa's wooden front railing is a bit like the reservoir's stone wall. The two photographs play off each other—*Croton Reservoir* returns to the obsessions of White's early career.

The spying of beauty for White is always a chaste civic project. Looking down into her book, Miss Grace is embraced by the swirling paths of her mind, a reservoir of sentiments no more traceable in those graceful lines than the content of a telephone call would be by staring at the wires. The mind is a treasure of resources, tapped back to hidden origins, a luxury as pretty as velveteen, parchment, and lace. The mind is also a civic project, an infrastructure, as important to the operation of civil society as a good supply of water, the manicured grounds of parlor and reservoir alike a model of middle-class reserve, of passions carefully channeled and

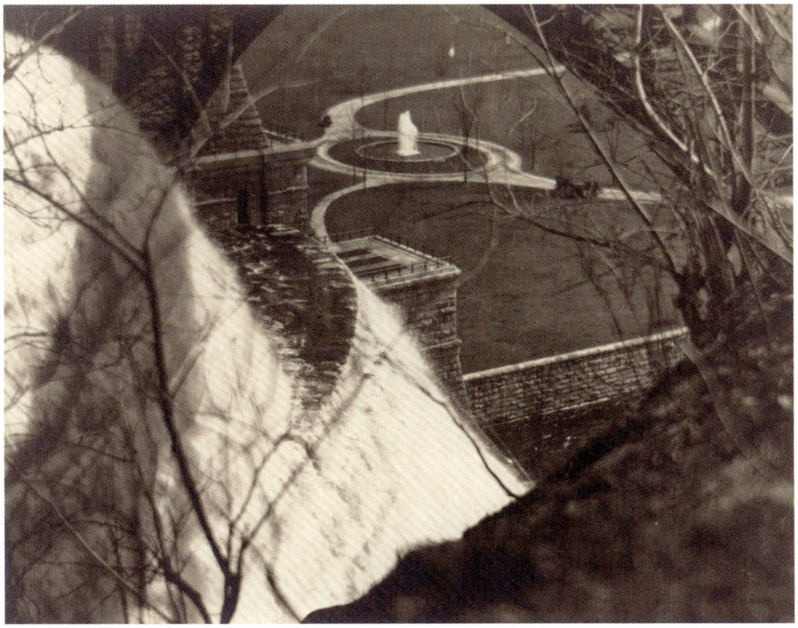

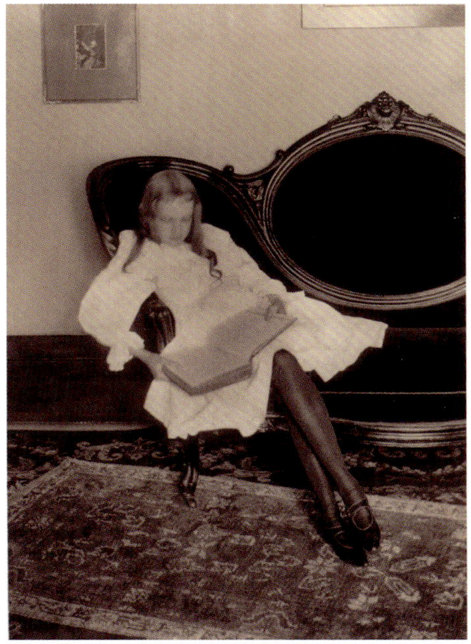

pure. Yet the furtive freedom of an erotic mythology shows through, too, recalling the nudes that White also photographed. The contours of *Croton Reservoir* imply a maiden dipping an earthen vessel at the origin, a modest nymph beheld at her bath, the branches pulled back so that Actaeon might take a peek, terror-free, at a chaste stream in its virginal seclusion.

And the mind is an ancient rampart, like the Indian earthworks running in a sixty-mile network in and around the Ohio towns where White grew up. He and his older brother Pressley used to play among the Newark, Ohio, hills as teenagers, intimate with the contours of the earth there, part of an idyllic growing up. To judge by *Croton Reservoir*, White's attraction to these boyhood earthworks stayed with him as a primeval experience his whole life—he made the new Croton Reservoir recall the site of his own ancient past. The secret of the reservoir is that it repeats who one was, stating the mystery of the past as a cryptic earthwork, a record of lost civilization. For *Miss Grace*, likewise, the ramparts and earthworks of primitive childhood would require a Freud to excavate, a mental archaeologist to trace the neural filaments of thought patterns grooved so elegantly in their paths, the habits and accustomed routes, the garden parks of genteel space, lovely and remote.

Fig. 55
Clarence White, *Croton Reservoir*, 1925.

Fig. 56
Clarence White, *Miss Grace*, ca. 1898.

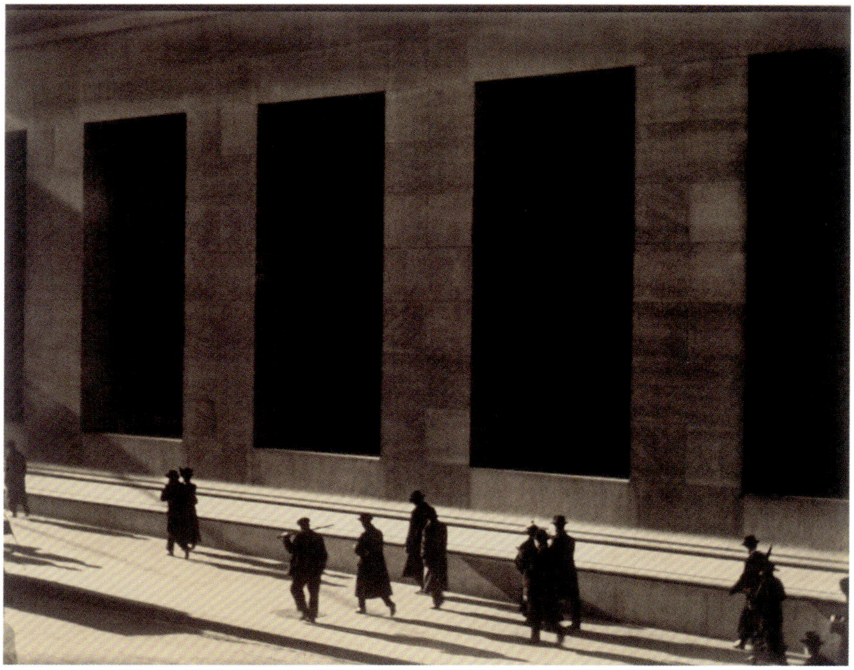

Fig. 57
Paul Strand, *Wall Street, New York*, 1915.

White thinks of the falling away of who we were. The blur-faced girl is a flat pattern, a retreat—the maker of her own lost world. *Croton Reservoir* is equally retrospect. Made the year White died of a heart attack while leading a photography class trip in Mexico City, it predicts the architectural ruins he must have wanted to photograph in that ancient place. Working upon his designs, White pressed life into patterns of rigorous formal clarity, finding that if looked at closely it will yield the raised edges of archaic signs.

What then was the architectural present? Paul Strand made it indelible. In *Wall Street, New York*, taken in 1915, Wall Street workers move along the sidewalk with such chill grimness that their alienation becomes an enduring glamor (fig. 57). Boldly picked out in the cold morning light, casting shadows like an army of souls, they shed their rich individualities while paying no mind. And above them, of course, looming like the mother of Hine's factories—a colossus of all the brick mills in dusty towns that Hine did or ever could photograph—is the blind black arcade of a building owned by the great financier J. Pierpont Morgan. The drumbeat of voids is a pattern of permanence, helping to ink the workers in the fixation of their march. Once recorded, the moment cannot be erased. It is one day but a day for all time.

But the present moment of Strand's teacher, Lewis Hine, was a much more fleeting operation. In his photograph of workers going to the mill at Opelika, Alabama, one morning in 1914, Hine settles for a random data of sociological notation, perhaps as compensation for not being able to get closer to these faraway people (fig. 58). What he shows is all in passing, even the things stock still. The dirt yard, the stunted foot-high shrub at the center, the iron upright in the right foreground, the fence posts flanking the lead group of workers—all amount to a dutiful shorthand, a reporter's scribble that also manages to get more emotionally salient details such as the long diagonal line of morning shadow falling across the bricks that separates the two children at the rear from the main group.

Strand, if he looked at this photograph, must have understood that he could strengthen it in so many ways. Modest Lew Hine might even have assured his protégé that it could be bettered, and Strand moved directly to accomplish the task. Poor Hine—he was so much less suave. He could not make pictures as Strand could, simultaneously as assured as socialist cartoons and infinite works of art. Hine was always making photographs of brick walls in the sunlight, and who knows but that the scrabbly little bush in Opelika caught his eye as a forlorn detail whose destitution was its charm. Even in much better photographs than the one he took at Opelika, he could never get his laborers to trudge like Strand's doomed souls. Hine's workers instead walk with individual gaits, a notation of calico, bare feet, and suspenders, unlovely in the sun. Strand's photograph is to Hine's what Ernest Hemingway's prose is to Sherwood Anderson's. As Hemingway made fun of his mentor Anderson, parodying Anderson's sentimental portrayal of small-town life, shredding Anderson's studied Ohio locutions in the terse simplicity of his remarkably pared-down sentences, Strand made short work of Hine's eye for scattered local details and mysteriously inconsequential lives.

But Hine's focus on what is not there—rather than what is—made his moments devastating in a way that Strand's are not. The isolated figures and empty space at Opelika call to mind Giorgio de Chirico paintings such as *The Piazza*, also a work of 1914, when de Chirico was living in Paris (fig. 59). De Chirico's picture is dreamy, a cryptic array of nostalgia and morbid presentiment. The puffing train, the two figures standing on the piazza, the stone town-father gesturing to them and the train from his pedestal—these are the long shadows of a psychological episode,

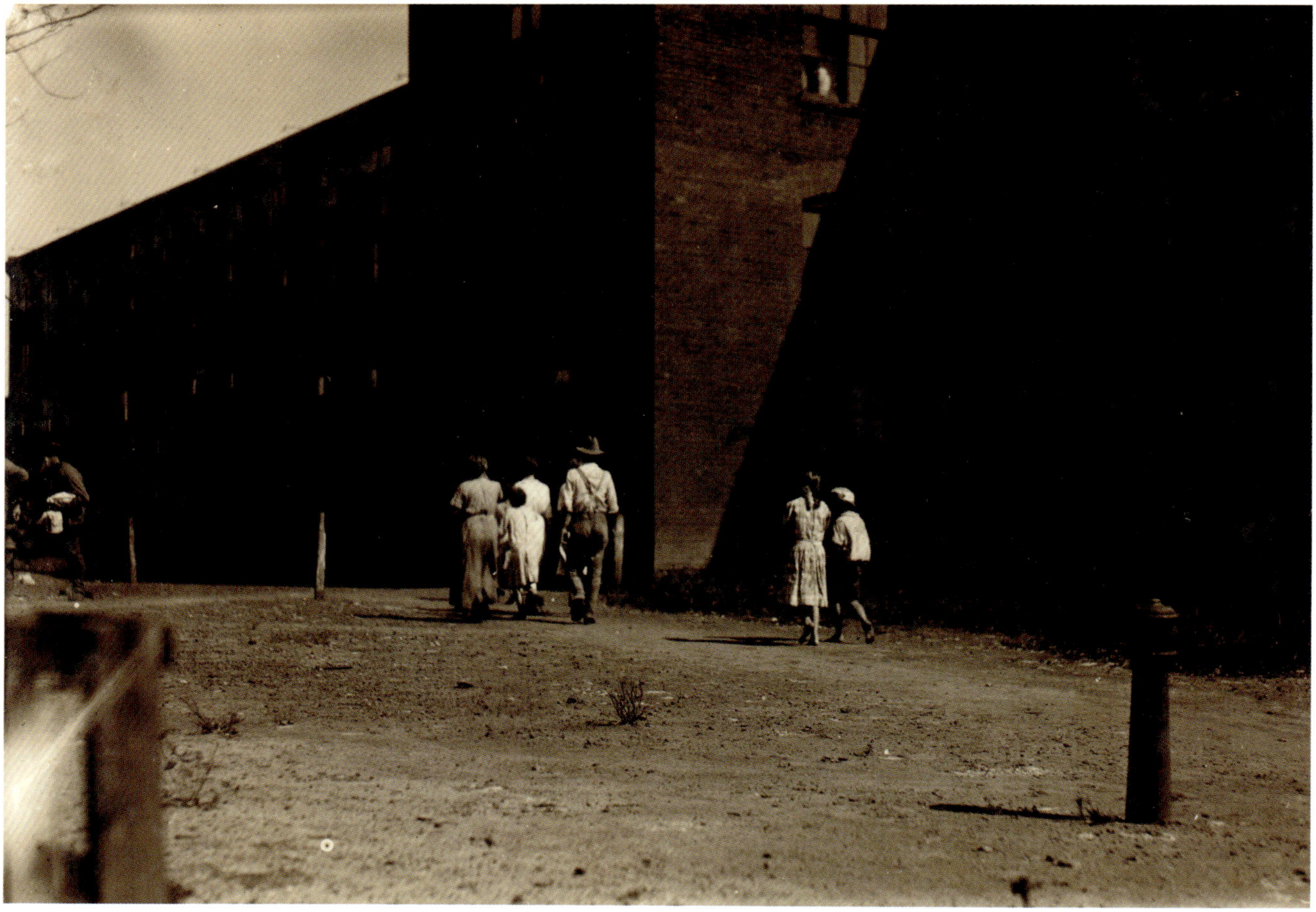

Fig. 58
Going back to work. Youngest boy is Richard Millsap. The family record in bible says he is 11 years old—born Jan 22, 1903 (doubtful), and father says 12 years old. He appears to be under 9. Works every day at spinning, and has been working for some weeks. Boss saw investigator photographing him and whistled to him to get out. This photograph was gotten as he went in to work. October 1914.

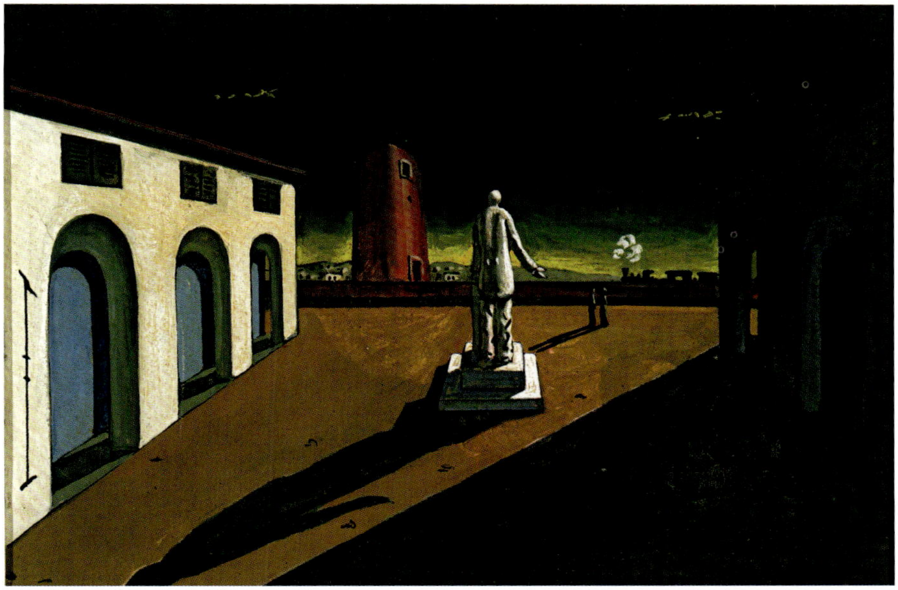

Fig. 59
Giorgio de Chirico, *The Piazza*, 1914. Oil on canvas, 13¼ × 20 in.

some dismembering scenario of elongations, phallic journeys and churning drives, all overseen by the nameless authority in coat and baggy pants, trousered lord of the emptiness.

Hine's feeling for space was not the erudite blankness of de Chirico—his enigmas were not so portentous. Emptiness for him was not hypochondriac and neurotic, yet it was equally despairing. Hine's was the revelation that, if looked at closely, moment to moment, the American scene contained ... *nothing at all.* A moment photographed really well would reveal that there was nothing there to see. Even when a subject might appear before Hine more vividly than in the Opelika photograph, a pretty millworker or handsome doffer staring straight into his camera, the feeling of a presiding emptiness might still be the spirit of the place he would hope to catch.

To do so would require a leveling of Hine's own propensities to symbolize, to quote, to draw a moral. In 1845 Henry Wadsworth Longfellow had written his beautiful poem "The Ropewalk," in which the bourgeois narrator muses on a factory interior, imagining the mill as a farm and a school and a ship and other things before pleasantly reawaking to the mill's reality. The imaginer-poet is overprolific in his dreams, each one exquisite, but Hine's photographs make a point of eroding his own intelligence. They annul the suavity of metaphor as a cheap indulgence.

Strand's gorgeousness—had Hine ever been able to approach it—would have been equally beside the point.

What metaphor there is in the Opelika photograph falls like an impersonal array of forces. The jagged line of light splitting the first group from the second is a sundial, a marking of time decisive and blank. But the warm blade falls on the bricks as if careless that even a gesture so precise should mean anything at all. The world only "falls" and "casts," just a dumb show of forces that photography in its mechanical literalness is suited to show. If Hine's photographs sometimes resemble de Chirico's paintings, it is from the other side of the painter's erudition, a nether world where the photographer and the world conspire to meet in a trapezoidal zero, a rock-strewn yard where the *lack* of signification, of Freudian and other investments, starts to show as a feeling about the emptiness of moments themselves.

Like this: Hine attends to the word *absence*. Ever the educator, he understood the daily and weekly hours of child laborers in Alabama—up to eleven hours a day and sixty hours a week in 1914—and he knew the limited schooling of children such as he shows at Opelika. The fallow yard is like an empty mind, absences of different kinds adding up to make the human waste Hine's posters direly predicted. Even the paltry few landmarks (the iron upright, the fence posts) have nothing to teach.

But the absence goes beyond an educational wasteland. It says this: the moment, revealed in an American place, is as uncultured as its location. We could as soon imagine de Chirico setting foot in Alabama as we could a mill called the Enigma Cotton Company. There is no enigma, no mystery of widening vistas, only the distinctive *lack* of these things that starts to make itself felt as a curious and even poignant absence showing through—and as—the American scene truthfully beheld. Show a gas station at rush hour, or a field at dusk, or a river levee of weathered bricks and rusted iron chains—whatever it is, in whatever era—and there would be, as an understructure, some blankness wafting through it. Double the effect if the scene is of a plaza, a civic array of pleasing parade, for these gladsome indicators of a day fully lived and sportively represented would only better make visible, by their very attempt to hide it, the absence lurking within it all. The genius of the place is that there is no genius.

What was there to save in the emptiness? Back in 1910, three months before he came to Bennington, Hine visited St. Louis, Missouri, then one of the largest cities

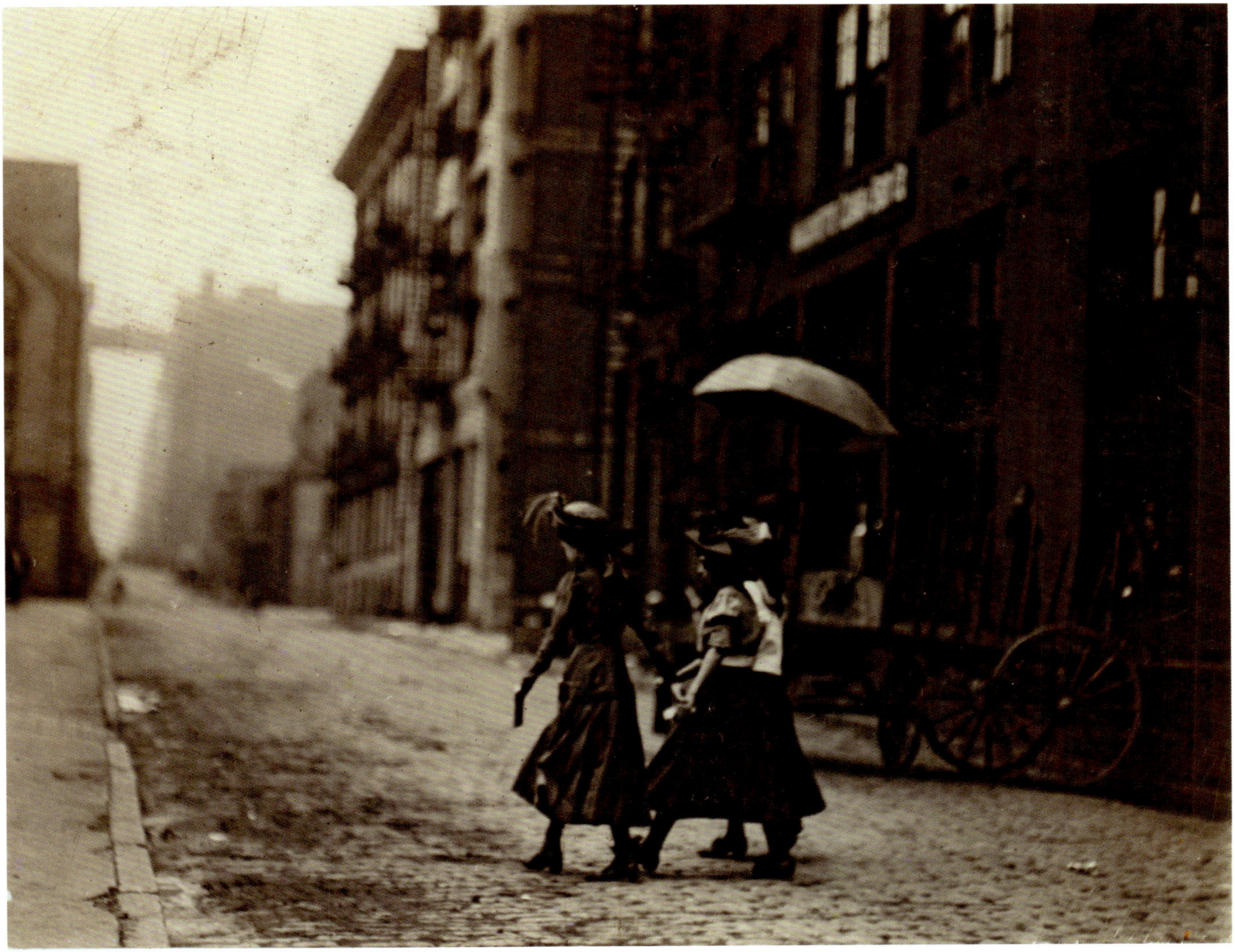

in America, where he made photographs in the days prior to the National Conference of Charities and Corrections held there that May. One of his photographs shows three girls walking across a deserted downtown street at noon, leaving work for lunch (fig. 60). No other soul occupies the scene, save maybe a distant pedestrian on the sidewalk at far left, a blotted bicyclist on the street farther in the distance, and a man or two standing dark against the bricks at right.

Fig. 60
3 girls working in Salvan Medicine Factory and in a Seed store. Olive near 14th St. Noon, May 12th, 1910. St. Louis, Missouri.

In this blank world the girls measure their steps. The one on the left, the leader of the group—the most forward—takes the middle girl by the hand and

Fig. 61
"If You Had But Three Days to Live," *St. Louis Post-Dispatch*, May 15, 1910.

advances with purpose, her left arm swinging, but also with caution. She looks down and steps gingerly, careful not to catch her high-heeled boots on the cobblestones. The empty street tilts up, and on this upward wayward path the girls are exposed. The large pale canopy above two of them is not really a parasol, as a casual glance might suggest, but part of the cart parked a few yards up the road. The girls go without coverage, save their plumed hats, sallying forth to walk the streets with too much independence, too much uncertainty.

If you had asked them, the girls would have told you the end of their world was in the air. Hine took the photograph on May 12, six days before the closest approach to earth of Halley's Comet—visible in the heavens that month for the first time since 1836. The comet's tail would pass across the earth on May 18, and because the tail contains traces of cyanide, some people thought that it would destroy life on earth. "If You Had But 3 Days to Live," asked a *St. Louis Post-Dispatch* headline on May 15 accompanied by a cartoon of the comet striking the earth and a reproduction of Adolf Hirémy-Hirschl's apocalyptic blockbuster painting *The Souls of Acheron*, which the paper called *The River of Death* (figs. 61–62). The headline subheading calmed the nerves, somewhat: "What would YOU do IF All the Old Superstitions Regarding Halley's Comet Were on the Verge of Being Fulfilled—Which, of Course, They Are Not!" And true, the world did not end—newspapers such as the *Post* said there was no danger—and, true, to judge by the news stories leading up to May 18, few people were especially concerned in the first place. When the comet made a feeble appearance in the evening sky on May 20, the delegates to the National Conference of Charities and Corrections took time out from the speeches to gaze at the vast fireball that two days earlier had brushed the earth with a harmless tail twenty million miles long.

Even so, the article of May 15 could not let the thrill of Apocalypse go, asking readers to envision a scene something like Hine's deserted street of May 12: "Can You Imagine What the Earth Would Be Like With Every Human Activity Stopped?—No Trade, No Gas, Electricity or Water, No Street Cars, No Newspapers—Nothing!" The disaster the girls walk through is not something that *has* happened but something that *will* happen. It is not a literal disaster, of course—the streets were certainly busy those days, to judge by other photographs Hine took then—but this one picture activates impending fatality like none of the others Hine took then and there. "Suppose—just for the sake of a very serious question—that the comet should slip its trolley this time," the *Post-Dispatch* asked,

pg. B5

IF YOU HAD BUT 3 DAYS TO LIVE

What Would YOU Do IF All the Old Superstitions Regarding Halley's Comet Were on the Verge of Being Fulfilled---Which, of Course, They Are Not!

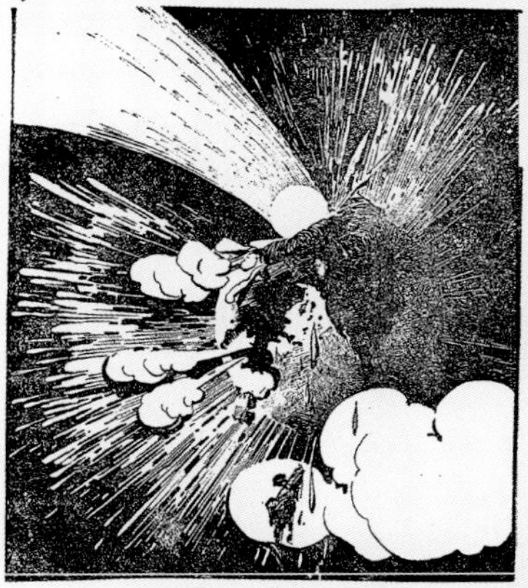

"The en[illegible] all had come."

Can You Imagine What the Earth Would Be Like With Every Human Activity Stopped?---No Trade, No Gas, Electricity or Water, No Street Cars, No Newspapers ---Nothing!

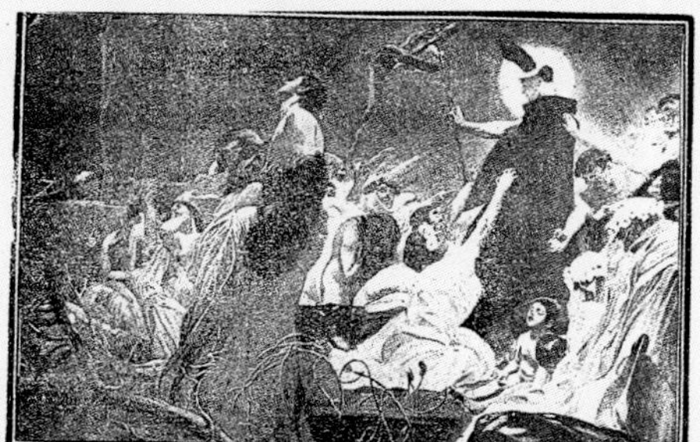

"THE RIVER OF DEATH"—from a painting by Adolph Hiremy Hirschl.

MAY the fifteenth! If the alarmists had struck it right, but three days would remain before this old earth would be knocked into smithereens by that gigantic mass of gas known familiarly as Halley's Comet! Three days—seventy-two hours, four thousand, three hundred and twenty fleeting minutes!

Of course, no sensible person believes that anything of the kind is going to happen. Halley's Comet is a big affair, goodness knows, with a head about 200,000 miles in diameter, and a tail some fifteen or twenty million miles long; and that same tail is going to sweep across the face of this earth during May 18, but the astronomers assure us it is quite harmless.

Yet, suppose their calculations should prove to be wrong and suppose the comet should slip out of the orbit so carefully laid down for it by the wise men of the telescopes, and bump against this unoffending planet?

Suppose—just for the sake of a very serious question—that the comet should slip its trolley this time, and, instead of sweeping peacefully over us, come into collision with us—suppose you knew for certain that this was going to happen, and completely gave yourself up to the event. In that case, between now and May 18, when the thing would happen, would you not be apt to be rather busy?

Whole Fear of the Comet Has Ruled.

THIS is not the only time in the history of our spinning old world when men have considered the end of all things. Only a few weeks ago, in Hungary, the population of many villages absolutely gave itself up to the belief that Halley's Comet was sure to strike our sphere and wipe everything out of existence. The people went mad, money was scattered in the streets, wine flowed literally like water, for the wine vats were broken open. There were days of hysterical wildness, and then—well, Hungary is still on the map!

In the Tenth Century the benighted people believed that the end of the world would come in the year 1000. Crops were neglected to such an extent that when the scare was finally over there was nothing for the people to eat, and a great famine ensued.

As this paper has already described in detail, every visit of Halley's Comet has caused a scare and, strangely enough, its every visit has been followed by some remarkable event.

Of course, we do not live in those benighted days, nor in the rural districts of Hungary. We are thinking, reasoning folk, yet if we were sure that the new appearance of the comet, with its gaseous tail, meant certain destruction for all of us, would we look on the matter with more coolness than did our forefathers?

Just what would you do? If you were absolutely certain that May 20, 1910, would never come?

How would you spend the last three days of your life, under such circumstances? Think well before you answer, because the situation is a little different from any that has ever confronted a human being. And the more you think of it the less foolish and more perplexing the question will become.

The first idea that strikes your mind is about like this: "I would take those three days in which to settle up all my affairs, arrange for the welfare of those I leave behind me, and prepare myself for the judgment to be mine."

That would be a good way to do, if things were not as they are. In the first place, what would be the good of settling your worldly affairs? With whom would you settle them? There wouldn't be anyone left on earth to settle them for or with, would there? As for your family, if everybody were to be destroyed, what would be the use of trying to provide for them? Your insurance would be worth exactly nothing, because there would not be anyone to pay it to, to say nothing of the fact that there wouldn't be any insurance company worth noticing after the comet and the earth had met!

The millionaire who may have squeezed his fortune out of the public may have such terrific remorse for his ill-spent life that he will decide to do all the good possible and to make all the amends in his power, during the 4,320 minutes of grace left him. What would be the use of all that? What good would it do the public to give it back any of its rightful own? What could the public do with the money? There wouldn't be any public in three days.

No, there would be no use in that.

Well, then, why not enjoy oneself during the brief space left for fun? Eat, drink and be merry! Yes, but where, how? Could the St. Louisan, for example, expect that Faust's or McTague's will be open and that the cooks and waiters would be working very hard to supply his appetite? Hardly. They also have to prepare themselves for the end! Why should they work? For pay. What's the use of pay? And the theaters! Imagine actors and actresses trying to be interesting and amusing for the sake of a crowd that is going to be wiped out of existence in a few hours! The managers, too, and the ticket speculators would probably have deserted the playhouses by the time you could get to your seats. No, the theaters would be closed tight; or, more likely, left open for any one to enter. Certainly there would be mighty little entertainment within the walls.

Of course, you could eat and drink free of charge in other places, because the merchants would surely leave their stores open and allow the public to enjoy itself free of all charge on wines, liquors and fancy groceries. The Meat Trust would no longer hold up prices, for there would be no use in that. The money would do nobody any good. You could eat all the chicken you wished and devour prime spring lamb for nothing. But your appetite would probably not amount to much.

Suppose you were one of those—of whom there probably would be few—who decided that there would be no danger and that you had as well go ahead with the ordinary routine of life. Would it be possible? That is not likely, for all the facilities and conveniences, particularly in the great cities, would be in a chaotic condition.

Suppose the employes at the water stations had deserted their posts? The water would be shut off and you would have none for drinking purposes, much less to cook with. This would also be true as to the gas and electric service. You would have neither gas nor electricity for lighting, cooking or heating. Night would be a time of utter darkness, no lights on the streets, none in the residences, offices, railway stations or elsewhere.

Telephone and telegraph service would probably be among the first abandoned were the end of the world actually regarded as imminent. You could not communicate with your family or friends if you were away from them, and if you were attempting to carry on your business affairs as usual you would realize once and for all what a tremendous part the telephone and telegraph plays in the modern world.

And it would be just as impossible to take up business on the basis that existed before the telephone and telegraph came into existence. Fancy attempting to get a messenger boy to do anything for you when such an important event as the end of the world was looming up just ahead of him! It's bad enough when there is a ball game or a circus.

Likewise, the mail service would be demolished completely and even if you could find anyone else who, like yourself, had decided to continue with his business affairs there would be no way of communicating with him. Banks, essential to modern business, would also be closed.

Another problem that would loom large with the end of the world supposedly in sight would be that of transportation. Perhaps, if you are the owner of an automobile, you have already had trouble in getting the use of it because of the proclivities of your chauffeur to go "joy riding," but that would be nothing in comparison to the eccentricities that autocratic individual would develop under the conditions here discussed. Recourse to the street cars would be impossible, for they would be out of commission. One can imagine them standing dead at intervals or in strings along the tracks where they had been deserted by their panic stricken crews. Railway traffic would similarly come to a standstill.

Newspapers would probably be among the last of the great modern businesses to succumb to the terror of the approaching crack of doom, for the organizations back of them remain intact through almost unimaginable calamities; but, aside from the contagion of panic they could not long survive the collapse of telegraph, telephone, light and power service.

Finally—for in considering this possible condition the mind's eye takes in every form of human activity—even the baseball games would be called off and if you had remained sane and stoical you could not even turn to that amusement and find it normal—although one can imagine a few fans gathering at the parks in the hope that a game might be called even in the face of a disruption of the universe.

As for license and debauchery among people whose sole desire is for such things, it would go unchecked, because there is little probability that the police would arrest anybody. Who would try their cases. The police and the jailers would be busy with their own affairs. No doubt heroes would be found to minister to the crazed populace. Such heroes always arise in any contingency; yet in this one it would seem bootless to exert charity or solace to people who were going to be wiped out of existence within a few hours. Probably, too, the sickest man or woman in a hospital would forget his pains and wounds and think only of his impending departure for the other world!

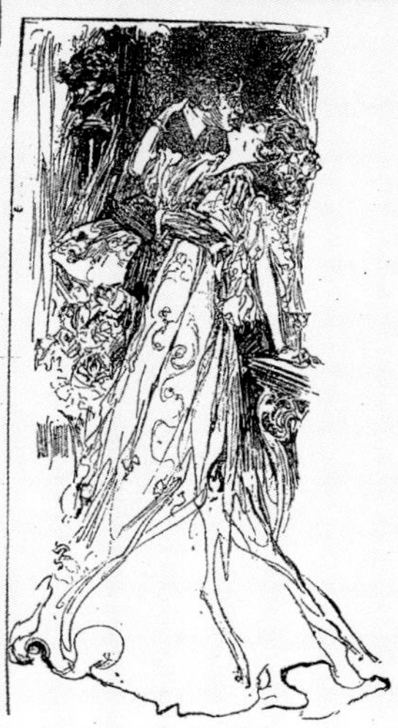

"For a last, fond embrace with a loved one."

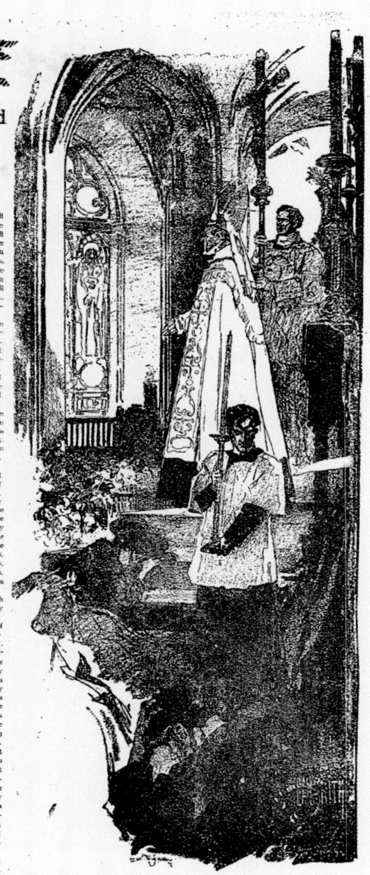

"Within the churches vast congregations of worshipers were on their knees praying to God on High."

It is absolutely certain that the churches everywhere would be crowded. The wretch sunk in deepest infamy would hardly dare neglect the opportunity to purge his soul under such conditions as would confront him. Millions of human beings would be on their knees offering prayers; millions more would be struggling to get into the houses of worship. It would be a wonderful scene of contrition! Prayers would ascend from hearts that had almost forgotten how to pray.

The ocean would present a strange sight with its great ships rushing to port as they had never rushed before, their passengers wild to reach home for a last embrace with the loved ones left on land. There would be riotous scenes at the docks, but unless the crews and officers happened to be on the side of the water away from their families no one could be found to man such ships as would be still in port and take them across the ocean.

Doubtless thousands of people would grow insane waiting for the terrible end of all things and would either run wildly at large or voluntarily end their useless lives.

You can imagine everything happening to any one else. There is no limit to speculation in that quarter. But how about yourself? Can you imagine what you would do? Most people cannot, for it is a matter beyond the self-knowledge of the human mind. You might sit down and plan, calmly, just how you think you would spend those precious minutes, but when you think it over more leisurely, does not almost anything that you could do seem almost useless?

Human endeavor is always measured by results and consequences. What could you do that would make for better conditions when no mortal was to be left to judge of your actions? It's a hard thing to think about! In all probability the world would first rush to ask forgiveness for its sins. But it could not confine itself to prayer and confession. Before the fatal three days were up the people would be forced to other thoughts. Unchecked hilarity, of a nervous, irresponsible character, would follow: moments of depression would be followed by moments of reckless gayety. Fear would be followed by happiness that all was soon to be over.

And then—when the last moments came! When the heat and light and noise of the rushing comet betokened the quick dissolution of everything, everybody earthly—Ah, well! It's something that we ought to be mighty glad is not going to occur, unless—unless the astronomers are all wrong and Halley's Comet is swinging in an orbit that they haven't reckoned correctly!

Then—but let us not worry! Let us go on and do just as we have been doing—and perhaps a little better—fully believing that we shall pass through the gaseous tail without knowing it, and shall wake up on the nineteenth of May as well as when we went to bed on the previous night. And the Sunday Post-Dispatch will be published next Sunday, as usual!

In the meantime keep your eyes on the skies, because they are going to be a wonderful sight!

Fig. 62
Adolf Hirémy-Hirschl, *The Souls of Acheron*, 1898.

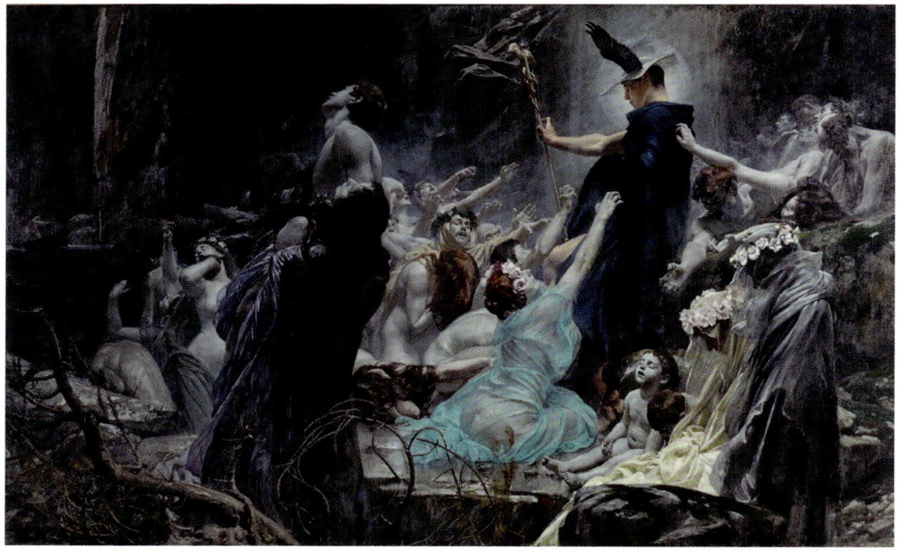

"and, instead of sweeping peacefully over us—come into collision with us?" There would be no actual trolley traffic in the days before Armageddon—"Recourse to the street cars would be impossible, for they would be out of commission . . . standing dead at intervals or in strings along the tracks where they had been deserted by their panic stricken crews." The crack of doom would be a cosmic traffic accident (fig. 63).

That was fun, but more serious was the chance to gain a heightened appreciation of everyday life—an opportunity to reflect on ordinary days as if they were your last or near to last: "If You Had But 3 Days to Live." Hine seems to have reflected on this same idea when he was in St. Louis, except from a grimmer perspective, as if the comet's light revealed how threadbare and pathetic and corrupt has been the daily life it would extinguish.

Take for example his photograph of a little boy standing outside Havlin's Theatre, at Sixth and Walnut, some eight blocks from the location of the girls walking across the street (fig. 64). The advertisements for Beulah Poynter in *Little Lord Fauntleroy*, emphasizing the matinee on Sunday, May 8, indicate that the photograph was taken early in the month, well prior to May 14, when the show closed. Hine's avowed purpose is to let us see how newsboys like this one waste their money on cheap and crude entertainments. Staged, the photograph lacks the dynamic spontaneity of his more elastic and comely depictions of space and place,

Fig. 63
"If You Had But Three Days to Live" (detail).

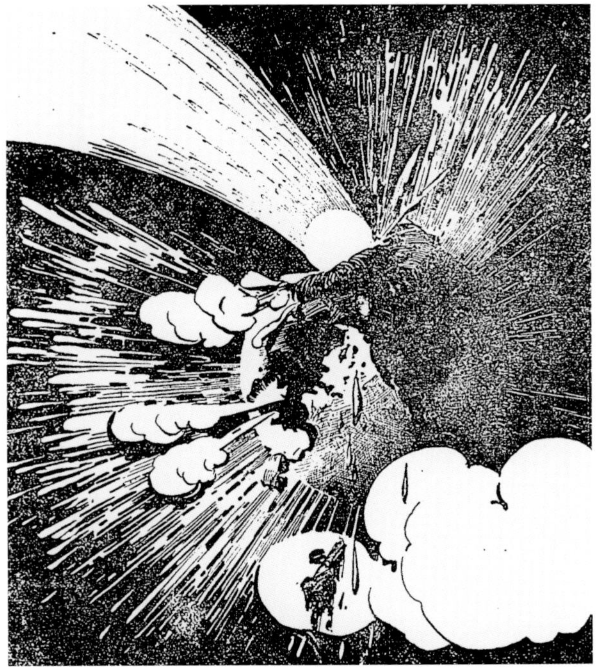

as if the clear moral had itself flattened it. But the meagerness of the everyday runs deeper than that. The loud call of the advertisements—the cheap and florid blandishments to come one, come all—invite a sense of the thinness of the daily thrills that beckon not just the little boy but all of us. If we had but three days to live would we go to see Beulah Poynter in *Little Lord Fauntleroy*? We congratulate ourselves that we would not. But maybe we would.

Maybe there was not much more than this unseemly parade of the everyday, where everything and everyone had a price. St. Louis exuded that feeling. Corrupt politicians had "sold the city," wrote the muckraking journalist Lincoln Steffens about St. Louis in *McClure's* in 1902. The crooks retailed "its streets, its wharves, its markets, and all that it had—to the now greedy businessmen and bribers." The visitor to St. Louis—such as Hine was to become eight years later—"sees poorly paved, refuse-burdened streets, and dusty or mud-covered alleys. . . . he turns a tap in the hotel, to see liquid mud flow into wash-basin or bath-tub." The city was filthy, down to the last cobblestone and the last moment, Havlin's no exception. In September 1910, four months after Hine took his photograph, the theater's manager was arrested, charged with having embezzled $27,840 from the box office

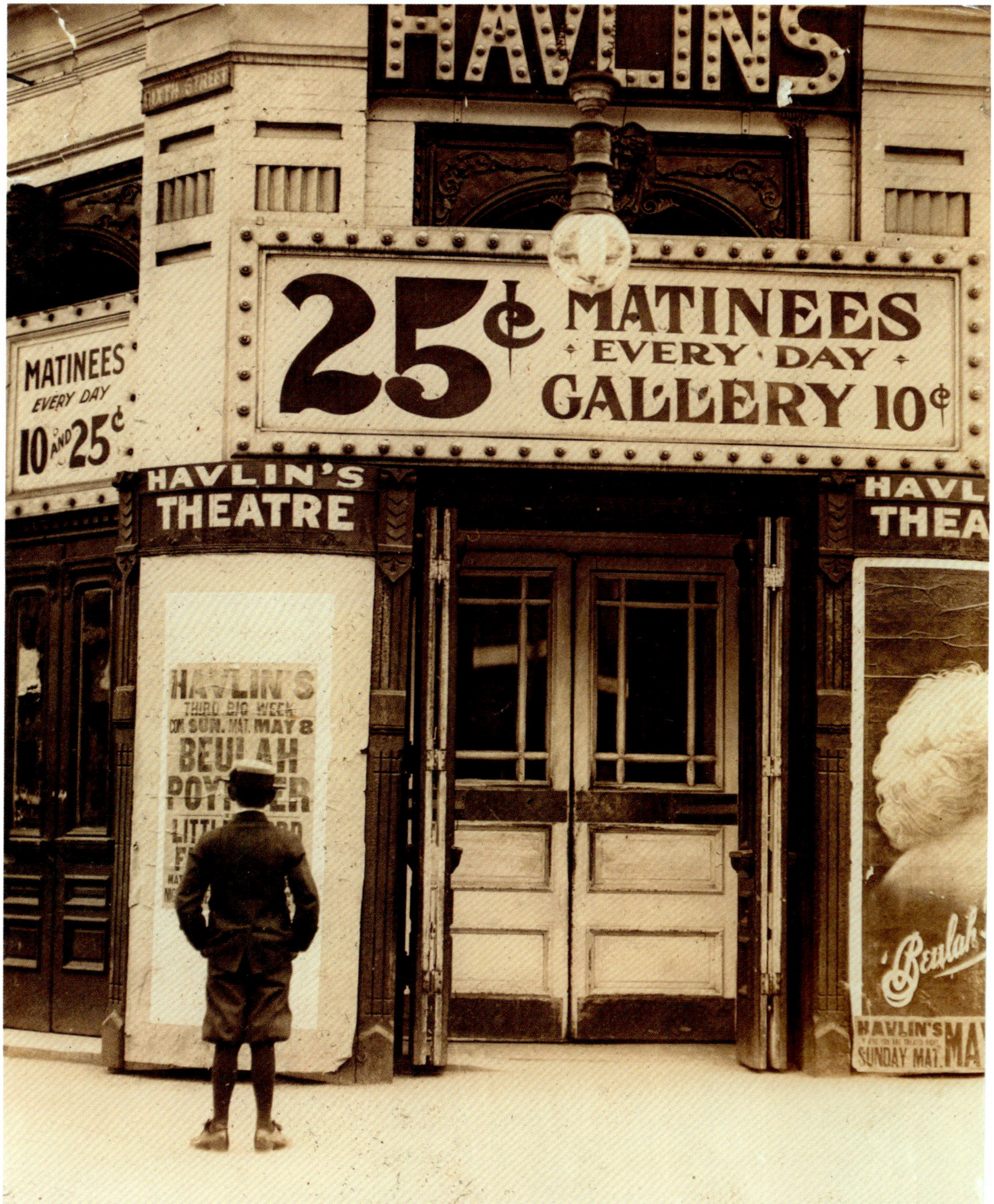
HAVLIN'S
25¢ MATINEES
EVERY DAY
GALLERY 10¢
MATINEES
EVERY DAY
10 AND 25¢
HAVLIN'S
THEATRE
HAVLIN'S
THIRD BIG WEEK
COM. SUN. MAT. MAY 8
BEULAH
HAVLIN'S
SUNDAY MAT.

in a long-term scam. Hine's boy, standing like Hine standing at the boy's back, doubles Hine's own pious incredulity before the wall-to-wall urgency of the daily, the forgettable—the expendable.

The ephemerality of daily life in the photograph makes it ominous. Havlin's would be razed in 1924 to make way for a parking garage, the solid walls and heavy timbers of the interior making it an especially hazardous destruction. The solid structure betokened the seriousness of the "heavy melodrama" that played there, as the newspaper called it—the downward drop of deep emotion that uplifted scores of patrons who climbed the steep stairs just behind the doors in Hine's photograph. But the ups and downs of the palace were no stay against the leveling disaster of time. And Hine's photograph, not knowing this specific fate, is well attuned to the wrecking ball, cosmic and otherwise. The theater, outside of show times, betrays the emptiness that haunts it at all hours. The comet will not destroy civilization. Beulah Poynter will continue in another role the following week, during and after the comet passes. But what the photograph makes clear is that had the comet come it would have found so little to destroy.

So little—yet something. Just prior to their walk across Olive Street, Hine took two other photographs of the same three girls. In the first, they stand outside a door in their shop-girl attire, two of them smiling back at Hine while the third, wearing a white sailor-like shirt with an enormous bow, shyly looks elsewhere (fig. 65). In the second, the girls turn the corner of Fourteenth Street onto Olive, the two more confident ones in lockstep, one of them still smiling back at Hine, while the other girl—tottering as if unsure on her high heels—extends her thin arms in balance as her skirt sways (fig. 66). In a moment they set sail on the long street in the photograph we have already seen. The trilogy of photographs (figs. 60, 65, 66) marks a departure—a taking leave.

What is lost is delicate. The feather hats and flounce make the girls a kind of exotica, a flower or butterfly that the photographer has happened to spy. He would save them but he is more attuned to how they will get away. To how they *must* get away. In fact this escape is exactly what he lays in wait for. And part of the process—part of what he must show—is that the children he will watch disappear must be invested with the souls it will be such a shame to lose. Who knows if the first two photographs of the girls preparing to make their way accomplish that soulfulness. I have seen better of Hine's pictures for doing that. But he has wanted to look at them—to give *us* a look at them—on the chance that before

Fig. 64
Where the boys spend their money. St. Louis, Missouri.

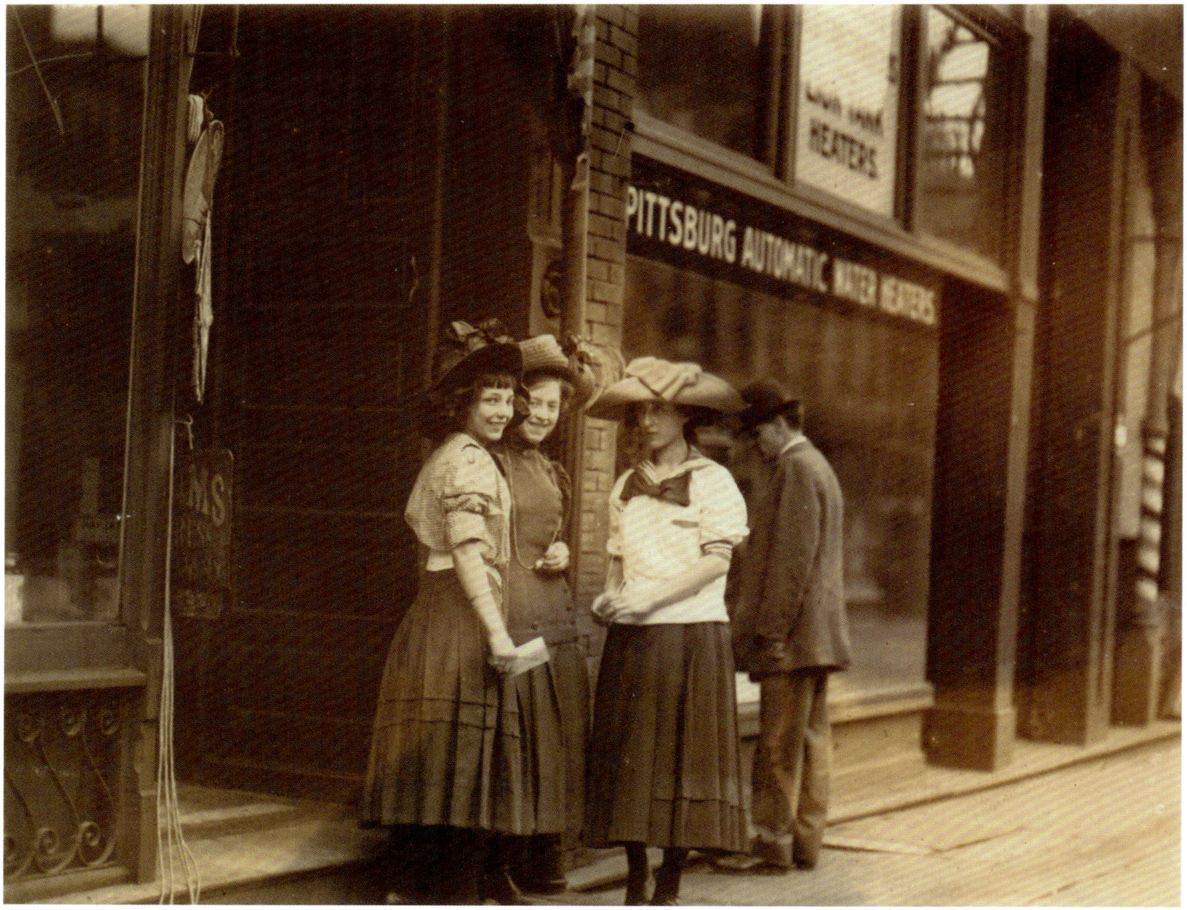

Fig. 65
3 girls working in Salvan Medicine Factory and in a Seed Store. Olive near 14th St. Noon, May 12th, 1910. St. Louis, Missouri.

they are gone they will window forth some glimmer of what's to be lost. You could even say he gives them every chance, and that hungrily, greedily, he watches them for the revelation of this inner life that will make their leave-taking a melodrama of the streets far greater than anything in the theater. We may all be damned, and the voyage out may be a setting-sail from which no one no matter the cuteness of their admiral's hat will survive. But a butterfly collection of curled hair and smiling glances becomes a proof that something precious really was lost. Pity that the photographer, the soulmaker, knew the fates of the figures he led into his trap of letting them escape. Pity that releasing them into the great long track of time, their souls safely extracted, he could parade them before our eyes as evidence that the

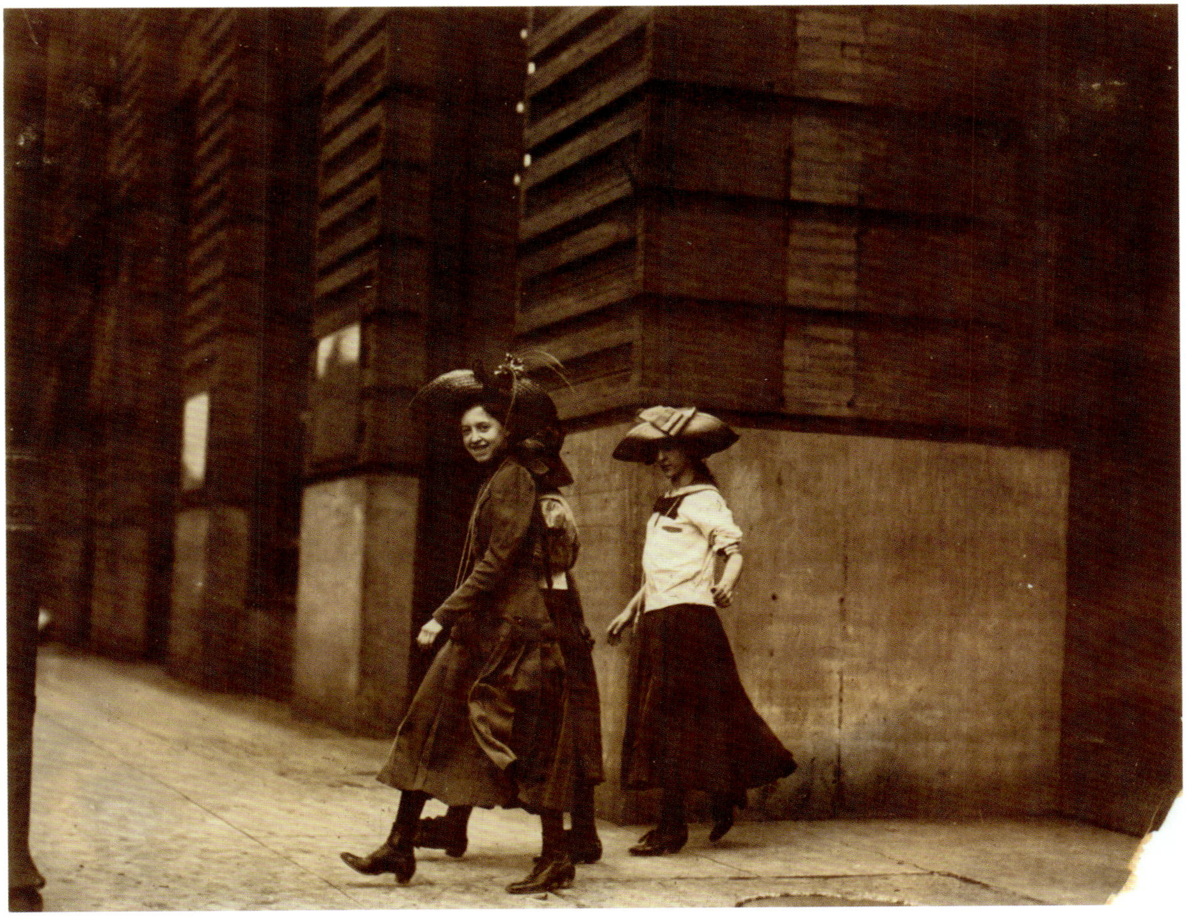

Fig. 66
3 girls working in Salvan Medicine Factory and in Seed store. Olive near 14th St. Noon, May 12th, 1910. St. Louis, Missouri.

end-world of cobblestone streets really did, once upon a time, hold something rare and beautiful.

Not that Hine's portrayals of time in American locations are always so empty and sad. On the contrary, he could show how ornately Americans of his era filled the hours and the minutes. A photograph he made outside the American Tobacco Company in Danville, Virginia, one morning in June 1911, shows seven women, six white and one black, walking down a sidewalk while a man sits on the curb looking at Hine and a little girl enters the factory (fig. 67). It is 6:45 a.m. and they are on their way to work. The sprightly march of the figures marks the procession of the time.

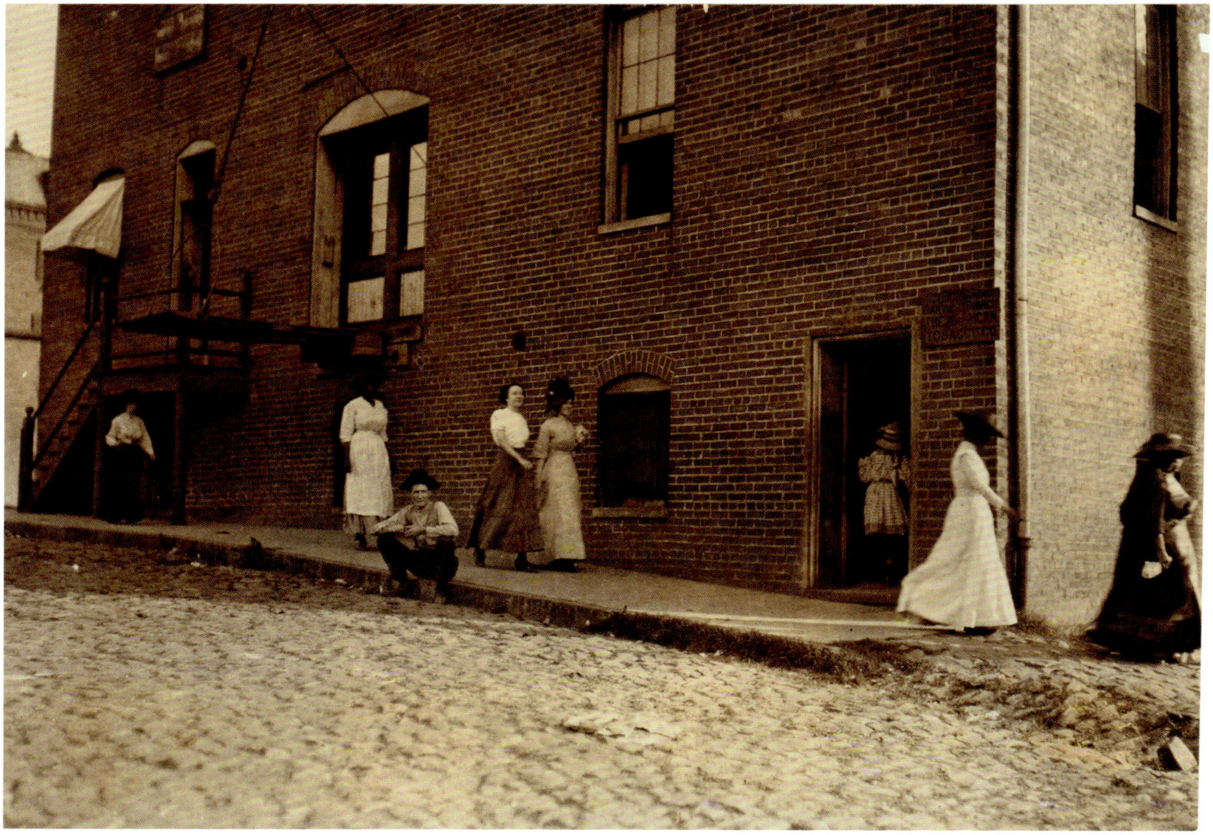

Fig. 67
One of the very little girls (going through door) that roll cigarettes in the Danville (Va.) Cigarette Factory. See other photos at noon. Taken at 6:45 A.M. Danville, Virginia. June 1911.

That's because the factory becomes a clock. In 1895 in Oshkosh the cabinetmaker Mathias Kitz completed the Apostles Clock, a large wooden timepiece in which, on the hour, Jesus appears from a central portal and the twelve apostles parade past him, emerging from an open door on the left before disappearing through another door on the right (fig. 68). Judas, the last in line, will turn away from Jesus instead of bowing to him as the other ones have done.

Kitz and Hine both portray the period's rituals of time, a religion of work that Max Weber, who visited America in 1904, would have appreciated. A strolling robed dignity structures the hours, investing the times of day with intimations and even outright declarations of piety and disciplined work. Kitz fashioned the apostles' revolving platform from a circular saw, the regimes of labor and apostolic goodness one and the same there in lumbering Oshkosh. In Hine's photograph even the repose of the lank old man seated on the curb is alert—he is early, mind-

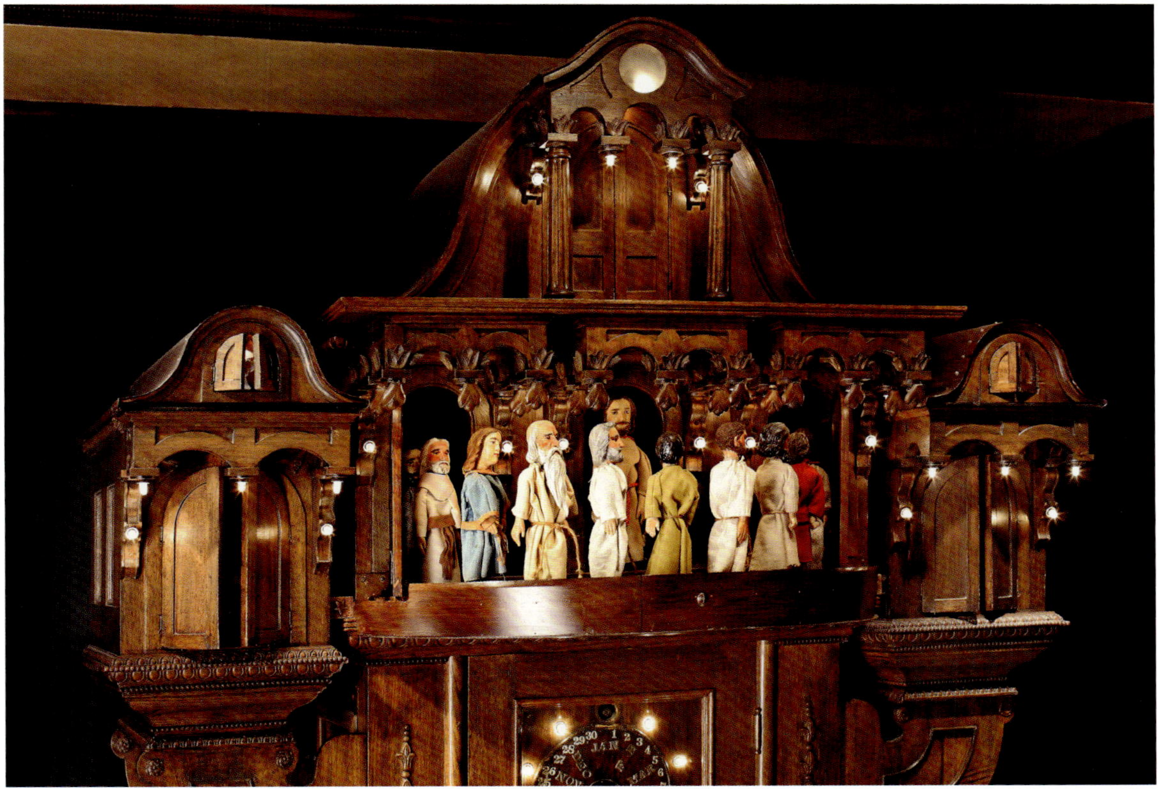

Fig. 68
Mathias Kitz, Apostles Clock, 1895.

ful of the livelong day, like the photographer he stares at. Meanwhile, the little girl enters the factory door like clockwork.

A few minutes later or earlier the factory clock has changed (fig. 69). Now the lank old man in the slouched hat looks to the right and a black man sits in a grilled window mostly obscured in the other picture by the walking black woman. A girl in a light plaid dress is about to enter the factory door, following a woman in white who steps the one step up into the darkened interior, just behind another long-skirted woman. Two girls emerge above at the open window level with the loading dock, staring happily at Hine.

The factory is a timepiece that tolls its own time, an edifice as elaborate and pious as Kitz's woodwork, all bells and whistles. In its motley assortment of windows and doors, figures appear and disappear. At the quitting hour, the peculiar Danville clock looks different yet again, as if there were a moment in the day when the apostles, freed from their daily round, could step outside and smoke one of the

Fig. 69
Going to work in Cigarette Factory. Danville, Virginia. June 1911.

Fig. 70 (opposite)
When the whistle blows. Closing hour at the Danville (Va.) Cigarette Factory. Danville, Virginia. June 1911.

Fig. 71 (opposite)
Noon hour, Quidwick Mill, Anthony, R.I. Anthony, Rhode Island. April 1909.

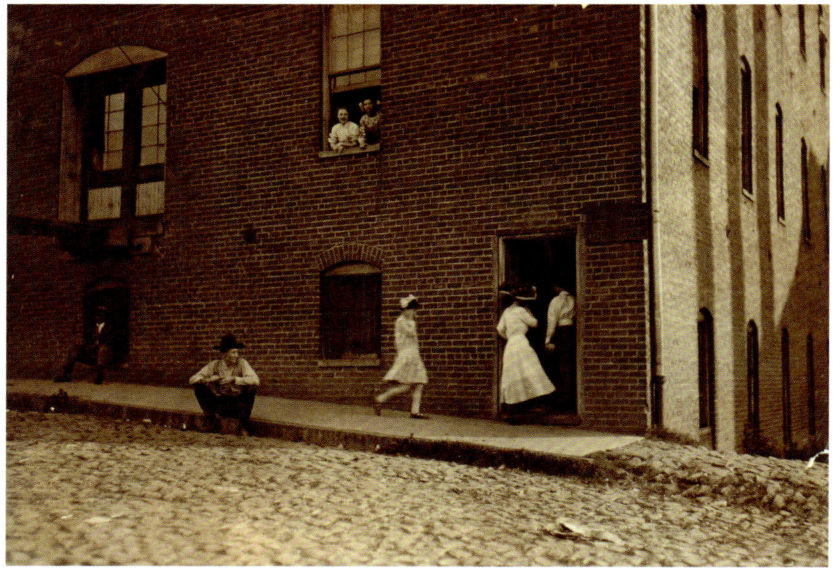

cigarettes they have been making all day (fig. 70). Every moment is different, and presence is grace, even a little girl named Grace.

Hine, like Kitz, marked time. At Quidwick Mill, in Anthony, Rhode Island, the workers emerge like clockwork from the darkened mill interior, each one neatly rendered by Hine (fig. 71). The time is noon on a day in April 1909. The swish of the woman's skirt, the conversation of the man and boy at center, the person at the picket railing on the second-floor balcony, the three little boys dispersing to the right—every figure is customized in fascinating detail. The precious ritual of time would be a blur unless each apostle of the hour is a figure to remember. The grooved track of their noonday custom is so lifelike that part of the pleasure is to look in vain for the mechanism guiding their remarkably individualized gaits and postures.

Hine's camera was a clock, but he did not slice the instants like a factory manager would. Instead, his shivering of time implies that the moment, if shown lavishly, does not freeze but disperses to a thousand incidents, each flowing away from the others, fluid and mysterious. Only the most remarkable clockmaker could give that moment not just a note of joy but of pagan eeriness, as of some garlanded ceremony that even he who fashions the figures cannot pretend to understand.

Out of the trite and the ordinary and the forgettable, the dross of the everyday, Hine made ceremonies of the hours as extravagant as rites of spring.

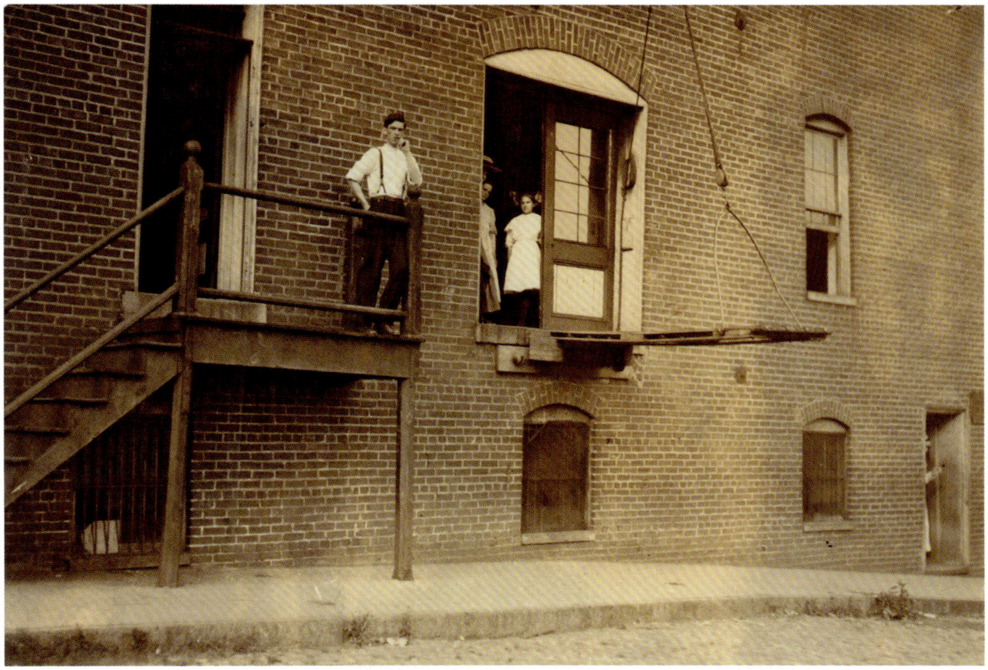

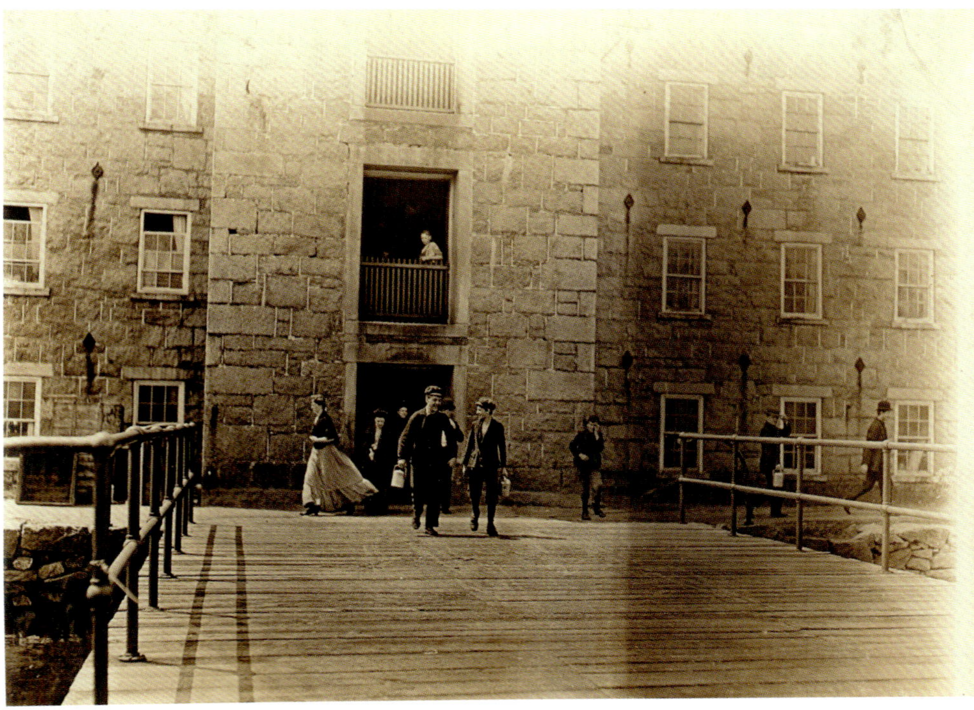

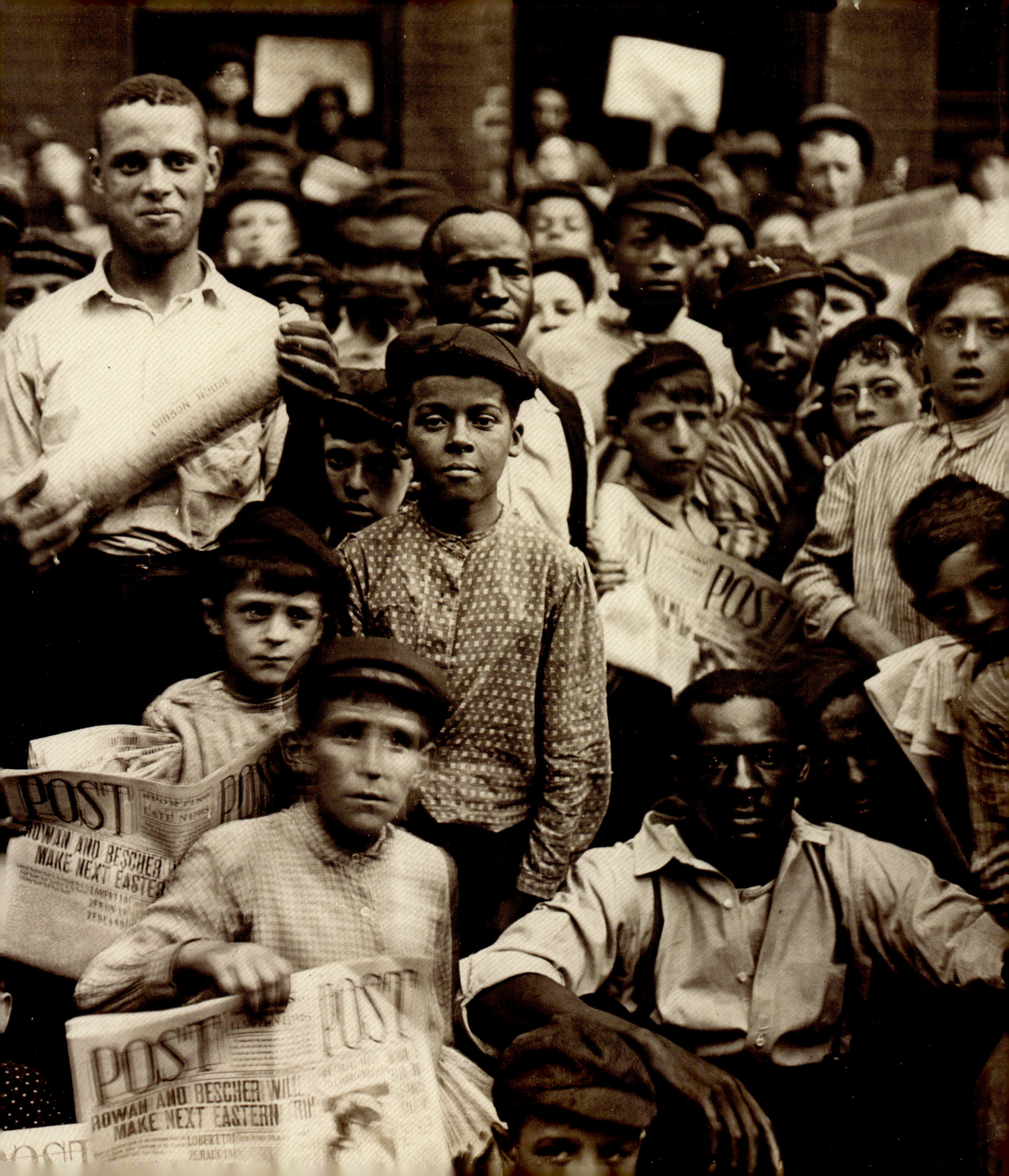

POST
ROWAN AND BESCHER
MAKE NEXT EASTER
POST
ROWAN AND BESCHER WILL
MAKE NEXT EASTERN
POST

4 PUT THE HEADLINES TO BED

Newsboys and supply men wait outside for the "base-ball edition" outside the *Cincinnati Post* in Hine's photograph of August 1908 (fig. 72). Three white boys at the front hold up the creased front page while a dark-skinned black man sits next to them at lower right, elbows extended to create room around himself. A lighter-skinned black boy in a workman's cap appears over that man's right shoulder and between the *L* of these two figures—seated man and standing capped boy—a group of boys, some black, some white, sweeps back in a bobble of craning necks to a far brick wall, where more newsies at window and door hold up the paper, the front page blank at that distance.

Back to the foreground and over to the left a wedge of white-shirted black men stands out. One at the far left holds a fan of newspapers at his waist while next to him, slightly farther back, a darker-skinned man appears to push back a little white boy, his face scrunched, who tries to squeeze between him and the man with the fan of papers. Two more black men in caps look on from slightly farther back, until the wedge of these supply men culminates in the striking strong forthright appearance of a lighter-skinned man, square to the camera, who holds a folded newspaper crosswise against his chest, cupping both ends of the tube in his large hands. Next to him, just behind the black boy in the cap, a much shorter and darker-skinned black man looks glumly back at Hine. Behind him an out-of-focus black figure swivels a twisting double-featured Siamese-twin head like a Picasso mask.

The photograph intimates violence. It is a raucous scene, halfway between pose and push. Most everyone crowds to the camera, keen to be included in the photograph, one of the first Hine took for the National Child Labor Committee—number three in the more than 5,300 photographs he ended up taking over the next ten years. "The boys get rough treatment from the negro supply men,"

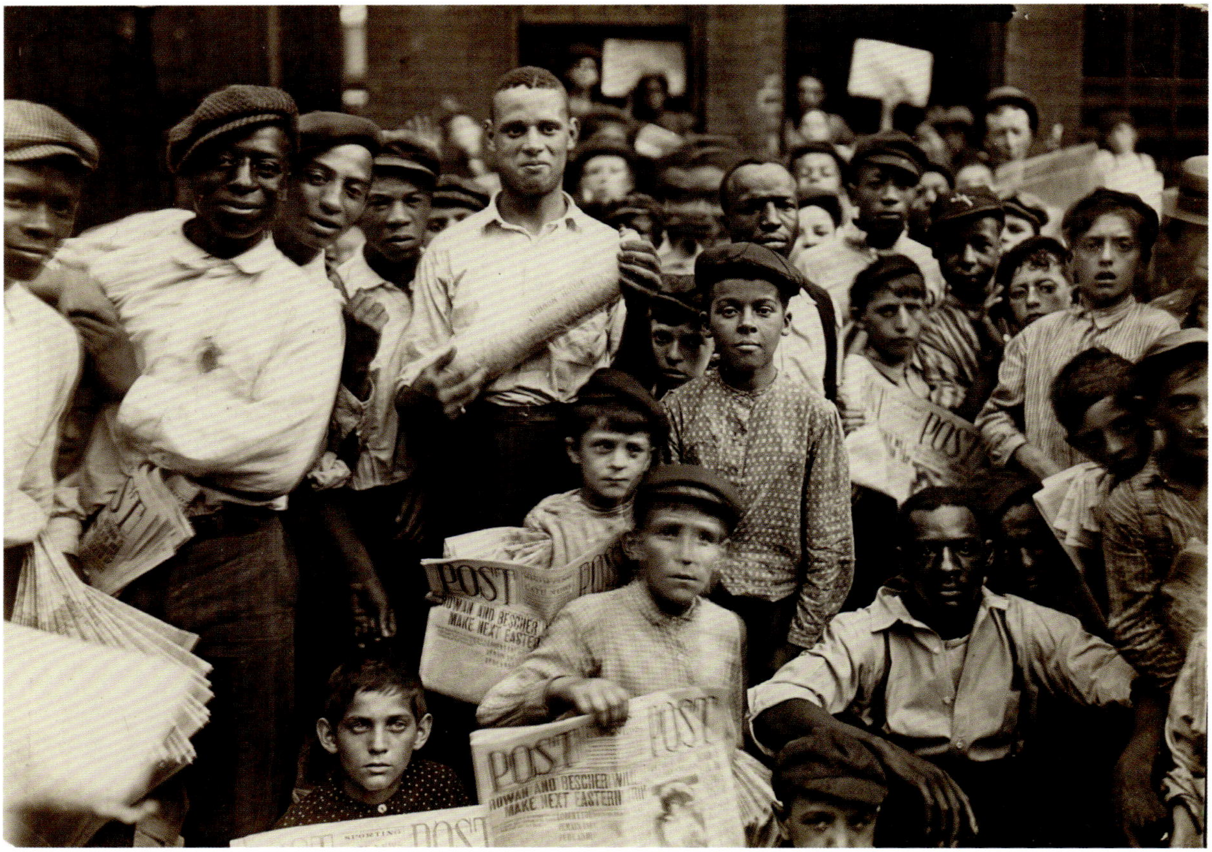

Fig. 72
Newsboys and supply men waiting at newspaper office for base-ball edition, 5 P.M. The boys get rough treatment from the negro supply men. The short negro without a hat is a pugilist. Cincinnati, Ohio. August 1908.

Hine and his witness, Edward N. Clopper, note in their brief written description pasted to the back of the picture. Here they single out the glum man: "The short negro without a hat is a pugilist."

The physical contact between the boys and men implies other kinds of violence. "The great majority of the supply men employed to wholesale the papers to the newsboys have criminal records of considerable length, while the character of their crimes makes them unfit for contract with young children," wrote Maurice B. Hexter in a 1919 report, "The Newsboys of Cincinnati." "Affidavits have been made proving that negro and other supply men have practiced on newsboys vile and perverted sex offenses."

Hexter, the superintendent of the United Jewish Charities and a former newsboy in the city, continues, "The supply men, for the most part, have a boy they favor beyond all others. The little newsboys have such precocious knowledge of

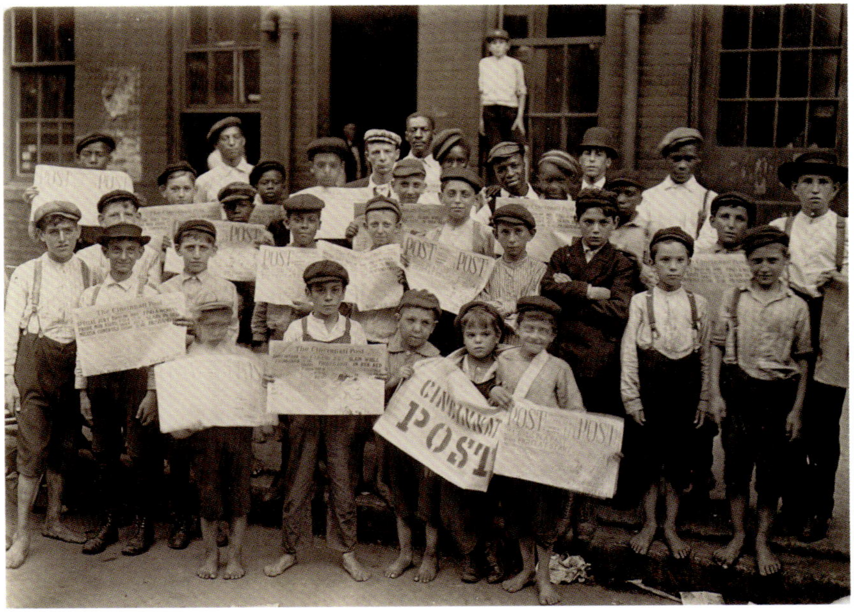

Fig. 73
A Group of Newsboys waiting at the newspaper office for the base-ball edition, 5 P.M. Cincinnati, Ohio. August 1908.

these affairs that they usually call such boys 'punks' (private property for immoral practices). The investigator on several different days saw one of the supply men take a white boy into the brothel on Longworth Street near Plum Street and remain within the house for about twenty minutes." Hexter goes on, "One affidavit is from a thirteen year old boy who testifies that he with other young boys were subjected to indecencies by the supply men and a man high up in the street circulation department of one of the papers. He further states that when he remonstrated he was slapped in the face by one of the negro toughs." The report cites another affidavit, "Supply men favor such boys who permit these liberties and . . . the circulation manager of one of the papers favors particularly the fat boys whom it is his custom to embrace." We look again at the boy squeezed between two men, a hand on his head.

What headlines do the boys hawk? It is difficult to read all the front-page headlines, but in a more orderly photograph Hine took at the *Post* on August 17, 1908, the boy in overalls in the front row holds up a paper with the headline: "Army Officer Facing Chair" (fig. 73). The story concerns Captain Peter C. Hains Jr., charged with shooting magazine writer William E. Annis to death at the Bayside Yacht Club in Bayside, Queens, as Annis's wife and children "and a group of fashionable clubmen" looked on. Hains had come home from his regiment in the

Fig. 74
Cincinnati Post, August 17, 1908.

Philippines, summoned by his brother Thornton, who reported that Annis, his brother's former friend, had been having an affair with his wife. Hains had filed divorce papers naming Annis "as the despoiler of his home" before killing the man, shooting Annis eight times as he disembarked his yacht after winning a regatta. Thornton Hains, who stood by to make sure no one interfered with the murder, allegedly urged his brother to commit the crime. The article quotes Mrs. Hains, who offers this opinion of her husband and his brother: "I hope they string them both up. They wronged me. It is true I signed a confession to my husband and his brother that I had been intimate with Annis, but only after they had forced me to drink a lot of whisky and nearly starved me."

The front-page headlines that day offer more violence (fig. 74). Over in the right corner the headline reads: "Slain While In Her Bed," with the subhead, "Husband of Dead Woman Is Locked Up." The story describes how a Cincinnati woman was found "lying unconscious on the bed, her face mashed almost to a pulp and blood streaming from her nose and mouth." Her husband, asked why he did it, replied, "I don't want her lying around here drunk." In the center of the front page is another headline, "Grand Jury Probes Riot." The story describes how Illinois state militia had been given orders to shoot to kill following weekend violence in Springfield, "home of Abraham Lincoln," where an elderly black man named William Dunnigan had been "dragged from his home Saturday night and hanged to a tree by a mob." A cartoon on the front page—under the heading, "Now wouldn't it make you peevish?"—shows a large man with "an iron jaw, protruding chest, and vise like grip" pursuing a fearful smaller man. A vignette below shows the same large man running over another pedestrian with a steamroller.

Violence was on Hine's mind in August 1908, his first month on the job for the National Child Labor Committee. Endangerment—from fistfighting to murder—might be the best way to show the plight of child laborers. Pictures of accident victims would turn out to be comparatively rare in the thousands of photographs Hine took for the NCLC, but at the start he saw violence. One of the photographs he made in his first two months shows Lawrence Hill, who "had 4 fingers mashed off by a stamping machine in [a] lamp factory" (fig. 75).

Hill, photographed at home, dressed up for the occasion in a plaid suit and polka-dot tie, stares coldly back at the photographer. Darkly handsome, he is backed into a corner, his chair pushed in front of a door. The spatial awkwardness resembles the arrangement of his emotions. Hill's white-bandaged club hand

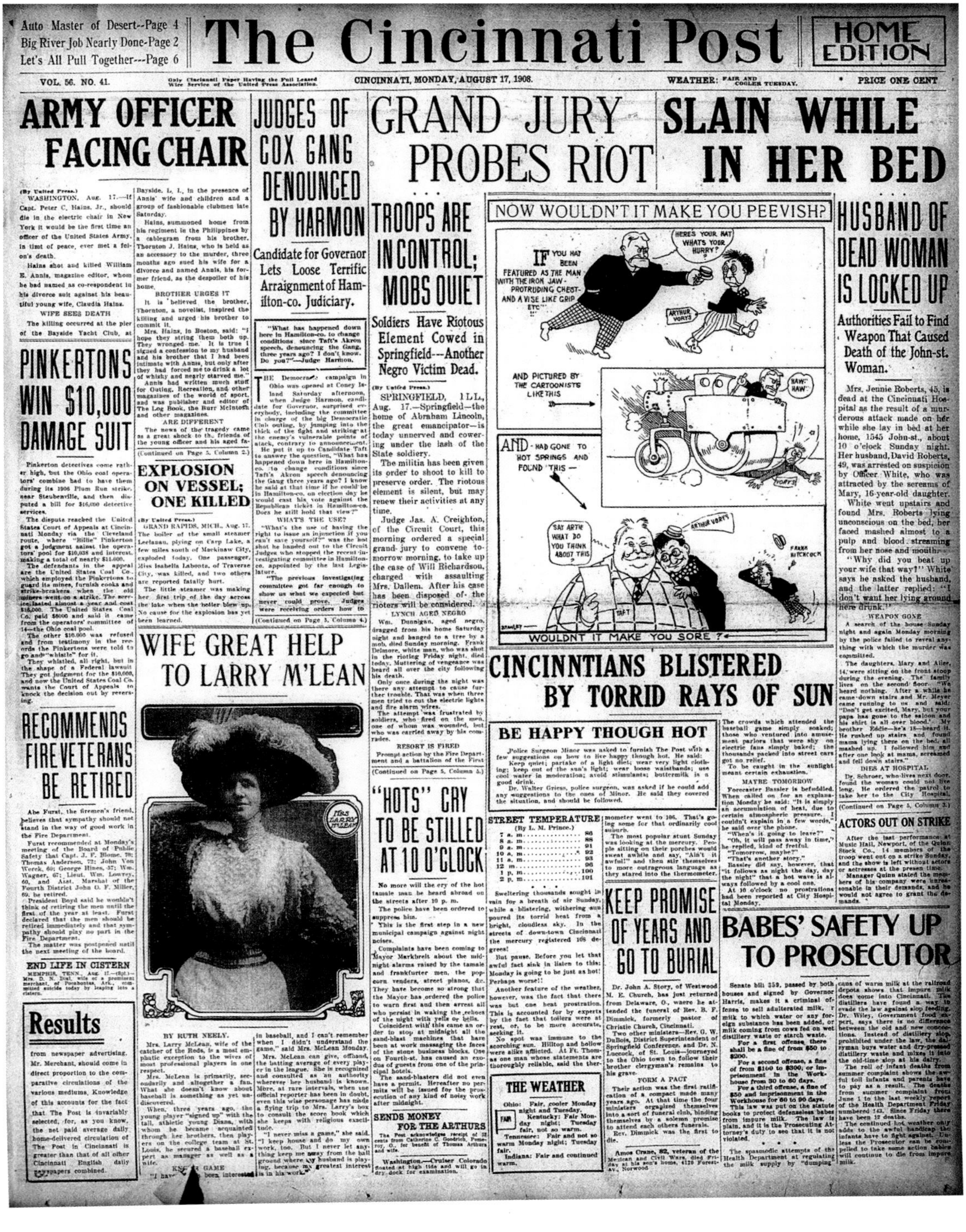

Auto Master of Desert--Page 4
Big River Job Nearly Done-Page 2
Let's All Pull Together---Page 6

The Cincinnati Post

HOME EDITION

VOL. 56. NO. 41. CINCINNATI, MONDAY, AUGUST 17, 1908. WEATHER: FAIR AND COOLER TUESDAY. PRICE ONE CENT

ARMY OFFICER FACING CHAIR

JUDGES OF COX GANG DENOUNCED BY HARMON

Candidate for Governor Lets Loose Terrific Arraignment of Hamilton-co. Judiciary.

GRAND JURY PROBES RIOT

TROOPS ARE IN CONTROL; MOBS QUIET

Soldiers Have Riotous Element Cowed in Springfield---Another Negro Victim Dead.

SLAIN WHILE IN HER BED

HUSBAND OF DEAD WOMAN IS LOCKED UP

Authorities Fail to Find Weapon That Caused Death of the John-st. Woman.

NOW WOULDN'T IT MAKE YOU PEEVISH?

WOULDN'T IT MAKE YOU SORE ?

PINKERTONS WIN $10,000 DAMAGE SUIT

EXPLOSION ON VESSEL; ONE KILLED

RECOMMENDS FIRE VETERANS BE RETIRED

WIFE GREAT HELP TO LARRY M'LEAN

BY RUTH NEELY.

"HOTS" CRY TO BE STILLED AT 10 O'CLOCK

CINCINNTIANS BLISTERED BY TORRID RAYS OF SUN

BE HAPPY THOUGH HOT

STREET TEMPERATURE

KEEP PROMISE OF YEARS AND GO TO BURIAL

BABES' SAFETY UP TO PROSECUTOR

ACTORS OUT ON STRIKE

THE WEATHER

SENDS MONEY FOR THE ARTHURS

END LIFE IN CISTERN

Results

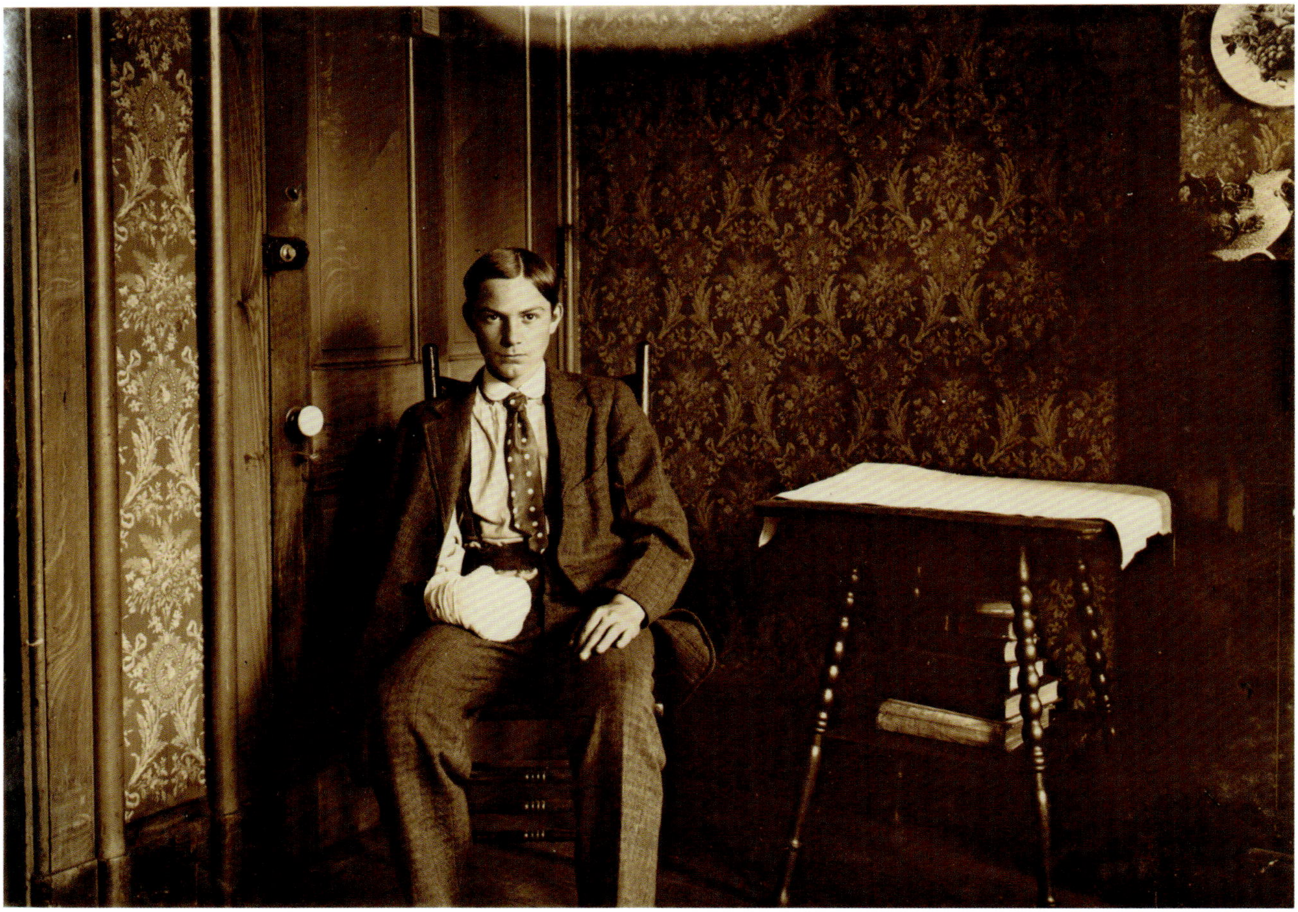

Fig. 75
Lawrence J. Hill—1125 Walnut St. 17 yrs. old March 1908. Had 4 fingers mashed off by stamping machine in lamp factory. August 1908.

suggests the white doorknob the hand cannot open. His eyes are like the keyhole. The only voyeurism he contemplates is a detailed inspection of his private thoughts, the injury of his forced seclusion, and now his coat-and-tie submission to the photographer.

Meanwhile, the cheap wooden end table to the right, a pyramid of books placed on its lower shelf, assumes a visual importance equal to Hill's own. Wearing what mother tells him to wear, posing for his photograph in front of the patterned wallpaper, stump-fingered Hill looks not only ill at ease but a fit subject to contemplate revenge. Depending on whether you wish to track the picture historically backward or forward, he sports either the baby-faced resentment of a Lincoln conspirator or the taciturn rage of a bootlegging gangster.

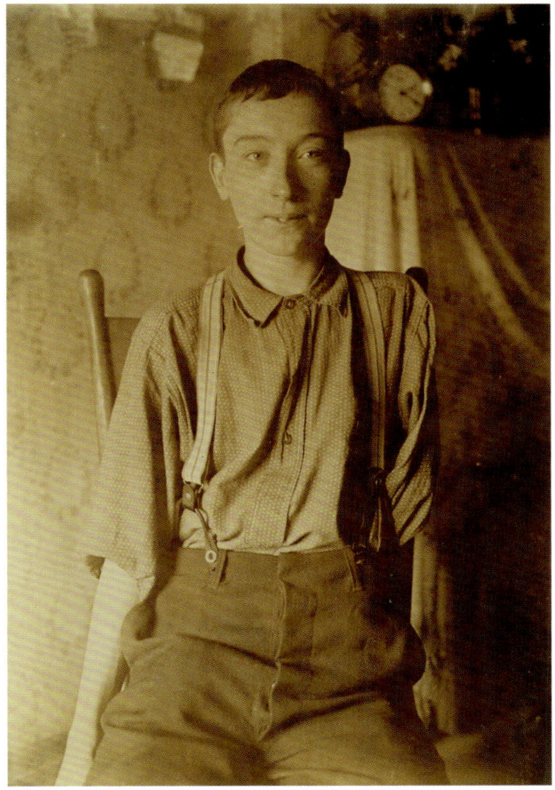

Fig. 76
Harry McShane—134 B'way-Cin. O.—16 yrs. of age on June 29, 1908. Had his left arm pulled off near shoulder, and right leg broken through kneecap, by being caught on belt of a machine in Spring factory in May 1908. Had been working in factory more than 2 yrs. Was on his feet for first time after the accident, the day this photo was taken. No attention was paid by employers to the boy either at hospital or home according to statement of boy's father. August 1908.

Hill's thoughts are a house of dreams. The Chicago reformer Jane Addams described a popular lantern-slide show called "The House of Dreams" about a young boy vowing vengeance on the criminals who have killed his father and stolen the family fortune. The boy "follows one villain after another to his doom. The execution of each is shown in lurid detail, and the last slide of the series depicts the hero, aged ten, kneeling upon his father's grave counting on the fingers of one hand the number of men that he has killed, and thanking God that he has been permitted to be an instrument of vengeance." In Chicago theaters, according to Addams, writing in 1911, "the leading theme was revenge." Over in Cincinnati, pent-up Hill cannot count his intended victims on his bad hand, but you feel he would if he could.

Another photograph of August 1908 depicts sixteen-year-old Harry McShane—who "had his left arm pulled off near shoulder, and right leg broken through kneecap" in an industrial accident (fig. 76). A darkness in the lower right

Fig. 77
Marie Costa, Basket Seller, 605 Elm St., Sixth St. Market, Cincinnati. 10 A.M., Saturday, Aug. 22 [?], 1908.

Fig. 78
Marie Costa, Basket Seller, 605 Elm St., Sixth St. Market, Cincinnati. 9 P.M. Had been there since 10 A.M. Sister and friend help her. August 1908.

corner creates a notable void in the zone of the missing arm. The absent arm gives out more sensations in the draped angle of the furniture behind the boy, the edge channeling down the seam where the arm would have been, the drapery creased like the empty sleeve. The protruding chair finial above the boy's good arm makes us see the mostly hidden stump of the finial on the other side. The stripe of shadow down that side of McShane's shirt is another pocket of absence next to the missing arm, even as the brightly lit suspender emphasizes the boy's sunnier side. The clock, brightly lit behind the boy's face, 2:20 in the afternoon, is the chronometer of his bucktooth smile, the game cheer of his convalescence. But the missing arm reaches its sleeve into his pants, as if embarrassed about its own absence—not wanting to cause a scene, be a nuisance—or as if aiding compulsively in the boy's search for what he has lost. All hands are to be enlisted in a loss so dire, even the hand that is itself the loss.

The violence could be time itself. Two more of the photographs Hine took in August 1908 in Cincinnati show a little basket seller named Marie Costa poised at her downtown post on morning and night of the same day (figs. 77–78). No one has done her physical harm—no slings or bandages—but her face at night makes plain the weariness of the task. In the morning, sitting at her place beneath a lamppost, her left hand on an inverted umbrella, she recalls a fisherman at the rudder beneath the lone sail of her craft, her boat a little corner of sidewalk amid the swirling cobblestones. Steering her way through a clogged port, trawling amid the trolley-line wakes of bigger ships, she is a small citizen of private enterprise, trying to stay afloat. The woven baskets, like the patterned bricks of the street, reveal the simple intricacy of repetition, the accumulation of sameness in her corner of the world. At night, the baskets tip toward us, revealing their emptiness in a row of three that matches the three people—Costa on the right—poised above them. The taller of Costa's two companions stands at the gleaming lamppost while the two little girls, lower down, slump a bit like the tipped baskets. Time stacks and extends, gathered in the same place. And back in the dark, the whites of their blouses and dresses caught in the photographer's flash, the customers slide as if on tracks, back and forth, coming and going in mechanical grooves, so different from the photographer's main concern, which is the way time is woven to a sturdy throwaway fragility in one place that stands still.

And in a West Virginia coal mine the next month Hine pursued this idea of waiting in one place. A photograph he took then shows a boy named Vance sitting

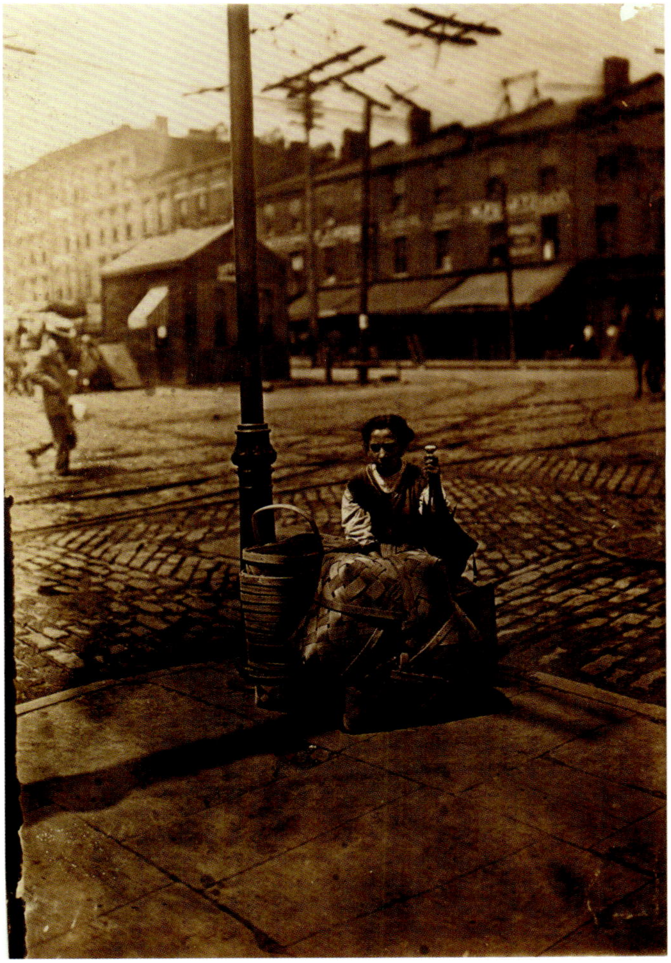

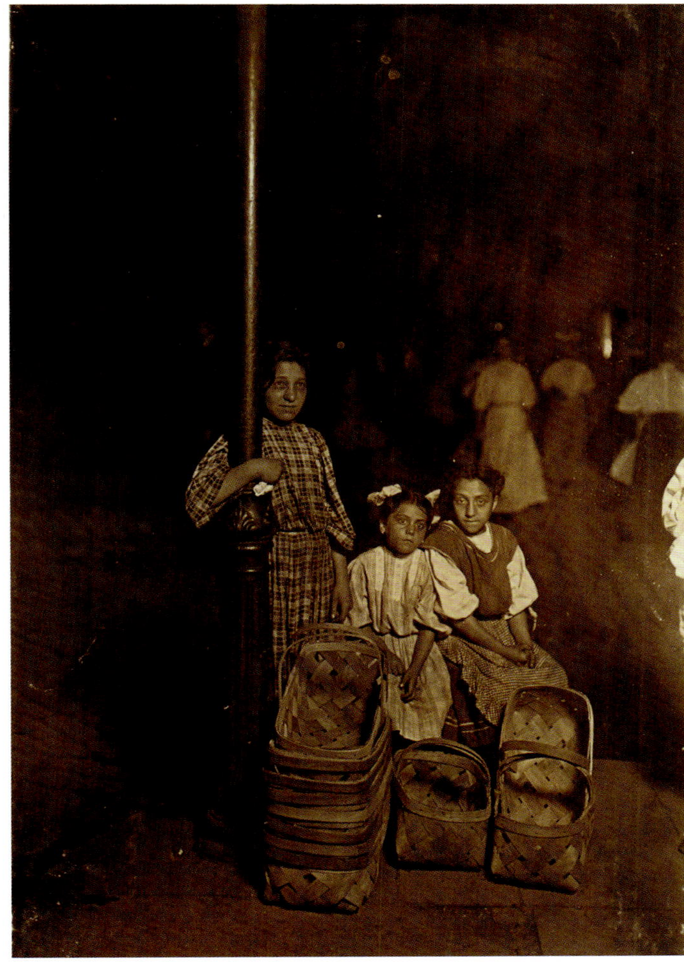

at a door he was employed to open and close throughout the night, letting coal cars in and out of the mine (fig. 79). The flash, illuminating scrawled writing on the door, suggests the mental darkness of the boy's world, a full picture of his thoughts, signed by him twice with a signature and once with his initials (V.P.). In chalk a flock of diving birds skims toward Vance as if homing to their master, birds and boy alike sightless in the blackened subterranean world in that place where flights and closed doors are one and the same. It is not exactly a sleep of reason, more a soporific daze of ornithological darkness. Mental flights in cripple-wing chalk are a migration of poisoned souls no one can see—not on this graveyard shift. And the hole in the wall behind the boy's head is a mental deterioration, as if his sheer boredom is daily eroding the walls. The sense of punishment reaches Dostoyevskian proportions: "You see, once again I positively maintain that this peculiar quality exists in much of mankind—this love of torturing children," says Ivan to his brother Alyosha in *The Brothers Karamazov*. "It is precisely the defenselessness of these creatures that tempts the torturers, the angelic trustfulness of the child, who has nowhere to turn and no one to turn to—that is what enflames the vile blood of the torturer." Shut up in his stupor of shiny filth, Vance endures his imprisonment silently, a helpless victim of human depravity.

This was the harsh time of child labor. Even before Hine got to Cincinnati and went on to West Virginia—back in 1907, when he was doing freelance work for the NCLC—he was portraying a newsboy's night as a Stations of the Cross exercise in temporal disaster—from 7:00 p.m. to 4:00 a.m. a gradual deterioration as the boy makes his rounds, consorts with colleagues of the street, and eventually passes out on a doorstep. But I suspect that Hine knew early on that he would have to find another kind of time than just the portrayal of disenchanted drudgery. Otherwise his photographs would merely portray the degradation instead of envisioning the soulfulness, peeping out, escaping, transfiguring, that alone could make the degradation appear such an outrage.

The little girl at the Singer gate in South Bend, photographed in October 1908 (see figs. 40–43), is a first successful attempt at finding this otherworldly time. But it was not until Hine visited the mills of North and South Carolina in November and December of that year that he started really wresting the other time—the soulful time—away from the daily toll. At first the efforts were more contrived, more a self-conscious "statement" than an intuitive discovery. His photograph of a spinner in a Lancaster, South Carolina, cotton mill, taken in Novem-

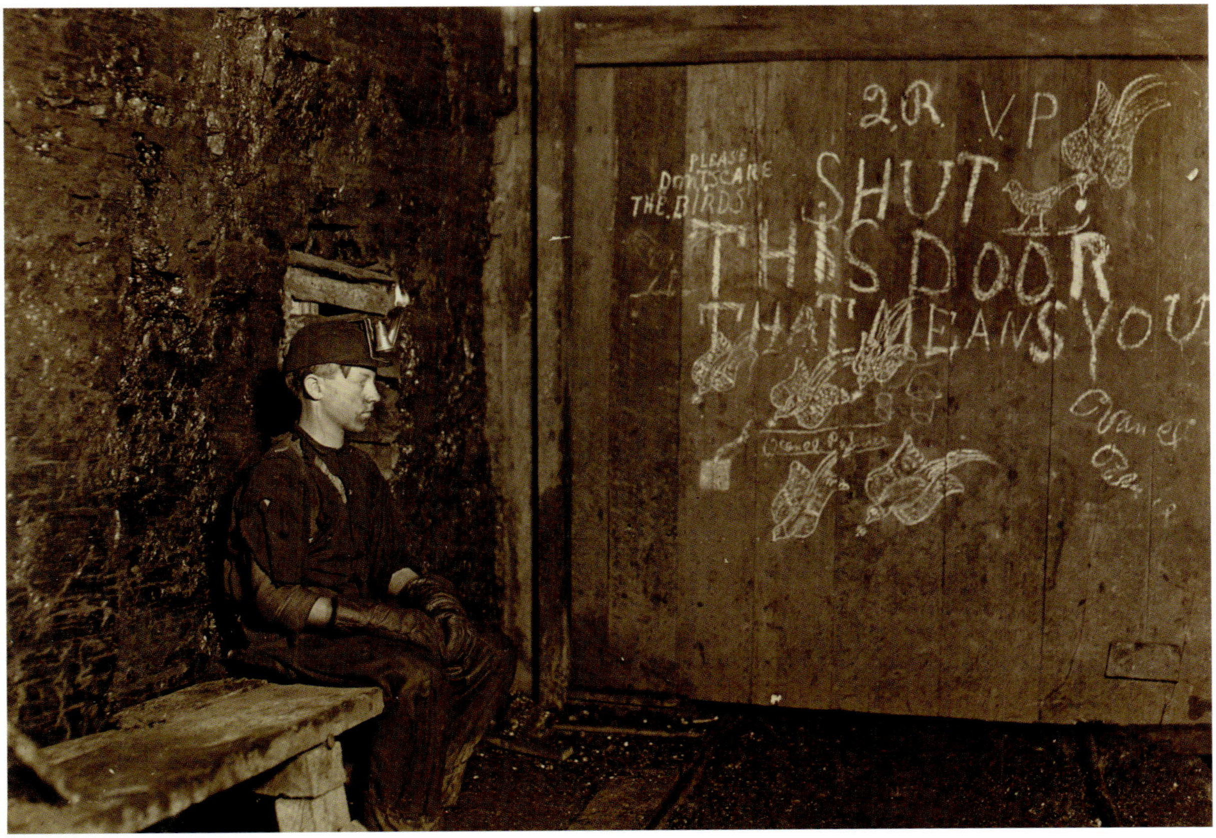

Fig. 79
Vance, a Trapper Boy, 15 years old. Has trapped for several years in a West Va. Coal mine. $.75 a day for 10 hours work. All he does is to open and shut this door: most of the time he sits here idle, waiting for the cars to come. On account of the intense darkness in the mine, the hieroglyphics on the door were not visible until plate was developed. September 1908.

ber, shows a little girl grasping the rounded iron component at the end of one of the long rows of bobbins (fig. 80). Photographed at close range, the girl looks up as if at the photographer's request, the sweep of her pinned-back hair emphasizing her upward look.

We are seeing an awakening, a realization. The girl grasps the iron form as if pushing it away from her, rejecting the star-centered heraldry of the mill for a more beatific vision. The taller young woman in the background, hands on hips, evidently unacquainted with the mystery, looks on as if today is just another work-day, the taking of the photograph a moment like any other. But Hine would have it differently. He imagines a "Change," to cite one of H. G. Wells's socialist words. The Change is what happens at the end of *In the Days of the Comet*, Wells's 1906 novel, when human beings wake into goodness after a comet releases a mysterious beneficent gas over their previously toilsome and hateful lives:

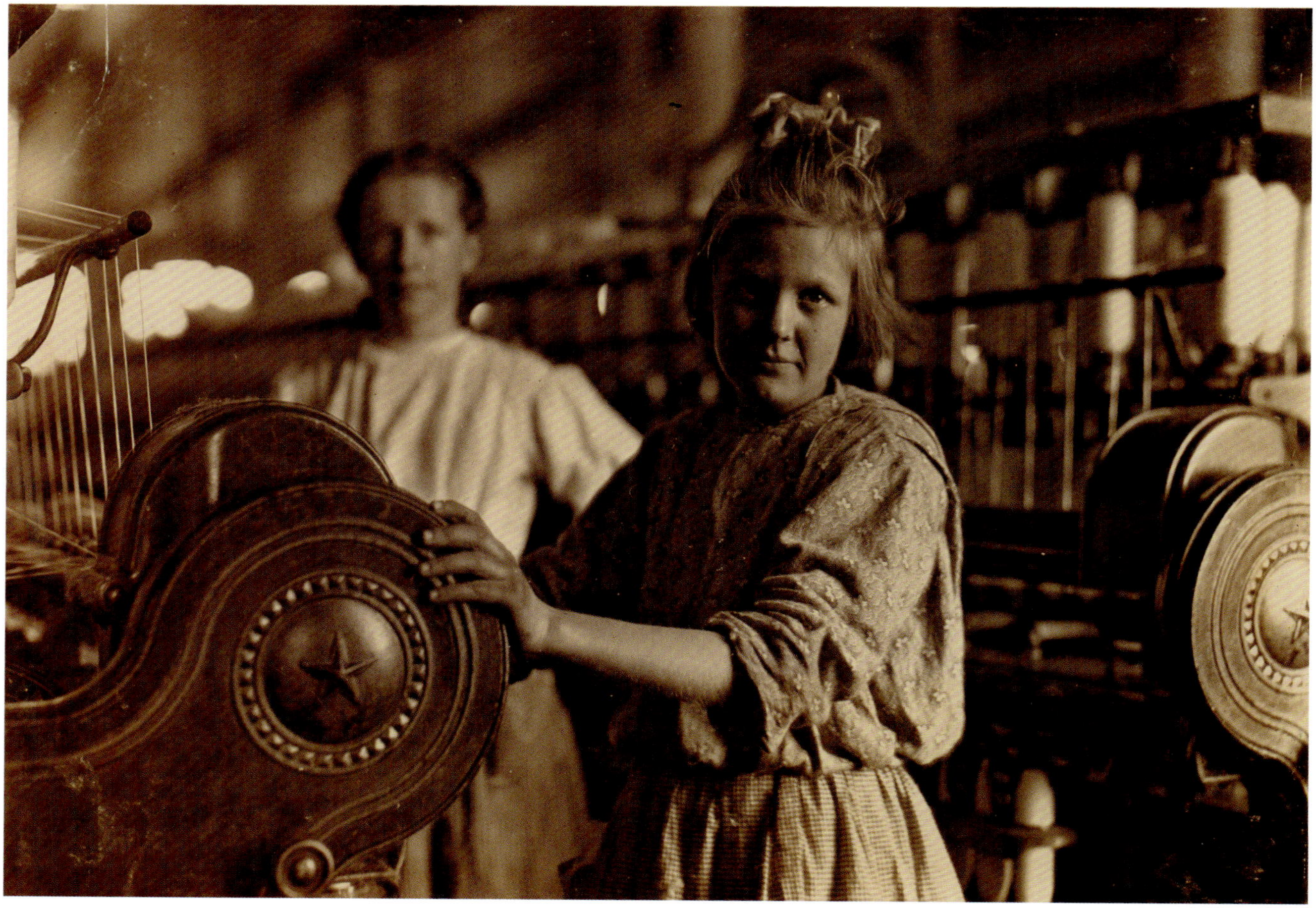

Fig. 80
A typical Spinner Lancaster Cotton Mills, S.C. November 1908.

We knew before the Change, the meanest knew, by glowing moments in ourselves and others, by histories and music and beautiful things, by heroic instances and splendid stories, how fine mankind could be, how fine almost any human being could upon occasion be.

The Change makes that goodness permanent—"men stood up; they took the new air into their lungs—a deep breath, and the past fell from them; they could forgive, they could disregard, they could attempt." Maybe Hine's spinner awakens to a similarly permanent new world.

But a more occult energy works through the scene, something that Hine cannot control. He had to learn to be on the lookout for what he could not anticipate.

What he did not expect to find would be the elusive spirit of something escaping—and finding its way back into—his designs. This unexpected visitation would need to be more than a confirmation of social content—Vance's chalk birds in the West Virginia mine, no matter how surprising, only confirmed the squalor of a scene perfectly apparent without these notations. No, there had to be something a little wilder, more flighty even than the birds.

The glowing lights in the background of the Lancaster mill, over the right shoulder of the bystander, suggest a mysterious and ephemeral grace. These circles of confusion, as scholars of Vermeer call them, owe to the capabilities and limitations of Hine's camera lens, but they are something stranger, too: a Pleiades of apparitional signs, as weird as a cluster of UFOs in the night sky. We see no spirit signs and other roguish trips of séance. The crystal ball and the levitating table are not in the bag of this patter-less magician in his search for truth. He is after what cannot be planned or named, even by himself—a momentary feeling without the imprimatur of a star, minus the stamped designation of trademark and authenticity, all the vaunted signs of material purpose and industrial definition that run and rule the world.

That feeling is some connection between the photographer and the girl, a specialness that is not built on anything other than their chance and brief interaction. It is as if Hine sensed that it is the interaction itself—not him, not the girl, but their momentary acquaintance—that contains the seed of what is special, separate, and elusive in the person he will portray.

It is an Annunciation of a kind, something to be found in the pregnant power of thin air. Mills were miracles of creation. The boy worker in Jack London's "The Apostate," the story from 1908, is born on the mill floor where his mother worked. John Spargo's aptly named *Bitter Cry of the Children* devotes several pages to women giving birth on the factory floor. Herman Melville's story "The Tartarus of Maids," published back in 1855, tells of young women working in the snowy mountain fastness of a New England paper mill who stir the pulpy creamy mass of woven rags in great trays of albumen, an ovoid generation of a writer's stuff observed by a quietly awestruck gentleman visitor. And at Amoskeag in New Hampshire, one of the young mill workers spent two weeks thinking she was pregnant because a flirting boy had touched her on the shoulder. But the connection between Hine and the girl in Lancaster is a virgin birth, a mysterious union different from the mill's stamped star of labor.

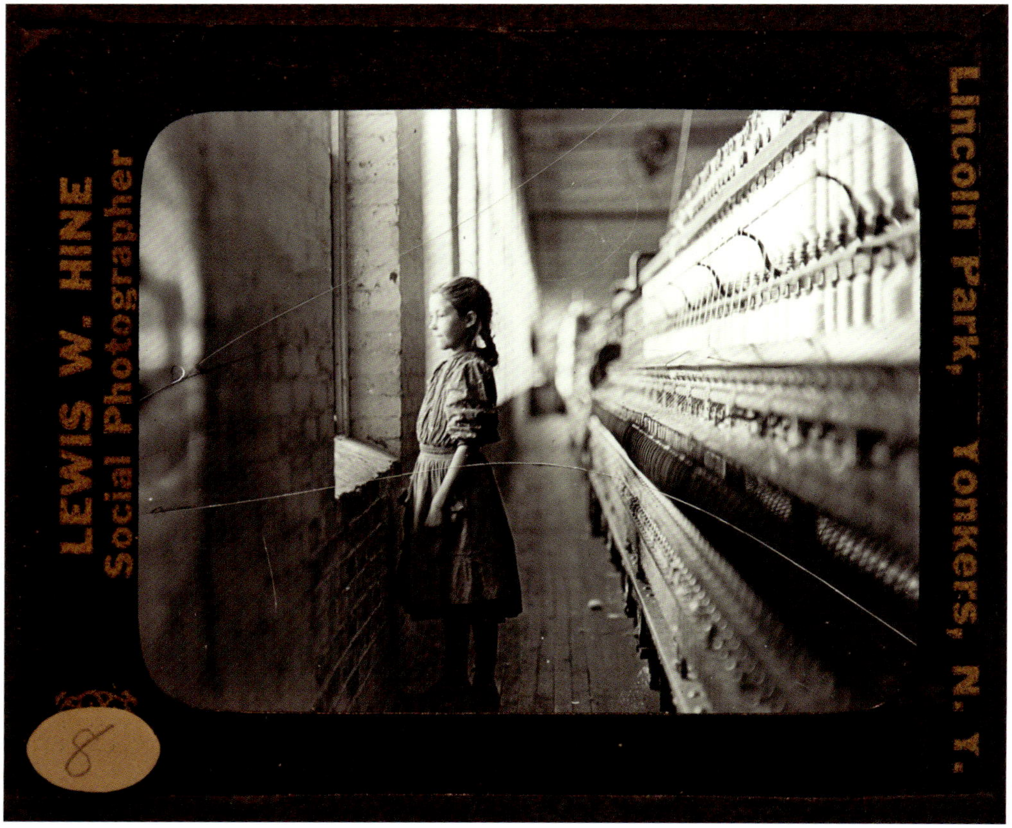

Fig. 81
Rhodes Mfg. Co., Lincolnton, N.C. Spinner. A moment's glimpse of the outer world. Said she was 10 years old. Been working over a year. November 1908. Lantern slide.

Hine was loosening the girl into the improbable floating world that is the soul he has found for her. He was discovering an allegiance to some burble of sunlight, scattered on the wall, that not in a million years he could hope to display as the badge, proof-positive, of who she was and what she did. The next month he made the photograph of the Whitnel spinner (fig. 1).

But another premeditation works through these scenes, another aggressive calculation that Hine had to overcome—the designs of advertising. Decisive, strong, peremptory, advertising was itself a form of violence—and Hine always remained enamored with it as a model for his work. The Lancaster girl's pose with the star-embossed iron is an advertising gesture. She looks like she is holding up a premium sack of flour, or pushing the biggest perambulator in the world. Truly, she is selling her awakening. Front and center, the girl illustrates what Hine meant when he told an audience that it was important to "advertise" the plight of child laborers. "To the range of advertising there is no limit," he said in a lecture he gave in 1909. "I wonder, sometimes," he told his audience, what an enterprising manufacturer would do if his wares, instead of being inanimate things, were the problems and activities of life itself, with all their possibilities of human appeal. Would he not grasp eagerly at such opportunities to play upon the sympathies of his customers as are afforded by the camera?

Such lectures, illustrated with lantern slides of photographs such as another one of November 1908 that shows a little girl spinner seeing the light (fig. 81), were noble and important. They got the word out as loudly as possible, trying to rise above the great clamor of other hawked goods. "Where all are tooting the loud bazoo," Hine said in his lecture, "the problem of any one making himself heard is no slight one." That is why "Advertising is art; it is literature; it is invention. Failure is its one cardinal sin." Hine's National Child Labor Committee posters are his own homemade effort to spread the word (fig. 82).

It all seemed so simple. A photograph Hine took of a classified ad from a New York newspaper in March 1912 isolates the plaintive appeal of ad and photograph alike (fig. 83). Showing the classified cut from the page and glued and centered on a tan cardboard background, the photograph dramatizes the sudden and personal attraction of a single set of lines in a sea of print: a personal invitation, no matter how anonymous ("Help wanted—Female"), stands out for the viewer, catching her eye as she scans the page. Evoking an older form of advertising, the kind that Raymond Williams notes was nearly the only kind until the late nineteenth century, when corporate capitalism began more aggressively to create needs and wishes, the humble classified portrays the workings of desire and necessity at the personal level—as Hine wanted his own photographs to do. They too would single out their viewers, soliciting interested citizens with "the problems and activities of life itself."

But of course it was never that simple. The classified, like the drooping cotton boll explosive with fluff that Hine photographed perhaps the same year (fig. 23), is an eye-catching but deceptive abstraction of experience. Hard labor, down to the pain in the joints of individual fingers, becomes a generalizable slogan, a graspable definition, but only at the expense of the strangeness that Hine had such a gift of portraying. Indeed that strangeness is manifest even in the cotton and the classified. The very act of simplifying—declaring—advertising—emits a forlorn resistance to the come-on charisma. A downbeat force bends the stalk and isolates the paper. The simple documentary truth—this is what the world is, take a look, proof positive—turns by some magic force into an isolated cry for help: help wanted.

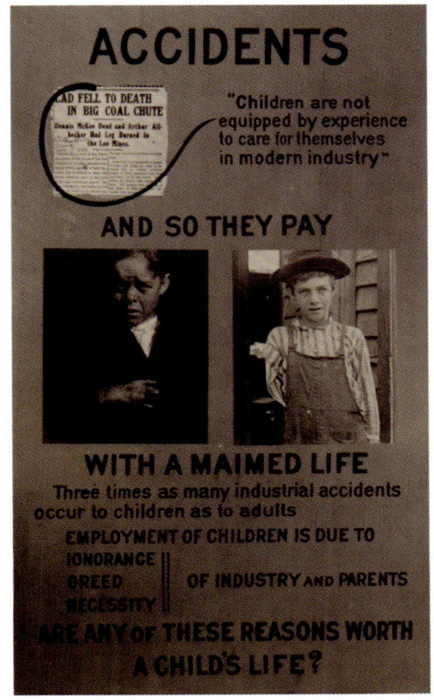

Fig. 82
Accidents. And So They Pay with a Maimed Life, ca. 1915.

Fig. 83
Photo of newspaper advertisement, calling for workers on hair-brushes. New York. March 1912.

Each emblem bleeds to a curious singularity, a lone fate, a lost soul. The bold appeal leaks a feeling of unknowable experience and unknown life.

Yet Hine never did fully escape the full-on allure of advertising. He was always interested in its directness. And as a socialist he should have been. In 1912 the national party office sent out more than three and a half million pieces of promotional literature—leaflets, pamphlets, and the like—and that was just in the first four months of the year. Hine too wanted to get the message out. But this was a problem, since advertising was a form of the daily violence—targeting people—that Hine's intuitive moments avoided.

Consider his photograph of twelve-year-old newsboy Hyman Alpert, taken in New Haven, Connecticut, in March 1909 (fig. 84). The boy stands before a sign, *Bought and Sold*, that Hine understandably appropriates for the message of his own photograph. Alpert too is a cheap good bought and sold. The only trouble is that amid the dispensable worlds of daily commercial transaction—books and newspapers, stacked and sheaved—the photograph becomes a transaction itself. Alpert is "used" by Hine—bought and sold by him, as it were—so that the injustice of his life, shut out from the knowledge he peddles, becomes a message as legible as the bookseller's come-on to the customer. Hine hawks his photograph, peddling

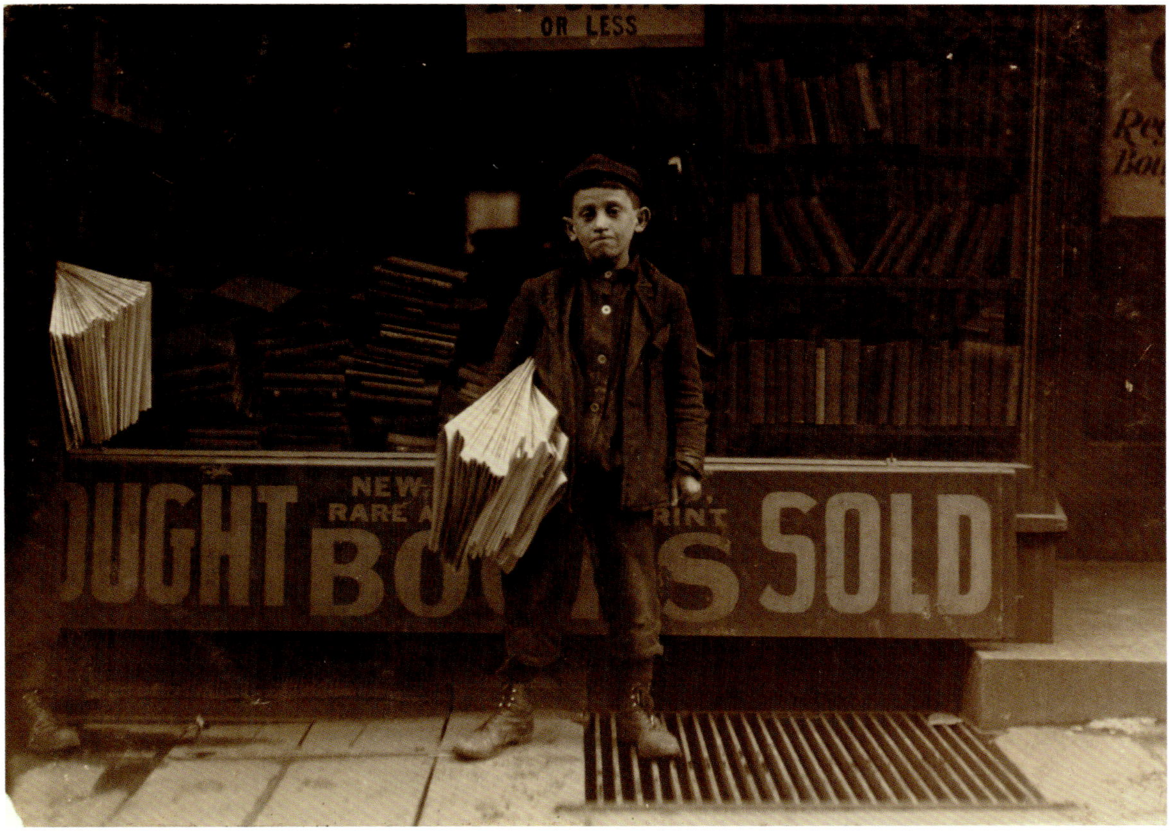

Fig. 84
12 year old newsboy, Hyman Alpert, been selling three years. Spends evenings in Boys Club. March 1909.

picture and boy as so many commodity-like products in a world in which even misery and sympathy have a cheap price. The drain grate is a grid like the books on the shelves—the rain and refuse that sluice down the hole are here today, gone tomorrow, yesterday's news, potentially like Alpert, like the photograph itself.

Yes, a scatter of unforgettable details makes itself felt. The boy's nearly lipless frown, the shining circular button at the top of his shirt, the gleaming eyelets and laces of the boots that seem obscurely to haunt his flared ears and sunken eyes—these are vivid enough. But they struggle to emerge amid the more whelming declaration of message. The temptation to sell Alpert's story is too good to pass up.

Hine's dilemma is understandable. Why should he be quiet amid the era's visual economy of everyday sensation? Blast his pictures into the public eye and the plight of the abused would ring as gutturally as the other afflictions that drew

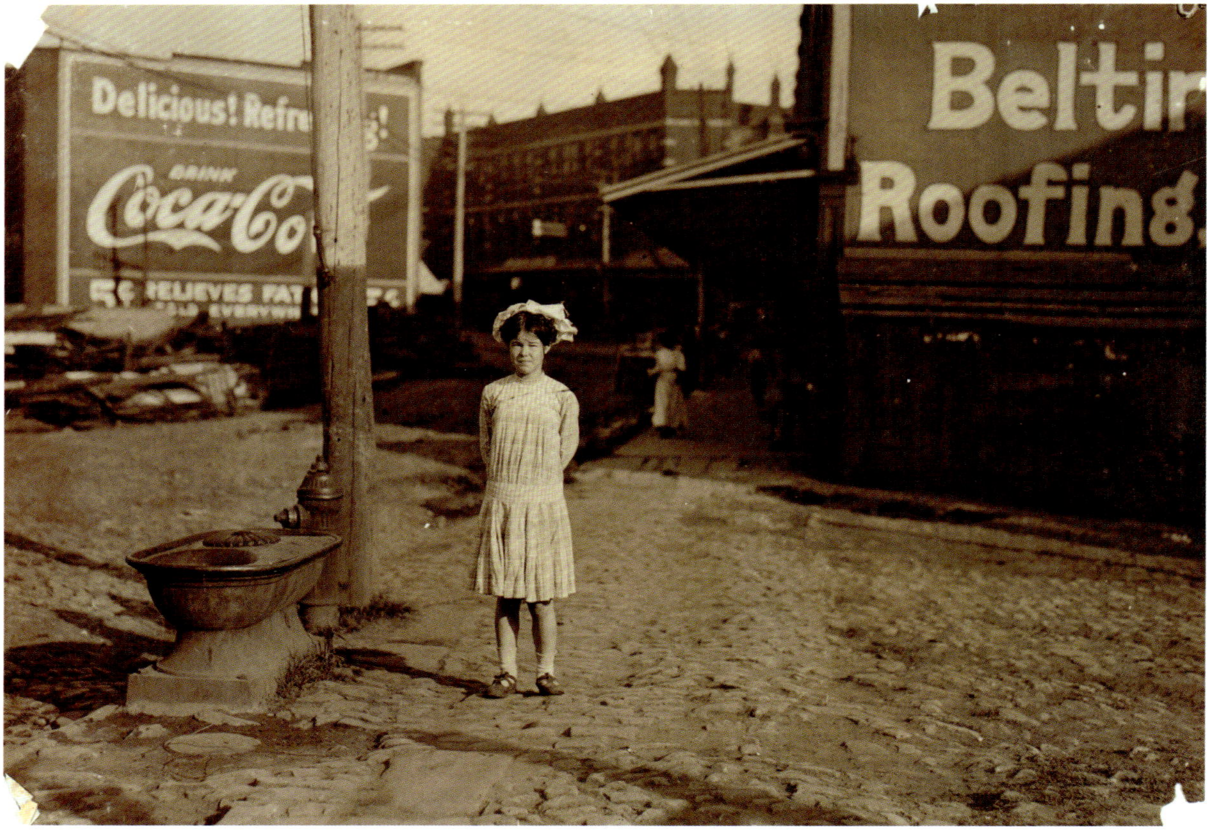

Fig. 85
Ethel Shumate. Has been rolling cigarettes in Danville (Va.) Factory for six months. Lives, 614 Upper Street. Said she was thirteen years old, but it is doubtful. June 1911.

a crowd. His picture of young Ethel Shumate on the streets of Danville, Virginia, taken in June 1911, shows the girl standing on a rough cobbled sidewalk, her hands behind her back, next to a trough, fire hydrant, and telephone pole (fig. 85). Across the street looms a large Coca-Cola billboard (Delicious! Refreshing! Relieves Fatigue 5 cents Sold Everywhere"). To the right we see part of another advertisement displaying the words "Beltin" and "Roofing." Hine's use of Shumate makes an equally loud statement. She may appear diminished in this loud atmosphere of buying and selling, a product herself, but Hine makes Shumate equally deliver the message of herself. The brightness of her dress and hat picking out the morning sun just like the swirling fonts of the advertisements, she catches the eye—the socialist bitter cry a brand as resounding as any large-lettered exhortations.

The Danville photograph even divines a choice between showy statements and sober responsibilities, choosing the former. The horse trough, fire hydrant, and

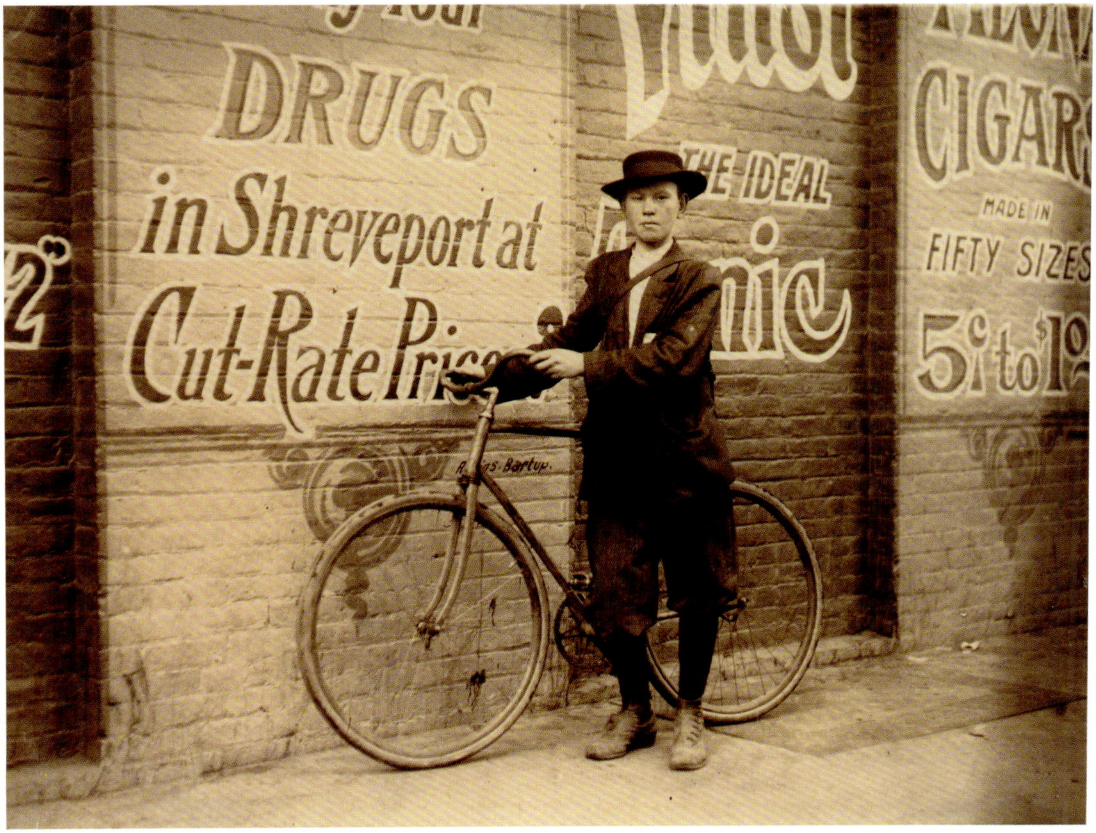

Fig. 86
Howard Williams, thirteen year old delivery boy for Shreveport, La. Drug Company. He works from 9:30 A.M. to 10:30 P.M.; has been here three months. Goes to the Red Light every day and night. Says that the company could not keep other messenger boys; they work them so hard. November 1913.

telephone pole come from a different world than the sprightly advertisements. The appeal of these solemn public utilities is subdued and unglamorous. An unsung trio of ugly accomplices, a boring entourage of necessaries, important but taken for granted, they are no match for the advertisements' loud grandiosity of immediate satisfaction. Hine, posing Shumate next to the public services as if debating whether to align her to them or not, prefers the glamor of the advertisements' immediate appeal, a morning sun as refreshing as the girl herself. Ethel Shumate is on her way to roll cigarettes in a Danville factory, and in Hine's picture she too is a stimulant, all but orally consumed, a bracing inhalation of sentiment. "We have got to arouse and marshal public opinion," Senator Beveridge urged on the Senate floor in his lengthy speech against child labor in January 1907.

Just so: In November 1913 in Shreveport, Louisiana, Hine took a photograph of thirteen-year-old messenger boy Howard Williams (fig. 86). Standing before a

Fig. 87
Bleach-room boy—Leon Halcourt [Valcourt], 34 Melvin St., 16 years old. Lawrence, Massachusetts. November 1910.

wall of painted advertisements (for drugs at "Cut-Rate Prices," for a tonic, and for cigars), Williams is no stranger to sales propositions. "Goes to the Red Light [District] every day and night," the caption says. Messenger boys frequently worked prostitution districts, according to Spargo, where they were "sent out to place bets; to take notes to and from houses of ill-fame; or to buy liquor, cigarettes, candy, and even gloves, shoes, corsets, and other articles of wearing apparel for 'ladies,'" and where "they cannot avoid being witnesses of scenes of licentiousness more or less frequently." In New York, Shreveport, and other places, the messenger boys possess "the most astounding intimacy with the grossest things of the underworld." Williams lives in a wall-to-wall universe of cheap fixes, restoratives, and any-sized masculinities, priced to fit the budgets of all gents under the sun—and they make the sum of who he is. Not to be outshouted, Hine promotes Williams among the promotions.

But the moment—unrepeatable, ephemeral—resisted daily shock and seduction. Lew Hine was one of the ones who sensed it was there and who found it as a kind of by-product of the messages he was supposed to portray. If the slaughter-men of Upton Sinclair's stockyards took "everything but the squeal" from the pig, the comparable managers of time pacing their factory floors had evidently missed a choice morsel of daily existence that Hine stumbled upon. Only an artist would care for a temporal scrap that could not be cooked up, canned, and sold. No matter if the artist was one who admired those very techniques of packaging and selling and sought to make them his own. Hine was not the first to be beguiled in wrong directions, seduced into misspent energies. The ease of an advertising statement seemed like a ready solution, even if it was not his best talent and instinct. Certainly Hine did not have a gift for sales like his fellow Oshkosh resident Carl Laemmle, the future head of Universal Pictures, who "learnt, not how to ascertain what the public wanted, but how to impress upon the public what he wanted it to want." For Hine, by contrast, it was only by avoiding the declaration, the statement, the come-on, that he was able to make his best work.

Take his photograph of sixteen-year-old Leon Valcourt standing in front of a tree outside the Pacific Mills in Lawrence, Massachusetts, on a morning in November 1910 (fig. 87). Together with eighteen-year-old Mike Kennedy, seated on the rail at left, Valcourt is a bleach-room boy at the mills, one of the nation's largest manufacturers of wool and cotton products, a complex that by the 1920s would include twenty-seven brick buildings sited along two canals running parallel to the

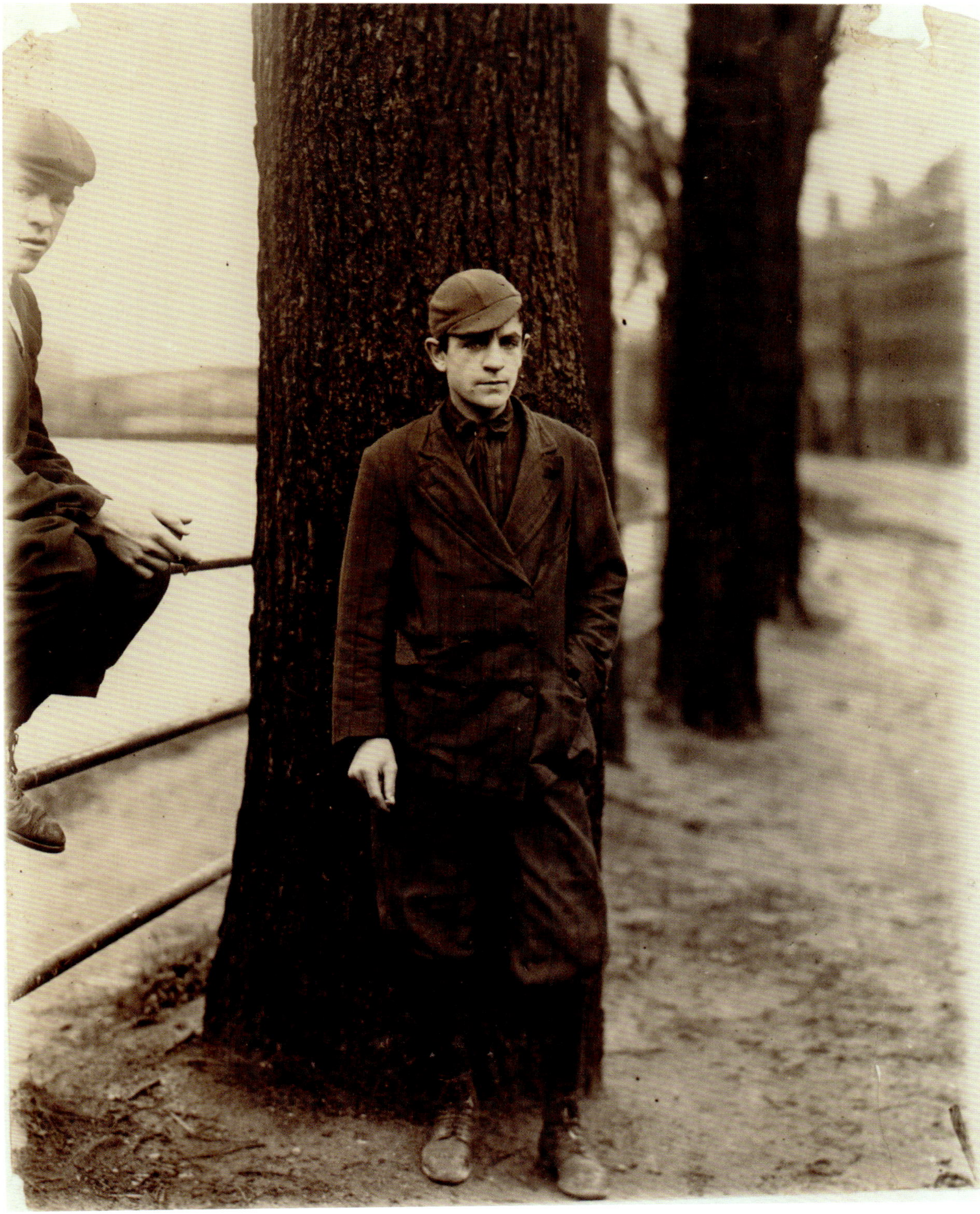

Merrimack River. Valcourt stands in the dirt path before one of those canals, sharing a smoke with Kennedy, the two of them both looking at Hine.

The picture shapes up to be clear, propagandistic. Valcourt stands before the tree, face and right hand stark against the backdrop. Like the messenger Howard Williams in Shreveport, except more so, Valcourt looks worldly beyond his years, a man who is still a boy. A photograph Hine took in the same few minutes, showing Valcourt, Kennedy, and a third boy, seventeen-year-old Daniel Crowley, is so much a picture of renegade youth, bad news waiting to happen, that these fellows might be the members of a 1960s band posing for an album cover (fig. 88). The Dylan-esque look of Crowley, the Mick Jagger intensity of Kennedy in the center, and the brooding songwriter-poet figure of Valcourt—leaning against the railing like a young Bruce Springsteen—these are the stuff of legends. The photograph invents the imagery of adolescent disillusion.

But the photograph concentrating on Valcourt is reluctant to be taken away from itself, to be conscripted into a story, even the very story Hine is there to depict. The reluctance is difficult to identify except as a sensation, felt as a certain trembling around the edges of the moment it was made, as if the instant *prior to* Valcourt becoming a photograph were what Hine wished to portray. This is a sentimental feeling not about child labor but about time itself—a desire, against the odds, to find and hold and suspend the quiver of the November day *against* the photograph that would inevitably be enlisted as the illustration of that day, that place, that person. The feeling is also jealous, a sense that this is *my* moment, or better *our* moment, Valcourt's and mine (and perhaps Kennedy's too), and that it is untrue to that small unit of time, unscripted, beautifully unknown, to drag it away from itself, virtually at the same moment it *becomes* itself, into a tale of what is already known and believed and hence hardly seen. Dwell in the details, the dark eyes and the little-billed cap, the one hand in the pocket, the other hand holding the cigarette, because in these episodes time itself might gather in some impossible staying pattern, as if delaying the script Hine himself is being paid to help write. "The meaning of the times," said Senator Beveridge in a speech at Yale on January 17, 1908, is "the organization of honesty," it is "the moral regeneration of American business." Maybe it was. But Hine was not so sure—both about the meaning of the times and whether or not a photograph should try to record it. What he found in those moments was not the times but time. That was because the moment, when invented, released strange intimations of the future and the

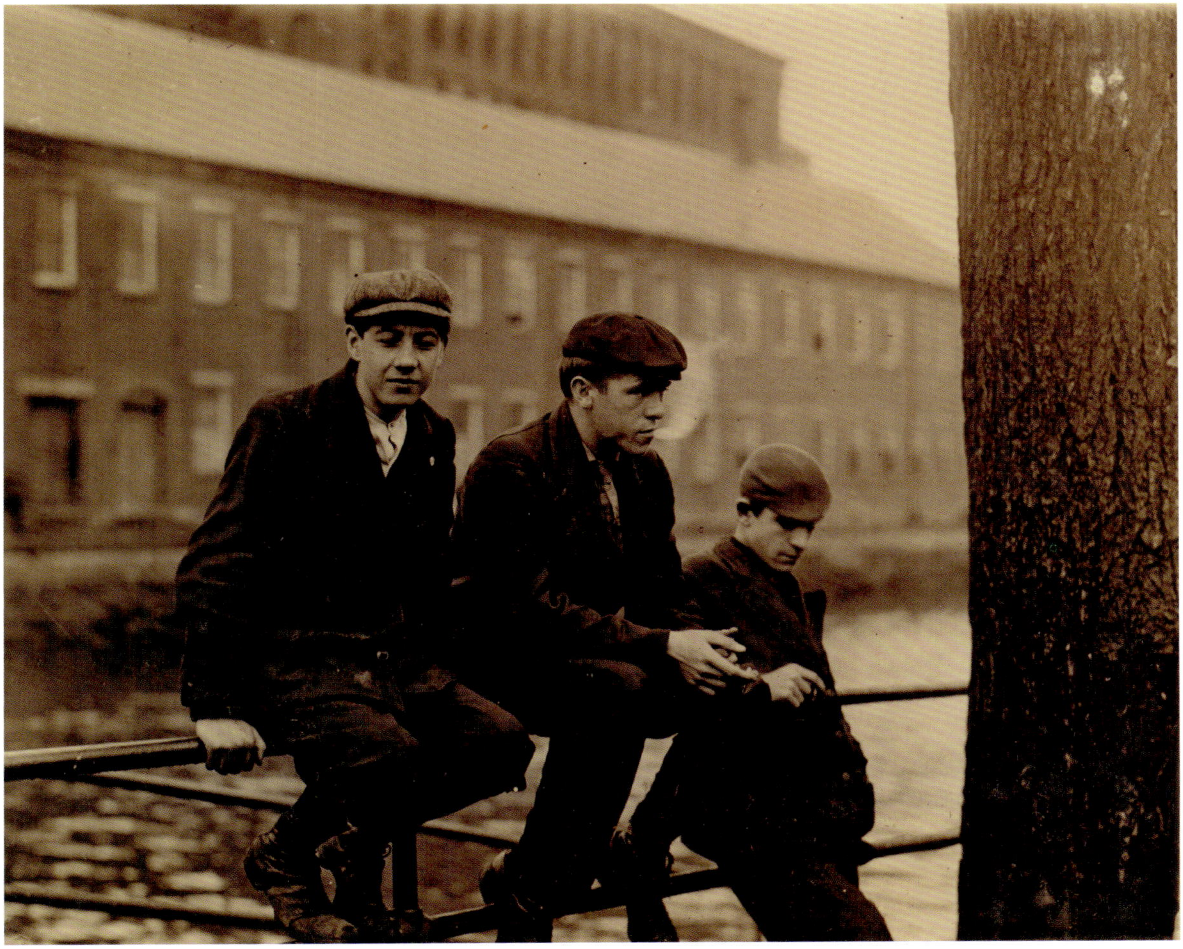

Fig. 88
Bleach-room boys Daniel Crowley 17 years, 358 Broadway; Mike Kennedy, 18 years, 40 Margin St. Pacific Mills. Lawrence, Massachusetts. November 1910.

past, as if who someone was, and who someone will be, could only be found in the utterly insubstantial instant where, by intuition and chance, a wave of time is made to pass across the person. Forget that "time" is not a medium, not a substance even of air, but rather think of it as a feeling—an emotion—of the photographer, almost too much preoccupied with historical distance and comet futurity, so that he nearly wills it into being as something "real" permeating the worlds of his people. How could Hine know that Valcourt would be killed in World War I, dying of his wounds at age twenty-three, south of Soisson on July 21, 1918? He could not. But moments are premonitions.

They look back, too. Hine's photograph of a young newspaper seller named Mery Horn, taken in Hartford, Connecticut, in March 1909, shows the girl on the corner to hawk the news, sordid and otherwise (fig. 89). She too is news of the day, as much as the papers she sells, her occupation making her a story of daily violence.

But we do not see the newspapers, and some vaster time opens up in their place. Jane Addams, in her book *The Spirit of Youth and the City Streets* (1911), describes how seeing a young orphan girl at Hull House made her think of

> the delicately tinted piece of wall in a Roman catacomb where the early Christians, through a dozen devices of spring flowers, skipping lambs and a shepherd tenderly guiding the young, had indelibly written down that the Christian message is one of inexpressible joy.

Mery Horn, driven to the underground of the streets, may be an enduring martyr to greed and corruption, subject to dangers and indignities great and small. Soft light may brighten the bricks, prison of solace and persecution, the troweled sentiments of her affliction and huddled faith. She may be Our Lady of the Masonry, face front, her body heroically small.

But she is quickened to enduring life by something other than pious goodness amid the violent stories she sells. Hine resists the imperative to make her a headline—another bit of violence imagined and moralized, innocence defiled or threatened. And he resists the Christian socialism that would install her in a catacombs gallery of heroic saints. Her immortality would be of another kind, staked all on the moment. Mystically, Hine thought of such moments as a breath, a fogging of the lens, some spirituous thing in the air, all or nothing, all *and* nothing, that a photographer could infuse into his subjects so that they would be neither yesterday's nor even today's news. The person to the right in the photograph—arm extended upward—is perhaps the flamboyance or indifference of time passing merely *without* ceremony, without gravitas, lacking the caryatid-corner grace of the girl at her post. For who says that all moments, discovered by the facility of the camera, should be equal in the eyes they invent to see them with? On the contrary, some moments stay, others do not.

The look on Mery Horn's face is hard to know—it is not a fixed emotion, packaged and ready, but some "unnamable sensation," in Fredric Jameson's term—an emotional transience. What Hine shows is what comes and goes before it has went—before it has come, too. And what is changeable is not only the expression in time but also the expression as it manifests the house-of-mirrors interaction between the photographer and the girl. In his novel *What Maisie Knew* (1897), Henry James describes a silent exchange of glances between Beale Farange and his daughter Maisie:

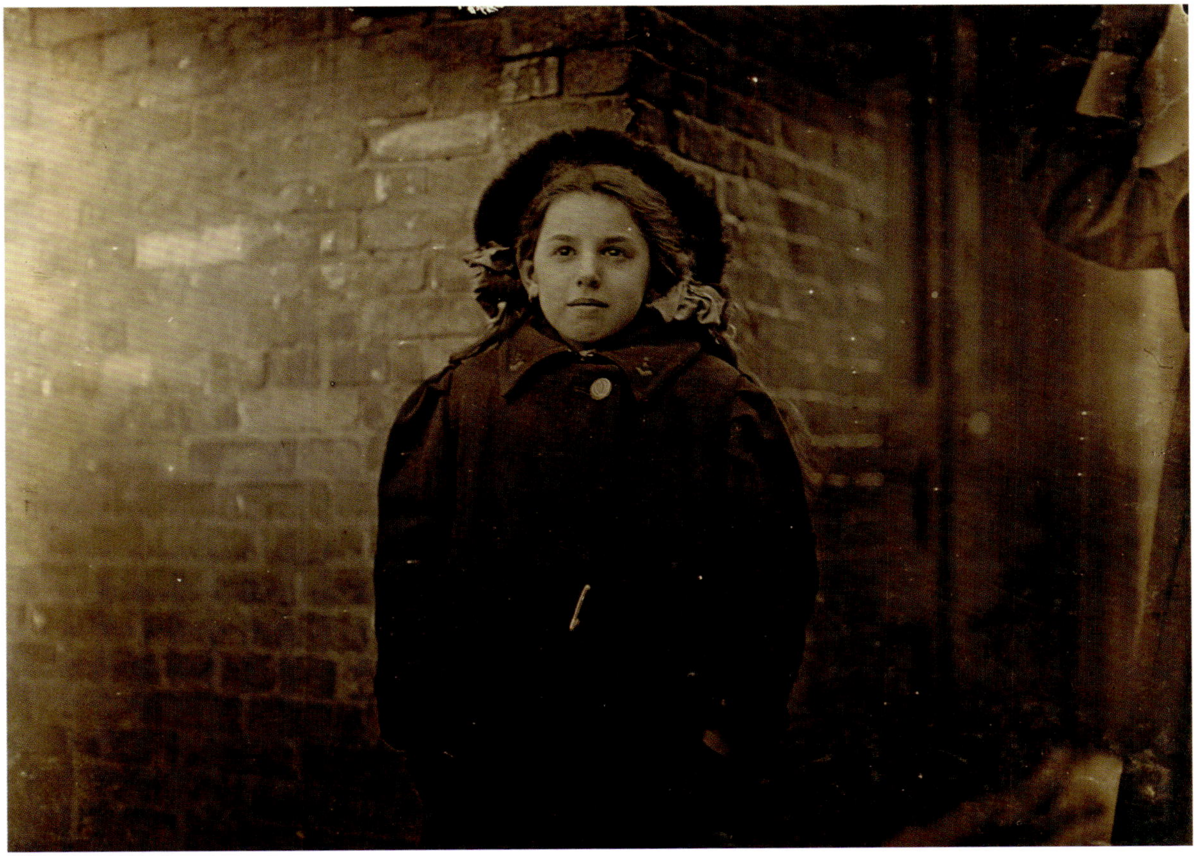

There was an extraordinary mute passage between her vision of this vision of his, his vision of her vision, and her vision of his vision of her vision.

Fig. 89
Mery Horn, a hunchback. The doctor told her it was a severe case and was being aggravated by the heavy load of papers she carried and so she must stop. She replied "But I need the spending money. I have to go to shows." Hartford, Connecticut. March 1909.

Maybe Hine is alive enough to show Mery Horn thinking of what he is thinking of her, thinking that he is even aware that she is thinking of just his thoughts of her, whatever they are. "Small children have many more perceptions than they have terms to translate them," James wrote in the preface to the New York edition of *Maisie*, published in 1908. What is assured is the momentary atmosphere, Mery Horn's expression at the center of it. And that moment, it would seem, is its own halo, perhaps because when an expression is as changeable as hers, the bankrupt eternities return as a glorious transience. A religion of the moment, call it, when something like a soul appears. Put the headlines to bed, because Hine intends that she will never die.

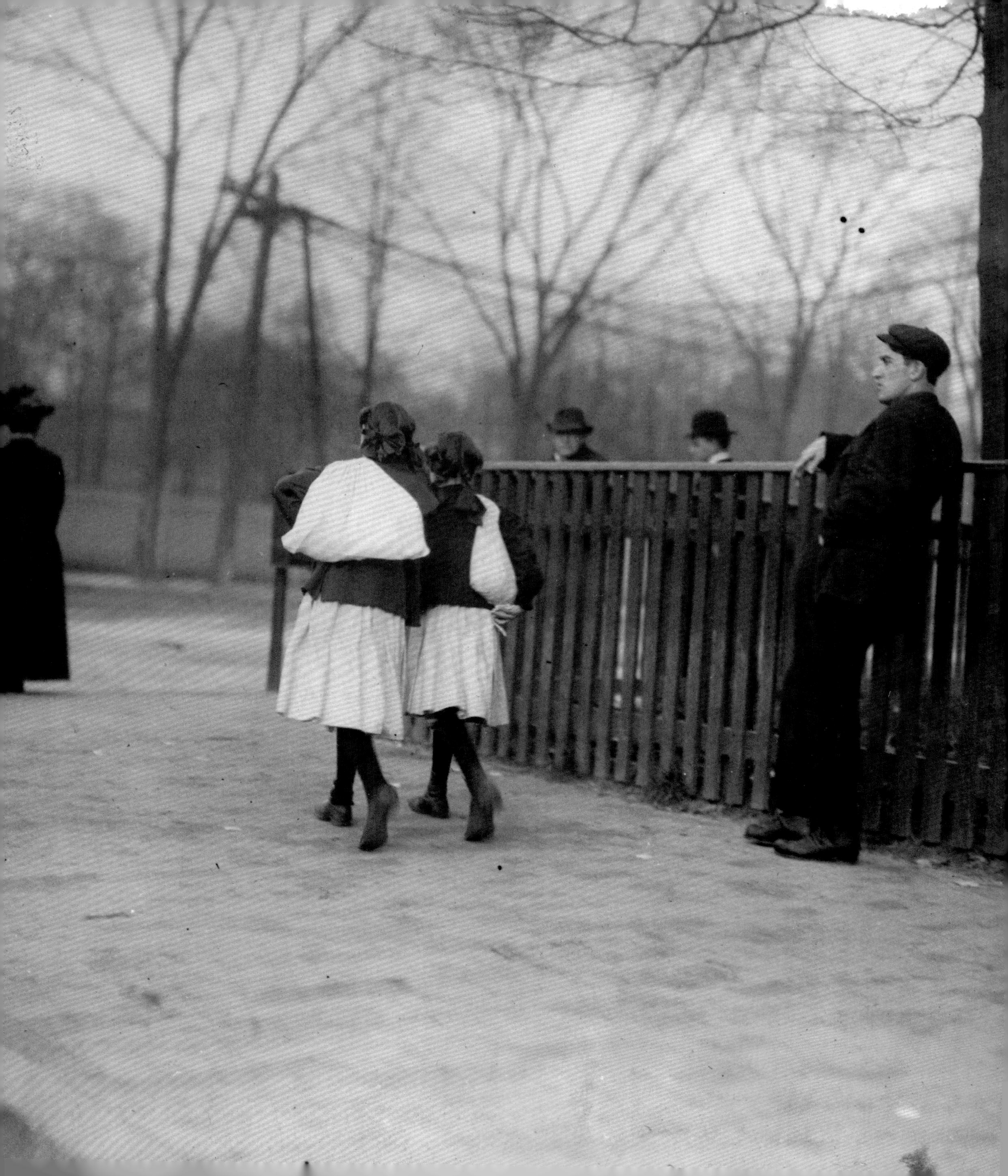

5 HAUNTED

Two dark-haired girls walk down a sidewalk, their backs to us, feet in step (fig. 90). Each carries a white satchel over the shoulder as they near a street corner at which two women wearing hats stand in front of them. One of the women faces away from us, like the girls, while the other woman places her left hand on her hip, her face occluded by the large metal stanchion jutting from the sidewalk. Two men also stand at the corner over to the right, only their heads and necks visible above the slatted wooden fence. One of them looks back in our direction. Nearer to us, a young man in a workman's cap slouches against the fence, his right hand resting on the rail, his gaze directed over and past the little girls.

The distance across the street, gray and latticed in leafless trees, appears on a level with the sidewalk, but it is also so vapory that it looks like a misty valley beheld from a mountaintop. The two women and three men at the corner wait for a trolley like travelers admiring the view from a summit. The girls proceed toward this edge where the adults stand, stepping forth in their matching outfits like the heroines of a fairy tale. Shoulder to shoulder, holding hands, centrally placed, they bravely make their way—youngsters setting out in an indifferent and cold world.

A folklorist could not have done it better. Hine, stationed there in the street, stages the scene, calculating the effects as any master storyteller might. "Make the story run a little hotter and swifter through your atmosphere," advised the young Willa Cather, then an editor at *McClure's*, counseling an author in 1906 to balance the twin journalistic imperatives of scene and plot. But Hine needed no such advice—he told a story and portrayed an atmosphere with equal skill. The two Worcester girls are riding-hood orphans setting out on a perilous errand into a mysterious wood—the heroines of one of those fairy tales that Felix Adler likened to "instantaneous photographs," stories that "reproduce, as it were, in a single flash of light, some one aspect of human nature."

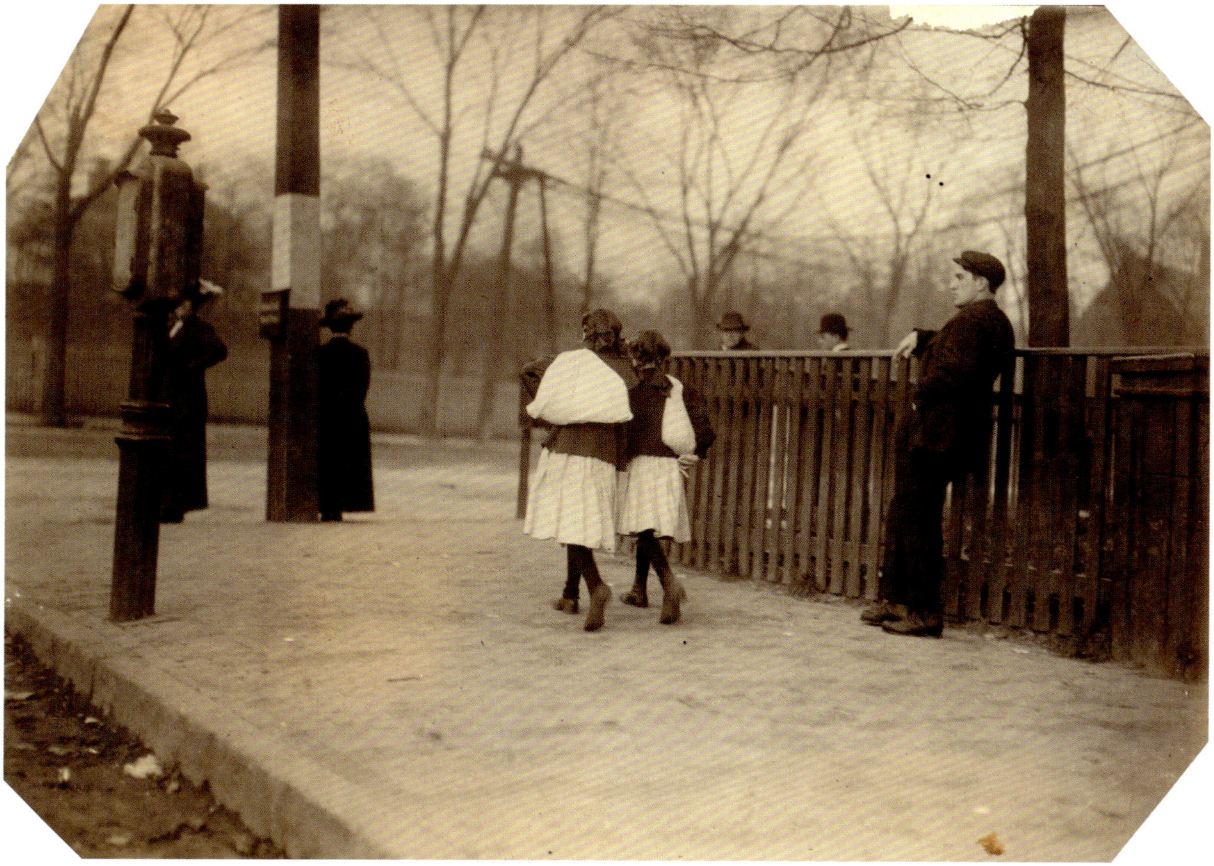

Fig. 90
8:30 A.M., Nov. 12, 1912. Two young girls, Murry and Westover, carrying home sacks full of hose-supporters for home work, from American Narrow Fabric Co., Worcester, Mass. Loads are heavy and distances long. They hurry so they won't be late to school. They have to stop frequently to rest. November 12, 1912.

The timing and staging had to be right. Letting the two girls walk past him, Hine waited for the right moment when their fairy-tale journey would be most resonant. The girls, knowing full well that Hine is there, contrive to appear as though they believe he is not. The sense of staging extends even to the adult bystanders. Almost all of them uninterested in Hine's presence—the one exception is the man in the hat who stares back at Hine from across the fence—they somehow all look posed, as if the photographer (a Gregory Crewdson before the fact) had commanded them to take their places. The insouciant stand of the man in workman's cap, profiled as he leans on the fence, is a model of adult complacency before the fact of child labor. He all but illustrates "the illusion of nearness," Edward Clopper's term for the way child workers on the street were so common that passersby did not even see them.

The theater of socialism drives the tableau, making it unforgettable. Eugene Debs, the great socialist politician and orator, gave a speech in Worcester during the presidential campaign of 1904 that made a lasting impression on a local boy named S. N. Behrman, who would go on to become a famous Broadway playwright, an effect like the impression the photograph aspires to make on its viewer. Age nine or ten, Behrman had been released from Yom Kippur services for a part of the day, absolved with his friends from participating in the *Yizkor* or atonement for the dead, and the boys "had run down the hill and were walking without objective on Front Street." Behrman and his friends came to the Mechanics' Hall, where they learned that "some feller Debs" was inside preparing to give a speech. For Behrman, going in and sitting in one of the front rows with his friends, the experience of watching Debs remained transformative some fifty years later:

> Though I cannot remember a single word that Debs said that morning to his apathetic audience and I never saw or heard him again, I am sure that this chance visit gave to all my later life an orientation it would otherwise not have had—a bias in favor of those who had suffered from cruelty or callousness. This was not because of any specific argument or thought that I carried away from that meeting. It was simply because of the overwhelming impression that Debs' personality made on me. Most of all, I remember his intensity and what seemed to me to be his quivering sensitiveness to pain. The latter showed up in his eyes, voice, and gestures.

Berhman went on, recalling the experience in his memoir *The Worcester Account* (1955),

> There was something about Debs's delivery I have never encountered since. He was tall and angular, and he leaned far over the edge of the platform, as if to get close to each of his listeners. His arms reached out, as if to touch them.

For Behrman, Debs's performance was real theater, where the performer's presence became so vivid that it stayed in his mind beyond—indeed instead of—any message that he spoke (and instead of the religious services that the young Behrman had been excused from). The earnest passion of the great socialist was a stark contrast to the other politicians Behrman eventually heard in Mechanics' Hall—milquetoast Woodrow Wilson, dapper in creased business attire (compared to Debs's "baggy, unpressed, cheap-looking gray sack suit"), or Theodore Roosevelt and William Howard Taft, both fulminators against tariffs and political opponents yet gentlemen who remained, at the end of their exhortations, "well

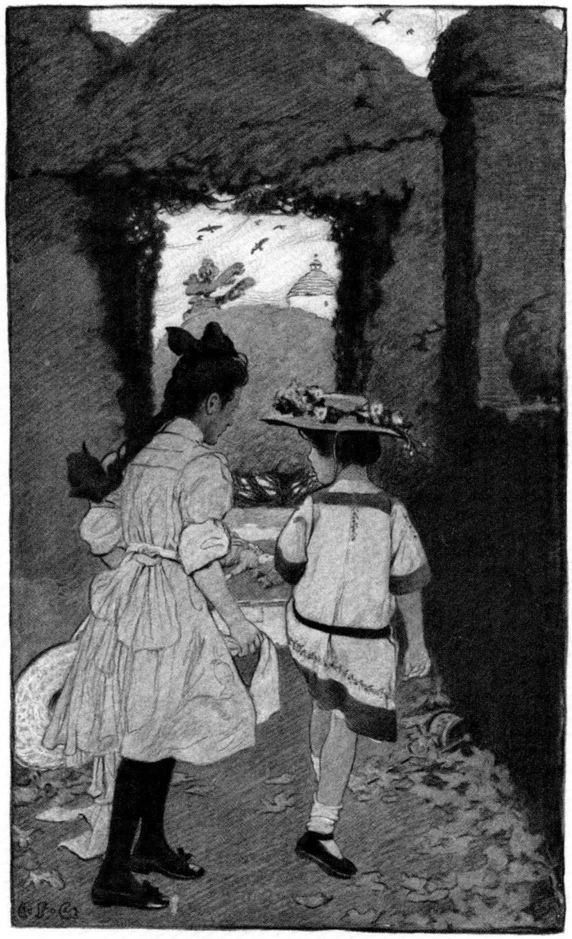

Fig. 91
Elizabeth Shippen Green, *Children have sharp eyes—one can't hide them from each other*, 1909.

fed and genial." Debs, gaunt, gave a performance not about the campaign or the platform but "the spirit of humanity."

Hine's portrayal of the little Worcester girls is as memorable as anything Behrman might have witnessed that day at the Mechanics' Hall. Some righteousness locks the little Worcester girls into place, as if the impression they make is a function of Hine's certitude, his social conviction, that to depict them in this way, highlighted and emphasized, is *the* way to show their solidarity and their plight. The clasped fixation of the Worcester photograph—every element structured as if inevitably—comes about partly because Hine was as convinced as Debs about the urgency of what he must show.

But some other spirit beyond socialism haunts the scene. It is a kind of temporality out of bounds. In Elizabeth Shippen Green's illustration *Children have sharp eyes*, reproduced to accompany Josephine Daskam Bacon's story "The Children" in the August 1909 issue of *Harper's* (fig. 91), two girls go into a garden to look for playmates who are not there. In fact the playmates do not exist. The girl-visitors have been led to believe there are such children in the garden by the mother of the house, a deluded widow named Childress (childless) whose one consoling fantasy is that she did have children, even children who had died, even though she and her husband had none, since then she could at least mourn them instead of being so alone. The widow ends up dying—of fright, of relief, of pain—when the little girl-visitors skip back from the garden and leave the impression that, yes, they *have* seen these purely imaginary children. Green portrays the girls about to pass beyond the dead leaves, through the looming garden gate, into some distant other world where arcing birds float in the sky.

At Worcester the adults in the photograph are so indifferent to the girls—truly not noticing that they are there—that for them the girls do not exist. So "not there" are the girls that it is like they have been superimposed from another photograph onto the sidewalk, "faked" into the scene, so that the adults minding their own business can better be shown as callous and insensitive. Hine creates a tableau of social blindness, yes, but of something eerier too. The fence across the street encloses the Rural Cemetery, Worcester's most famous burial ground. The dimly glimpsed sylvan woods and picket-slatted fence over there are the vision of another realm the adults understandably keep their distance from. The ladies and gentlemen wait at the corner, poised at the edge, contemplative or bored, passing the time, sticking to the nearby landmarks. The hazy place across the street holds them at bay, paralyzing them into stances of motionless isolation, even as they do their part to hold it back, standing sentinel lest it should come nearer. The girls alone stride forth toward that future, as if they envision what it holds. Children have sharp eyes. Who knows what thoughts skew through their floral bedecked imaginations. The governess suspects the worst of little Miles and Flora in Henry James's *Turn of the Screw*. "You little horror" the self-absorbed mother Ida Farange tells young Maisie in James's *What Maisie Knew*. There was no end of being surprised at the things children know, or the things you think they know. Joe Manning's research reveals that the father of the little Worcester girls was a long-time gravedigger. Hine, attuned to the otherworldliness of children, staged the drama of their private awareness—the way

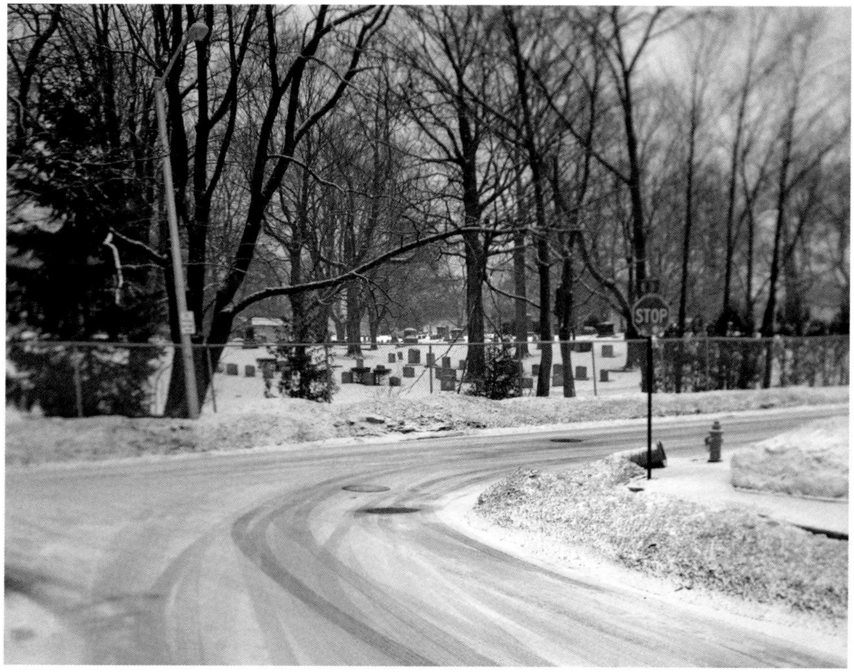

Fig. 92
Jason Francisco, *The corner of Milton and North Streets, looking toward the Rural Cemetery, Worcester, Massachusetts,* March 2015.

they walk away from him in the separateness of their lives. The temporal dimension they travel in is one that leaves him at the near shore—able to portray, but not to accompany, these girls he has made.

And where did they go? Consider Jason Francisco's photograph of that same corner in Worcester, taken in March 2015 (fig. 92). "I tracked Hine here and there, finding my way to his places, often to the very spot where he stood to make his pictures," Francisco writes, describing an epic 3,300-mile journey he took to sites where Hine had photographed more than a hundred years earlier. At these places Francisco contemplated the gap between Hine's time and his own, "never sure whether that interval is better understood as a presence or a withdrawal from presence." The past was there or it was not. Or it was there in some half-state—billowing into a gray storm of itself, even as it also left a windless calm of absence.

The Worcester street corner in Francisco's photograph is unremarkable. It presses on us the realization that were it not for our special knowledge that Hine had been there it would be a place we would walk right through, not mindful of any special past there. Nothing anchors or holds us by a telltale sign, a slender

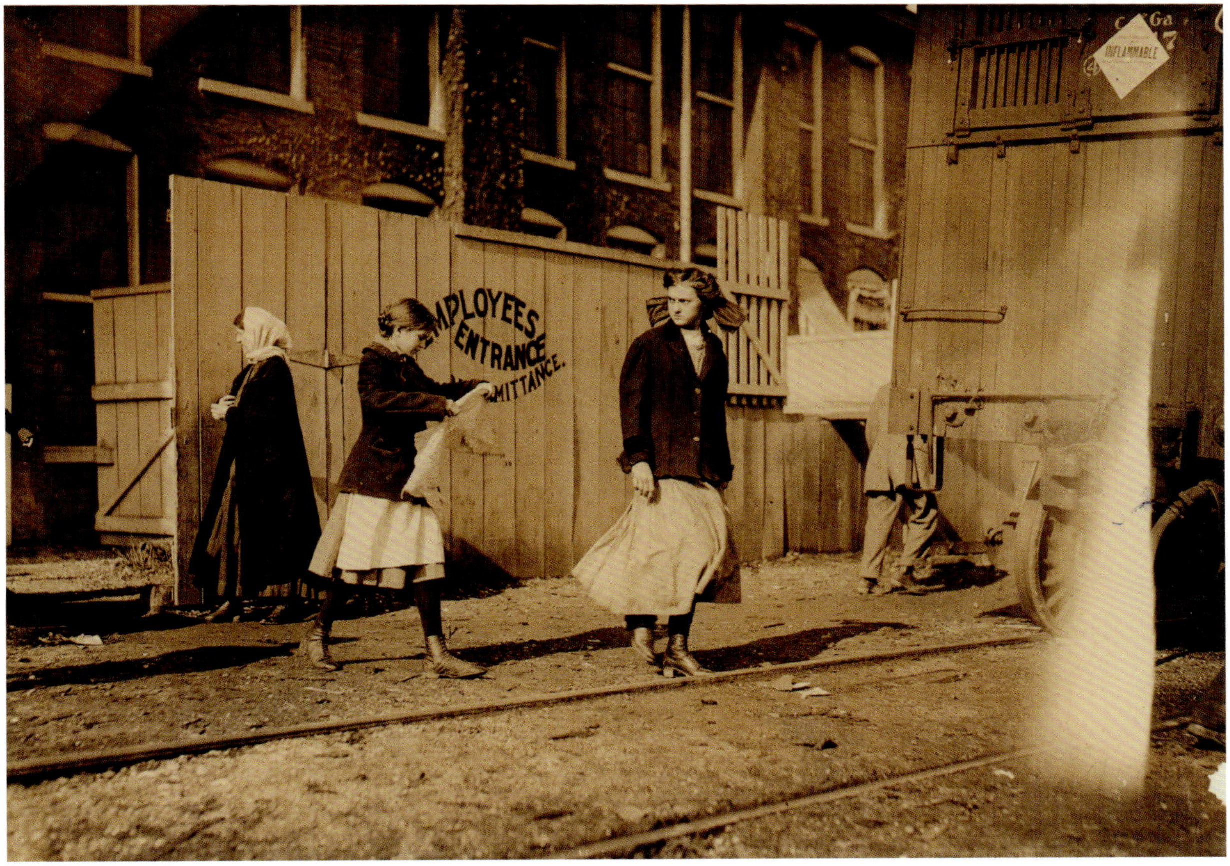

indicator that we should pause. Francisco's careful making of the picture—he used a 4 × 5 camera on a tripod, slowing the exposure and tilting the lens (for example, to get the blurring of the trees at upper right)—does however create a ripple of ceremonial strangeness, a feeling that we *should* stop, as he has done. Francisco, following in Hine's footsteps, makes emptiness animate the scene.

It is a feeling of extinction. At Rossville, Georgia, in December 1910, Hine photographed workers exiting the Richmond Hosiery Company at lunch (fig. 93). A young woman walks at the center, the strongest focus of Hine's attention. Set off from the other two prominent figures—a smaller girl folding a white kerchief, and a woman in a white headscarf waiting at the gate—the young woman looks keenly over her shoulder as she prepares to step over a rail spur. She is another Hine heroine, a personality. The desolate ground around the train tracks is not fit

Fig. 93
One of the young girls working in the Richmond Hosiery Co. Rossville, Georgia. December 1910.

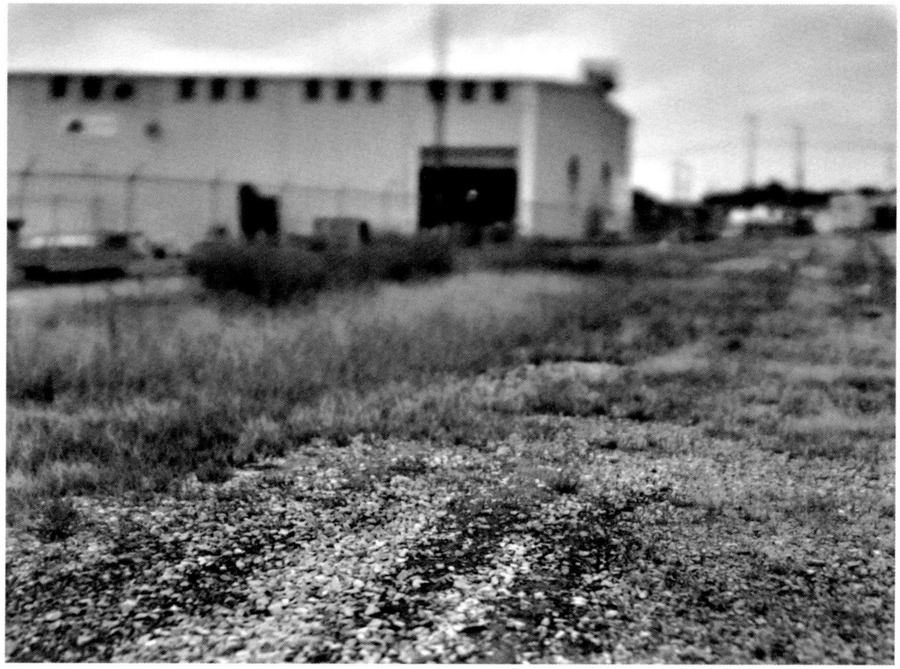

Fig. 94
Jason Francisco, *Site of the former Richmond Hosiery Mills, Rossville, Georgia*, September 2014.

to be beneath her feet, the filthy yard does not merit the impress of her boots. All of that is nothing, just a lot of squalor. But she is something. With her giant bow and exquisitely annoyed look, swishing her skirt in a way that uncannily matches the light leak in Hine's camera, she is a memorable figure, drawn out of nothing and nowhere, a moment of life itself. It seems impossible that there ever will be a time when she does not exist.

At the site of the Richmond Hosiery Company now, there is of course no trace of her (fig. 94). Torn down some ten years ago, the mill stood in the lot behind the barbed-wire fence in Francisco's September 2014 photograph. The scrub of weeds and gravel is where she walked. The space now is like a rocky beach at low tide. The energy of it has subsided. It has so much subsided that not only has the tide gone out but also the ocean is extinct and it is not clear, based on the flow of the fossils, just where was the surf and where was the shore.

Hine maybe aimed to make the girl memorable as a proof against this eventuality. The area around Rossville is full of commemorations—notably, at the nearby battlefield at Chickamauga, where Union and Confederate veterans began around

1880 to honor the spots where their respective regiments stood, making the place into a vast park of monuments by the time nearly the last of these solemn markers went up around 1930. And in Rossville itself, part of the monument diaspora around Chickamauga, a tall column dedicated to Iowa soldiers stands not a mile from the Richmond Hosiery Company. Then there is the John Ross house, home to the Cherokee chief, which even in 1910 was an unofficial memorial to his presence. At the mill itself it is as if Hine entered into the spirit of such recollections. The young woman marks the spot as if she would be the plenipotentiary of the place forever more.

But nothing grows there now. Does the photograph imagine the time in which she will be forgotten, her best defiance and pride vanished as if they never existed? At the Richmond Hosiery Company she made silk socks and stockings, the innovative foot- and leg-wear that replaced the coarse "leg-bag" hosiery of a previous generation. That hosiery got advertised in the pages of *Vogue* and other magazines that December, arrayed for the holiday season. The contrast between the cover of *Vogue* for December 1, 1910, and the Rossville girl on her lunch break could not be starker (fig. 95). The *Vogue* heroine—one of the illustrator Coles Phillips's popular "fadeaway girls"—has dropped a present. Her biggest problem in life is that there is no one yet to pick it up. Hine's heroine, meanwhile, walks the fallow ground of a place without gifts. She just makes the stuff. But the two young women share this: they both fade away—Hine's girl not only because her swishing skirt happens to match the camera's light leak but also because even more than Coles Phillips he practiced an art of disappearance.

Consider the next photograph taken that day outside the Richmond Hosiery employees' entrance (fig. 96). The woman in the white headscarf is still there, but the girl with the bow is gone. Naturally: she was on her way to lunch, making haste to get away from the mill. The center of Rossville was behind Hine as he made the photograph, and the girl looks like she is headed there. But the motion picture–type sequence of the two photographs opens up a set of time-effects that must have been curious in those years. People could be here one moment and gone the next, as if they had never been there at all. True, there was nothing automatically morbid about these effects, but there was nothing automatically indifferent about them either. The girl's disappearance is a dress rehearsal for the longer time when she will not be there. By the time Hine made the next photograph, centered on a

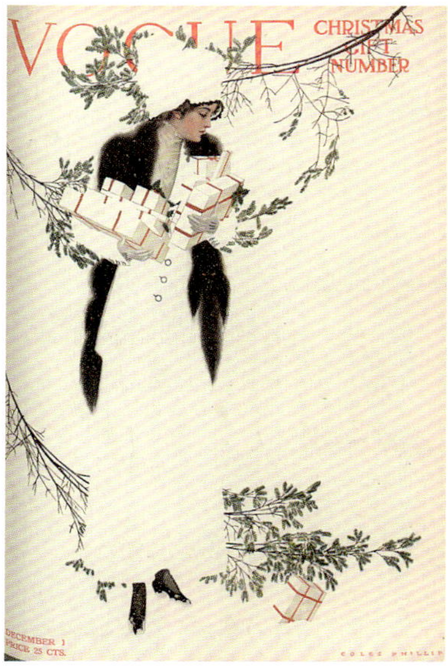

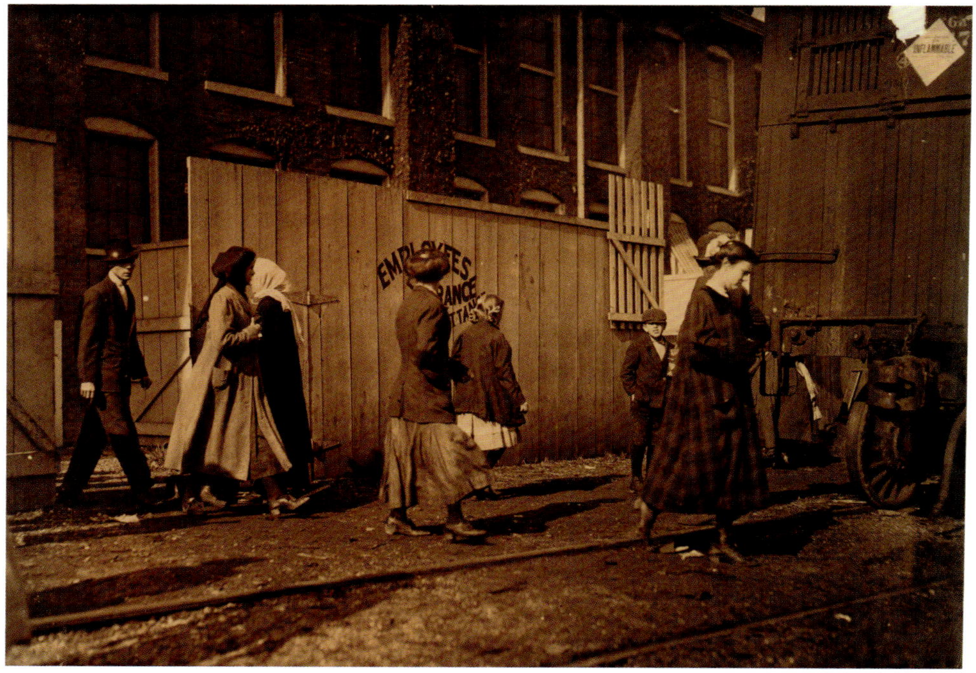

Fig. 95
Coles Phillips, *Fadeaway Girl*, *Vogue* (December 1, 1910).

Fig. 96
Noon hour Richmond Hosiery Co. Rossville, Georgia. December 1910.

decrepit man holding a lunch basket who stands a few feet from the torn paper on the ground where the girl was, the few seconds since she has been there are ancient history (fig. 97).

Erasure is what Francisco finds. At Spartanburg, South Carolina, in May 1912, Hine took a photograph of three boys leaving the Arkwright Mills one evening at 6:15 p.m. (fig. 98). The boys appear to be brothers, three ages with different dispositions to the man with the camera—the young one bashfully curious, the middle one suspicious, the oldest and lankest one turning away. They make a moment more various than an official history could describe. That year the long-time Democratic politician Coleman Blease, running for reelection as the governor of South Carolina, visited Spartanburg to rally the poor white mill workers who responded to his racist invective (not just a defender of lynching, he celebrated it). Hine might have shown the workers there without inflection—without doubt—as only a crude proletariat, but his moment, like the three brothers, takes different forms. Guileless children, not able to array themselves in proper guises, the brothers diffuse the time and place so that there is no such thing as "then and there" but only a dispersal of it in space. The tree grows and the mill stands, but we have no way of measuring what the moment is made of.

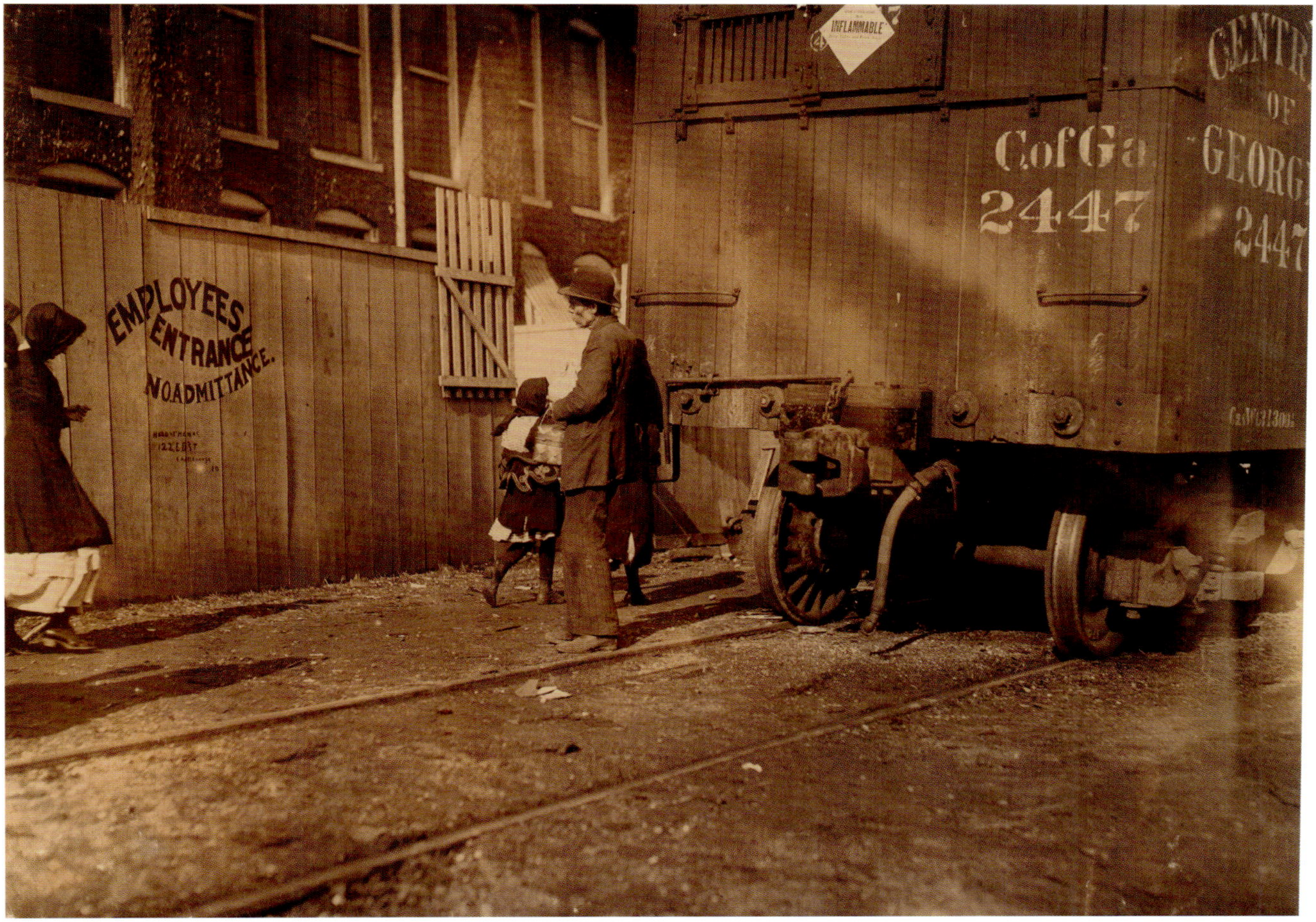

Fig. 97
One of the tiny workers in Richmond Hosiery Mills. Rossville, Georgia. December 1910.

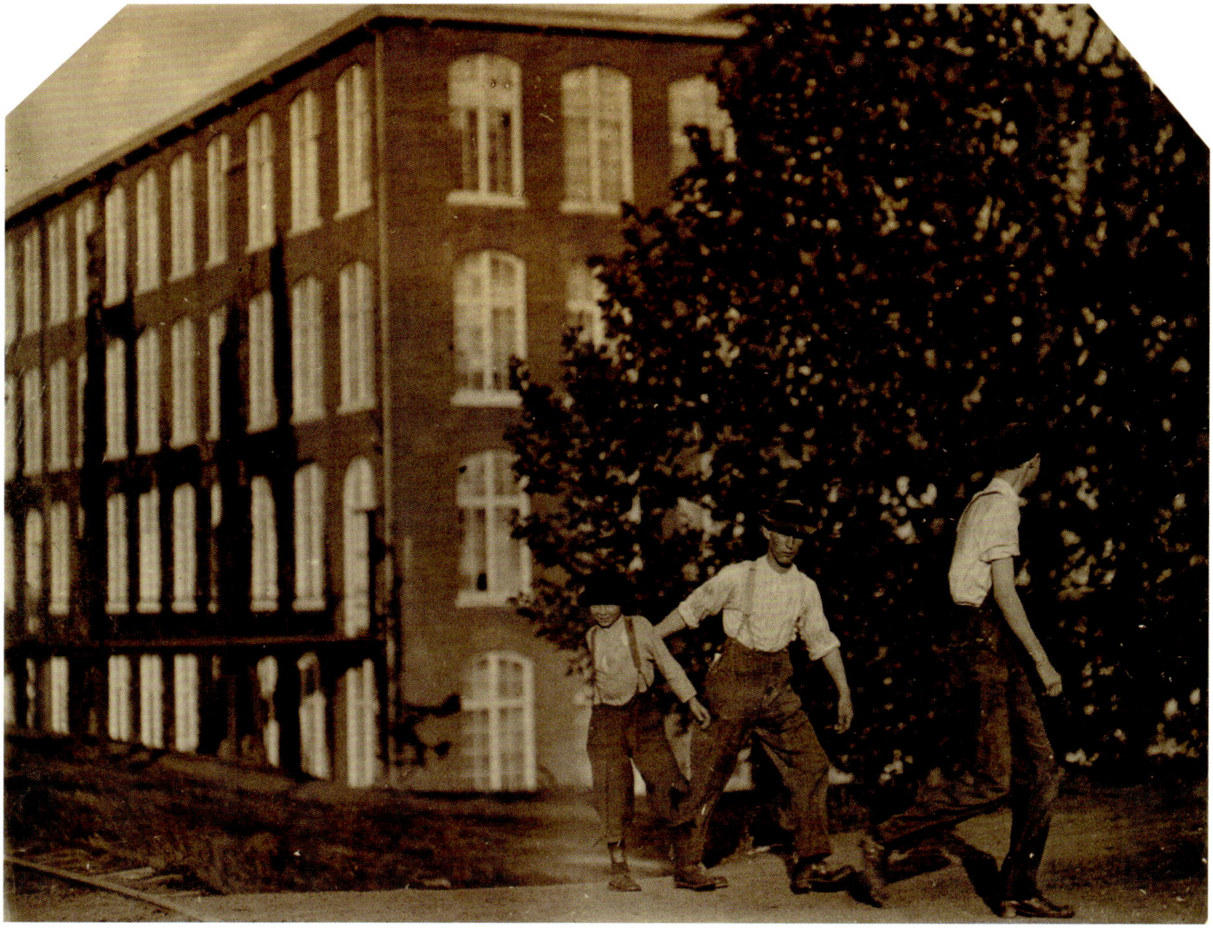

Fig. 98
6:15 P.M., Going Home from the Arkwright Mills, Spartanburg, S.C. May 1912.

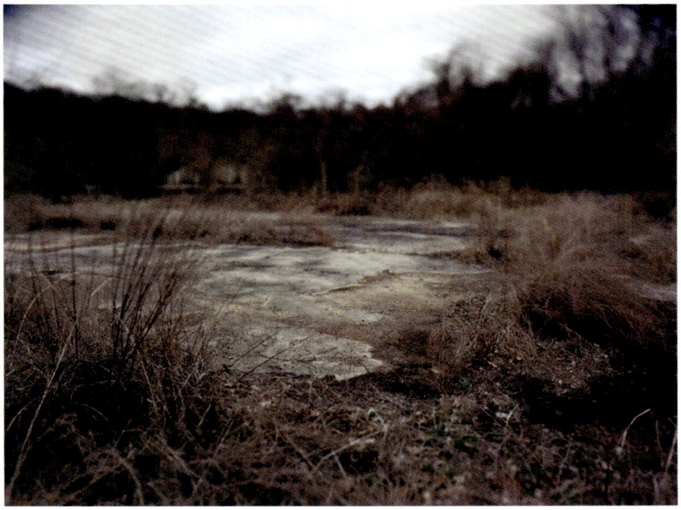

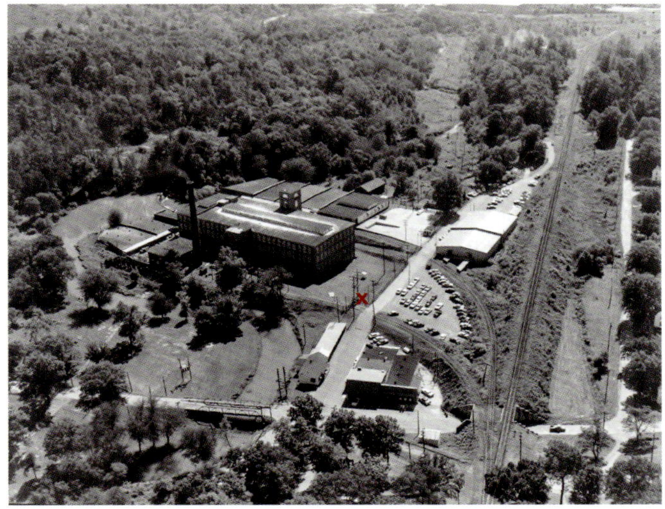

That moment you would never know now, looking at the site of the Arkwright Mills in one of Francisco's photographs (fig. 99). The mills have been demolished, though an aerial photograph of the building taken in the 1960s, which Francisco marked with an *X*, shows Hine's location when he made his picture (fig. 100). The place, in Francisco's image, is a blankness so complete that it is difficult to make contact with the past. As he wrote to me from Spartanburg, "Returning to Hine's locations now—not all of them but most of them so far—is not just to study change, but to study entropy, entropic loss, even abjection.... it's hard for me now to wrestle his sites in their afterlife back to the middle, as he did. It's as if the sites have been overtaken."

Fig. 99
Jason Francisco, *Site of the former Arkwright Mills, Spartanburg, South Carolina*, March 2015.

Fig. 100
Anonymous, *Arkwright Mills, Spartanburg, South Carolina* (x added by Jason Francisco to show Hine's location in fig. 98), ca. 1960s.

The slab concrete floor in the photograph, haloed in weeds, is a forceful platform that the photographer himself seems to conjure, as if by will, from the empty place. But the strength required appears too great, and all the magician of remembrance can summon, after several mighty heaves, is but this thin scrim of a past that begins to drown back down into the ground almost as soon as it is heaved up. Absence is now a hearty cliché of educated melancholy, a computer-generated phantasmagoria of once-there-now-gone effects—smiling predecessors vanishing in a cloud of digital effects—but Francisco comes by his absence the hard way: driving the highways to strange and forbidding places and photographing what is not there. It is as though his Spartanburg photograph is not just a portrayal of emptiness but a quotation of the computer-generated emptiness that his pictures overcome. Hine's boys are nowhere to be seen.

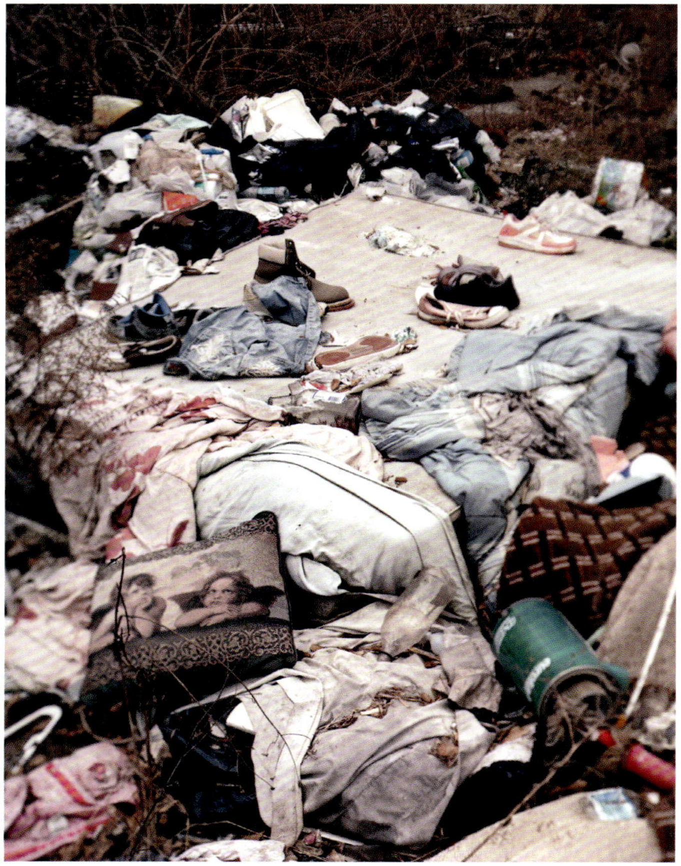

Fig. 101
Jason Francisco, *Dumping ground at the site of the former Arkwright Mills, Spartanburg, South Carolina*, March 2015.

It looks bleak. We search in vain for Hine's ghosts, or even for the feeling of being haunted by them. Despite the traces, Francisco's sense that "the sites have been overtaken" leaves him little to discover, even in the way of residual sensation. Worse still is the sense that Hine may have anticipated him, making his figures stride the earth only to test the grounds for when they will not be there. It is as if Hine knew the vaster emptiness contained in the ephemerality of a moment—the secret congress between the oblivion of a second and the deeper spill of forgetting, abandoning, and disappearing that is the flow of time across decades and now a century.

The nothingness is all the more frustrating because sites like Spartanburg remain, in Francisco's phrase, "unfinished memories." And as such they connect to other places around the world—notably, for Francisco, the places of the Holocaust in Poland and Ukraine, where he has spent much time photographing. He made his Hine trips in the latter stages of a long-term project called *Alive and Destroyed*, begun in 2010, that took him to different Holocaust sites where he made photographs clear and unclear, specific and ambiguous. And he began his Hine work not long after completing another Holocaust project, a piece called *An Unfinished Memory: Jewish Heritage and the Holocaust in Eastern Galicia*, commissioned by the Galicia Jewish Museum in Kraków for permanent display. No wonder the Holocaust seems to course through photographs such as one Francisco took at Spartanburg of abandoned belongings (fig. 101). The shoes and pillows and rained-on clothes in the weeds are not old enough to be ruins; rather they give off the new odor of the recently departed, a fantastic smatter of blue, pink, and sodden gray. No use in parsing symbols here—Raphael's dejected angels, sad on their throw-away pillow. Better to say that the junk is not yet junk but still someone's stuff, and that *the newness of the past* is Francisco's subject: the way items strewn here recall the freshness of other termini, seemingly more distant but really not, in Ukraine or Spartanburg. One ragged patch of forgotten stuff activates other more distant ones—the recollection of what is no longer there being always, somehow, fresh. Yet the feeling of *nothing there* remains.

It is a kind of telepathic mourning, strung together of wishful thinking and yet a deep sense—a photographer's sense, a writer's sense, too—that to be at the place is to invite some part of the past to come back to life. At Columbus, Georgia, where Hine took a photograph of a woman and a young girl walking across the 14th Street Bridge spanning the Chattahoochee River separating Georgia from Alabama (fig. 102), Francisco and I arrived around midnight to walk on the new pedestrian bridge fashioned from the old. The renovated bridge, part of a recent civic redevelopment project, is a postindustrial tour de force. Alluding to the iron-work era it has replaced, the bridge is a polished river walk trellised with girder-designs and other simulations of bygone industrial architecture. Neat iron railings and concrete pylons evoke the old bridge's iron superstructure. The smooth paths and bricks and brilliant lights convey the well-lit safety of a place where the past has been suitably commemorated and vanquished. Nearby in a little plot are the cornerstones of the city's mills, displayed in a kind of graveyard of recognition, good and buried, while a bit farther back down the street on the Columbus side stands a massive parking garage designed to look like a mill.

Does Hine's photograph taken at Columbus "know" any of this? Is its sense of time that capacious? The woman and girl walk away from the Muscogee Mill, where the parking garage now stands. The very stride of the woman and girl seems cadenced as if made for the rhythmic sound their footfalls make upon the wooden

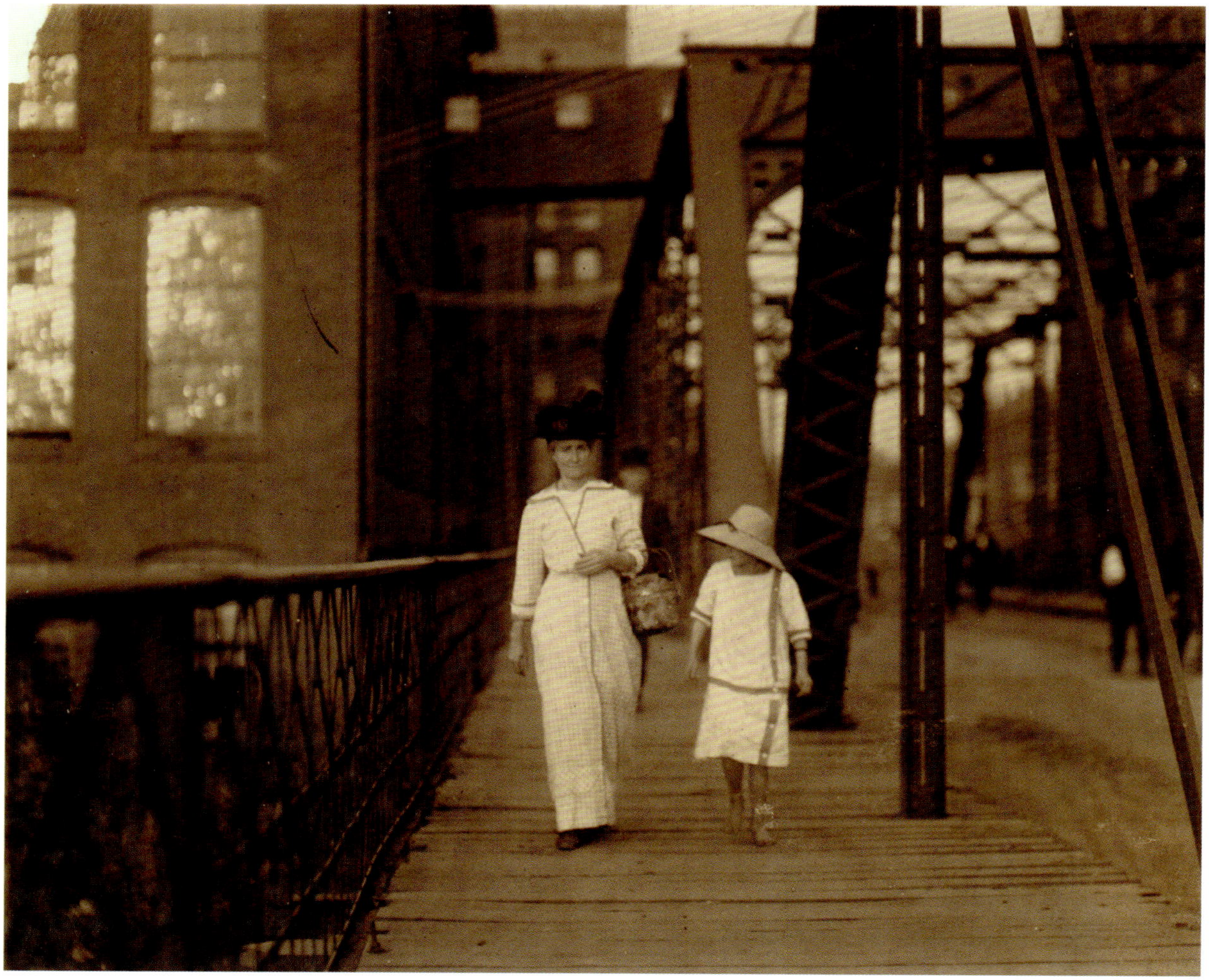

Fig. 102
I found some young helpers like this one in the Muscogee Mills, Columbus, Ga. April 1913.

planks. Shod and unshod, they distribute the time as so many sounds, louder and softer, spread behind them and ahead of them in gentle but firm reverberations. Above and around the woman and girl, the iron railings and beams convey the dignity of their pace, a ceremonial architecture of industrial splendor as grand as any triumphal arch through which an emperor might enter a welcoming city. Time—including the time of being photographed—takes on a regal formality, a pomp and circumstance, as if the bridge had bloomed there and then as an oxidized glory befitting the occasion. The big down-thrusting iron beam with its marvelous zigzag pattern emphatically channels down to the little girl—a lightning strike

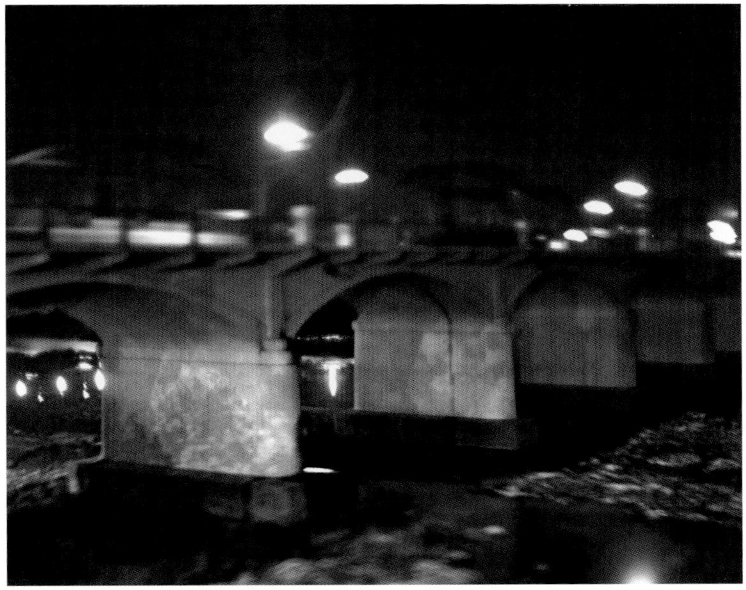

Fig. 103
Jason Francisco, *The 14th Street Bridge over Chattahoochee River, Columbus, Georgia*, September 2014.

fusing the figures electrically to that place. The moment, if sensed properly, reveals an ecstatic structure.

And if that structure were strong enough—if every last element of it were bolted into place—then maybe it could travel into a future where the very bridge becomes a memory. That is the ridiculous fantasy, the hope—time against time, 'til the end of time. Like the heroines of a science-fiction tale, the woman and the girl trust the man with the camera that the structure he has devised—some kind of photographic Zeppelin built to the latest industrial specifications—will encapsulate them and carry them forward. I think of Strobel's dirigible (fig. 31). Will it hold us? Is it sturdy enough? The girl looks toward the woman as if not sure it is all right. What is this "moment" thing, anyway? Is it okay to be in it? Neither the woman nor the girl really knows the moment like Hine knows it and can envision it—the elegant superstructure of a royal appointment. But the impresario appears to be a trustworthy fellow. And as the saying goes, it is the latest technology. So they go forward.

At splashdown the night Francisco and I were there on the new bridge we could not find much trace of what they traveled in. Unless it were the river itself purling beneath the bridge, revealed in a four-minute exposure Jason made that night (fig. 103). The photograph makes the river flow as well as William

Faulkner could make it run—a stagnant Styx lit in that long exposure made when Jason placed his tripod, and then himself, precariously on the river ramparts of the bridge. Then on this postindustrial castle with nothing to defend he looked down at what is still there, always there, but usually unseen. Back behind him as he made the photograph were the white cornerstones of different mills, including the Muscogee, set into their graveyard amid plinths and plaques, a neat and chiseled resting place. But the sludgy undercurrent is another past, a flow of time compounded of the water and the photograph's ribboned stretch of time. The two blur together, until what is felt is not a continuum between past and present but a sense that these durations—the photographer's and historian's principles of continuity between past and present—are themselves a kind of industrial by-product, a rhetorical waste, the remains of an era such as Hine's that thrived on sliced and carved and delineated time. What that era did not need it discarded, and among the things it did not need was the flow that Francisco and I discovered in Columbus. Maybe Hine, ever attentive to junk, knew that perpetuity was what his culture threw away.

At times the past takes an unbidden shape, half-jangled into a contemporary manifestation. At Knoxville where the two little girls cautiously strode out on the loading dock, Jason and I find the same building in a different form (fig. 104). The Volunteer Knit Apparel building, on that same site, looks at first like a modern structure built on the place of the old, but it turns out to be the same building that Hine photographed, just given a new front of stucco and metal cladding. Inside, on the day when we are there, garment workers are busy running huge swaths of green felt-like cotton through conveyor belts and silver steam machines—making sweatshirts for the army, they tell us. Around them as they talk we look at the interior brick walls—the same ones that were there in December 1910—concealed on the outside but visible in the steam. Back outside, the workers take breaks, checking their cell phones as they sit on picnic benches beneath a crude silver awning that keeps out the September sun. The work goes on, just as Francisco's mentor Allan Sekula always said it did, and Francisco asks if he can take the workers' photographs as they relax. Getting their consent, he waits until they forget he is there.

Out at the front of the building, the porch marks the spot of the loading dock. The area is all closed off, however—separated from us by a chain-link fence and barbed wire. Within that quarantined area, an iron railing makes a kind of

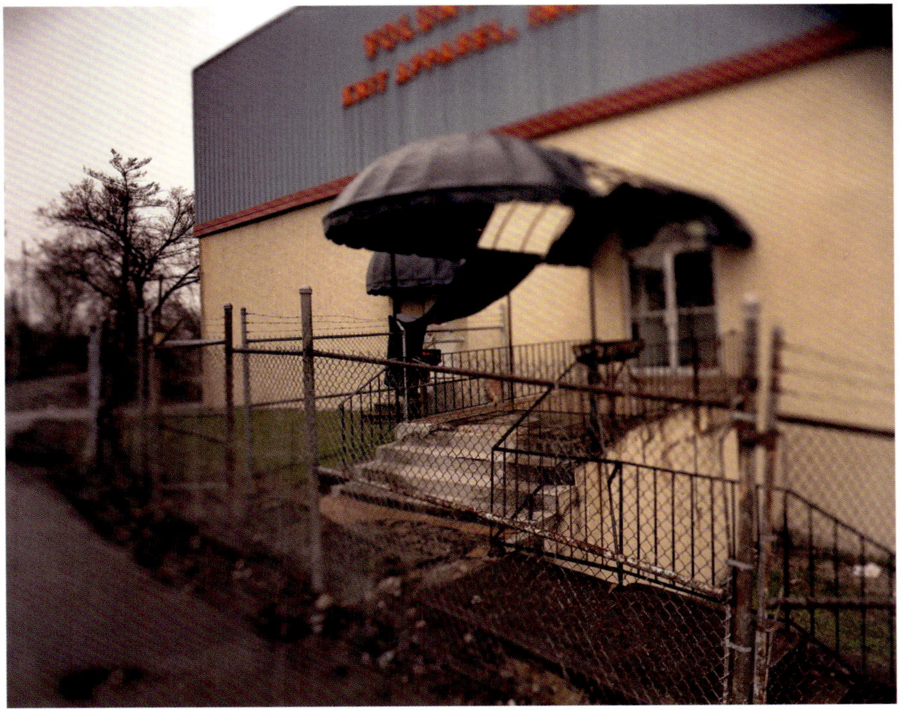

Fig. 104
Jason Francisco, *The former Knoxville Knitting Works, Knoxville, Tennessee,* September 2014.

additional fence, adding to the zigzagged separation of the past. The area where the girls walked (see fig. 27) is a no-trespassing zone. More than that, it resembles a failed magic trick, as if the summoner of the past, confusing his signals, instead of making it arise should have crossed his hexes so that what appears is actually this cubist lace of interference. A jumbled array of partitions arises, thrown together as if gathered from a back lot of props. It is like the enthusiastic handiwork of a master fence builders who, rising to the task, actually overdid the misplaced directive that the past be off limits.

But the place of the girls comes through. The porch is a quotation of the loading dock. The glass doors mark where the old doors were, and the awning is where the striped one used to be. The whole building keeps to the dimensions of the brick beneath, and the same railroad tracks run by on a recognizable curve. The exact location is a finality—we have found the place—though the question remains of what the meaning of "final" is.

That is because, at that same place, among the last of the photographs Hine took that day in December 1910, is one of all the mill's children out on the loading

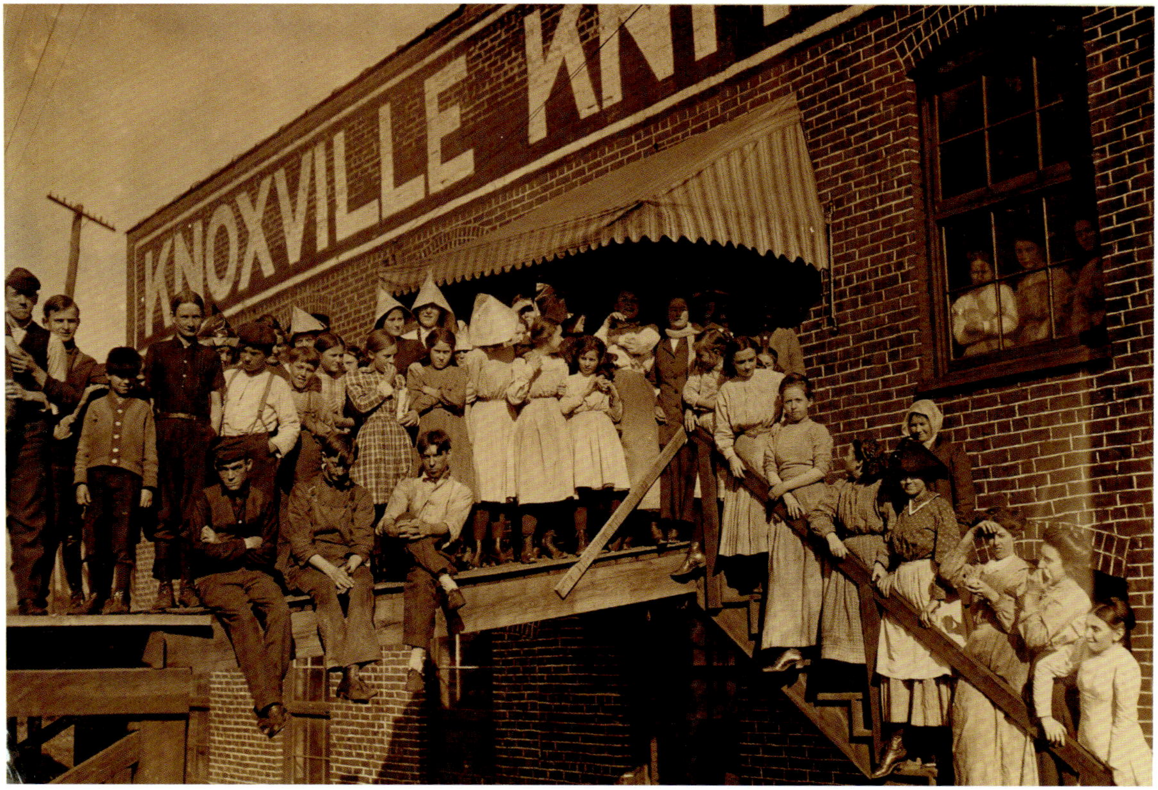

Fig. 105
All are workers in Knoxville Knitting Mills. Smallest boy "ravels," smallest girl is a steady worker. Knoxville, Tennessee. December 1910.

dock posing for him (fig. 105). From the tentative foray of the two girls to now this overflowing interest in the photographer—the final picture is a kind of curtain call. The children take their bows, as if acknowledging the performance Hine has directed. The show is over—the photographer's time is concluding there—and it is time to move on. The pied piper maestro must go, this episode of the socialist theater at an end. And as in any curtain call, a curious effect of reality obtains: the moment when the actors and actresses are finally themselves but still residually their characters. And that reality is made vivid by departure—soon the people we only now see as themselves will disappear. Then the aftereffect of an ephemeral moment—maybe what Hine has all along sought—begins to exert its power, crumpling the fences, bending the iron railings, closing off the present tense, as if "finality" were a kind of medium—even a philosophical principle—that Hine could wield and make stay, chained to that one spot, as the finish to a work that would never be completed.

Fig. 106
Jason Francisco, *The former Singer Manufacturing Company, South Bend, Indiana*, March 2015.

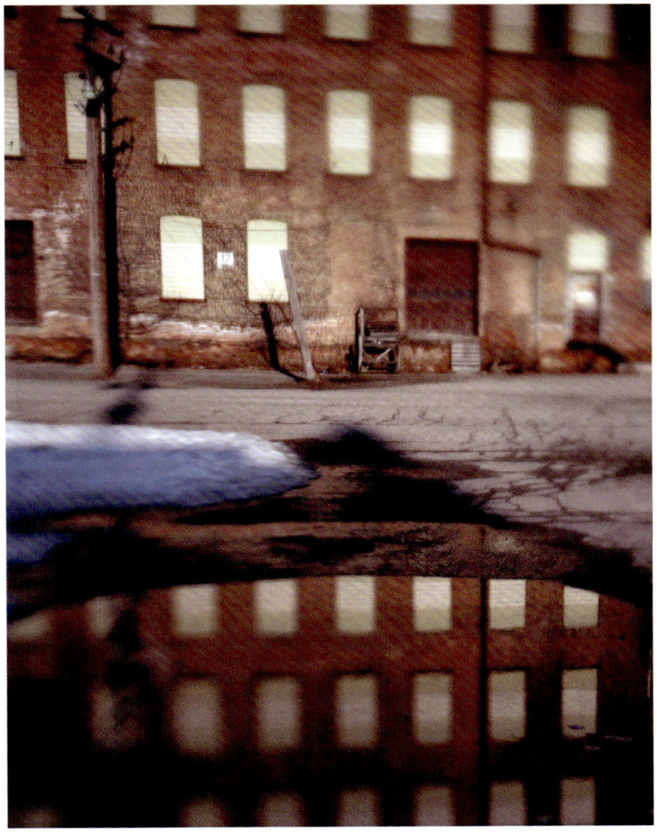

At such foreclosed, curtain-called places, it is a question of sentiment. At South Bend, where the little girl waited (and still waits) to deliver her lunch (see figs. 40–43), Jason photographs the abandoned Singer factory. Among the pictures he makes there is one showing a moribund building reflected in a puddle (fig. 106). It is a lovely adolescent gesture—full of fine sadness like what a teenager feels, a Holden Caulfield moment, a sense of exquisite chance beauty that a teenager believes has been set aside for him alone.

But down in the sorrow zone of these abandoned buildings, who is to say that an adolescent vision is not the proper medium? Puddles are the mountain lakes of the asphalt—secluded spots where the glacial runoff gathers in flattened pools. The site of the Singer factory repossesses itself, reclaiming its own image in a standstill of self-absorption. The photographer, happening upon the moment when the building in its decrepit spinsterhood is still admiring itself, chances on a poignant

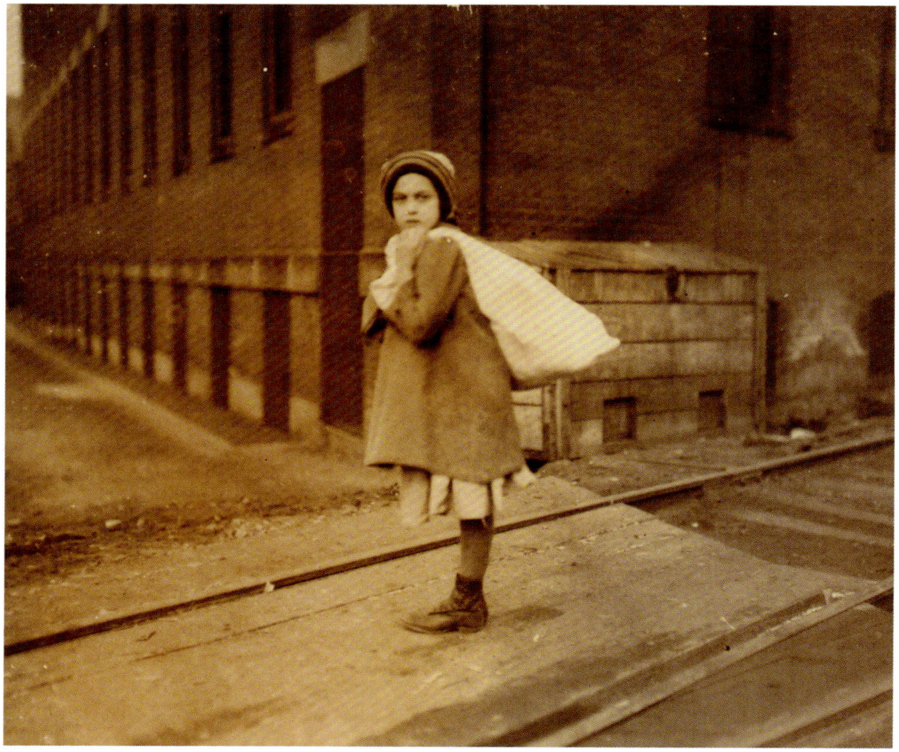

Fig. 107
Nearly 9 A.M. Girl (about 8 years old) carrying sack of hose supporters home, a long distance and she had to run to get home in time for school. Worcester, Mass. November 1912.

moment of loss. Interrupted in the circuit of its self-contemplation, the building hardly notices the traveler whose adolescent melancholy is the medium of its fretful reappearance. And down in the drowned deadbeat feel of the photograph is a sullen disillusion with the America of Hine, and now.

The visitor to such a place suffers the accusation that he is only a disaster tourist. He only indulges a fantasy, the criticism goes; he exults in pristine desolation. South Bend is his Chamonix. But the label is unfair. This pool of Narcissus is selfless. The Alpine traveler removes his cap and stares at a mirror where he does not appear. Going to a place where you are not there is a good working definition for fieldwork of this kind. Take it or leave it, because such places will surely take and leave you. They often have a toxic, half-life feel.

Francisco's Hine journey is a pilgrimage, not a vacation. The pilgrims to Santiago de Compostela in Spain stood in awe at the *Pórtico da Gloria*, a vast and intricate carving depicting the Apocalypse: Christ enthroned, the evangelists, the apostles, the instruments of the Passion, the souls of the saved and the damned. It is all there, an infinity, the End of Time. At South Bend the pilgrim finds another kind of church, a brick cathedral, where in scroll-less and blank walls, unwritten with sayings, he discovers a local Armageddon. Our Lady of the End of an Era, call it—a cathedral dedicated not to showing the destruction of the world but the destruction of itself. What the pilgrim to such places really finds, however, is *continuing* time, unfinished, pooled, standing, lost in self-regard. This continuing time is so abandoned that it finally seems to be consuming itself, having long since devoured all other rations, so that daily it takes a little more of its own life in self-consuming transfusions. The past wastes away, gorged on its own recollection, and the pilgrim goes to the spot as if witnessing the glut of time were a religious rite, an obscure responsibility.

It is a pilgrimage—it is also a quest. At Worcester one morning in November 1912 Hine photographed a girl holding a bag of fabric to take from the factory and work on at home (fig. 107). Her job is the same as that of the two girls striding at one of the city's corners. Like them, she looks like a wayfarer—a little wanderer with a satchel on her back, headed who knows where, a refugee from her own life and her own time, undergoing a Sebald-like deportation, even as the caption tells us she is just going home. When Francisco finds the spot where Hine made this photograph and makes a photograph of his own there, later saying that it is among the places where he felt Hine's presence the strongest, the picture suggests not only his pilgrimage to this chilly place but his mad quest (fig. 108). Call it Quixote-like. *Right there where nothing is, that's where she was, where she and Hine somehow still are*, I can imagine Jason saying, or I would say myself. A Sancho Panza alongside would correct us, pointing out that there is nothing there, not even a vestige, that it is silly to import such drama to a blank brick wall, no matter who or what ever existed there. But the quest continues, no one there to right it. When I am along with Jason it is though there are two Quixotes there and no Sancho Panza. Add Joe Manning, if he ever accompanied us, and it would have been three Quixotes and still no Sancho.

It is an idiot's pursuit, of course (fig. 109). The yellow shack stripped of its siding at North Pownal, Vermont, where Addie Card used to work, becomes … what? In Francisco's photograph it is a vision, like a hut that Quixote might insist is a quaint inn or country retreat, the touching abode of a wise hermit where we might learn word of the damsel we seek. At Bennington the Holden-Leonard Mill rises up as a specimen of industrial architecture and as a scarlet ogre, menacing on

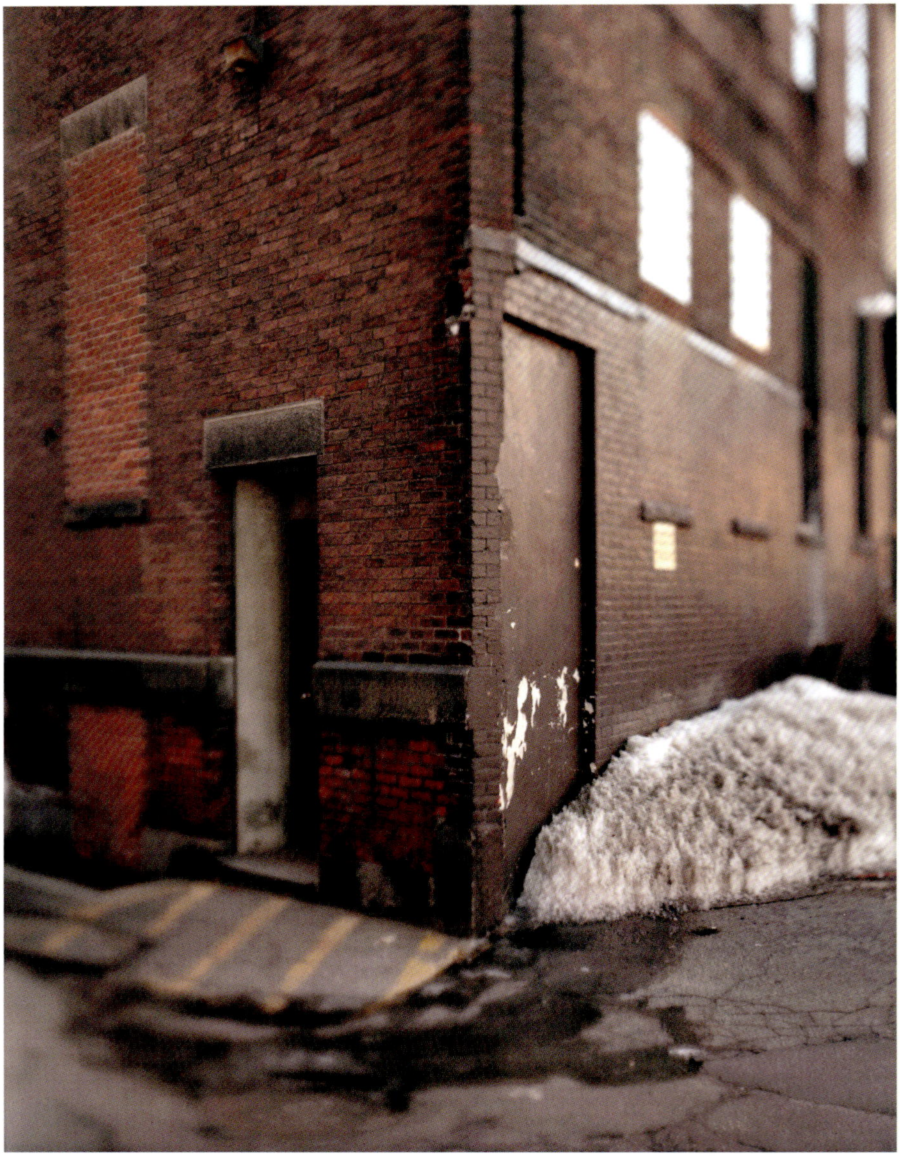

a bitterly cold day (fig. 110). Mirages like these portray the historian as Knight Errant: a person who sees what other people do not see, who believes that the past where those people once spilled out that door (see figs. 48, 50, 51) still exists. It cannot be that there is *only* a brick wall. It cannot be that imagination plays *no* part in historical inquiry. It cannot be that a cosmography of invisible presences does

Fig. 108 (opposite)
Jason Francisco, *The former American Narrow Fabric Company, Worcester, Massachusetts*, March 2015.

Fig. 109
Jason Francisco, *Forsaken house for mill workers, North Pownal, Vermont*, March 2015.

Fig. 110
Jason Francisco, *The Holden-Leonard Mill, Bennington, Vermont*, March 2015.

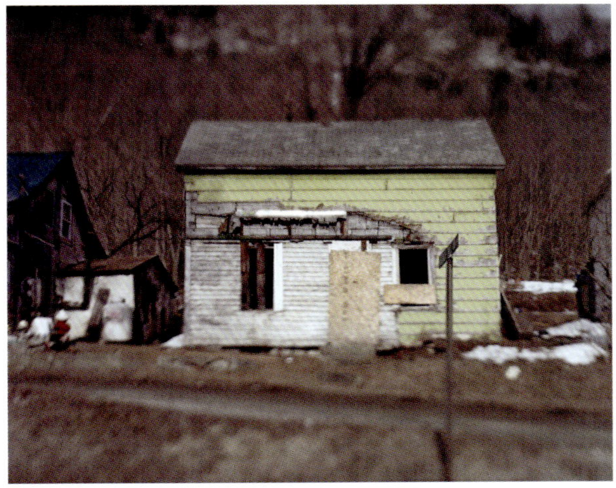

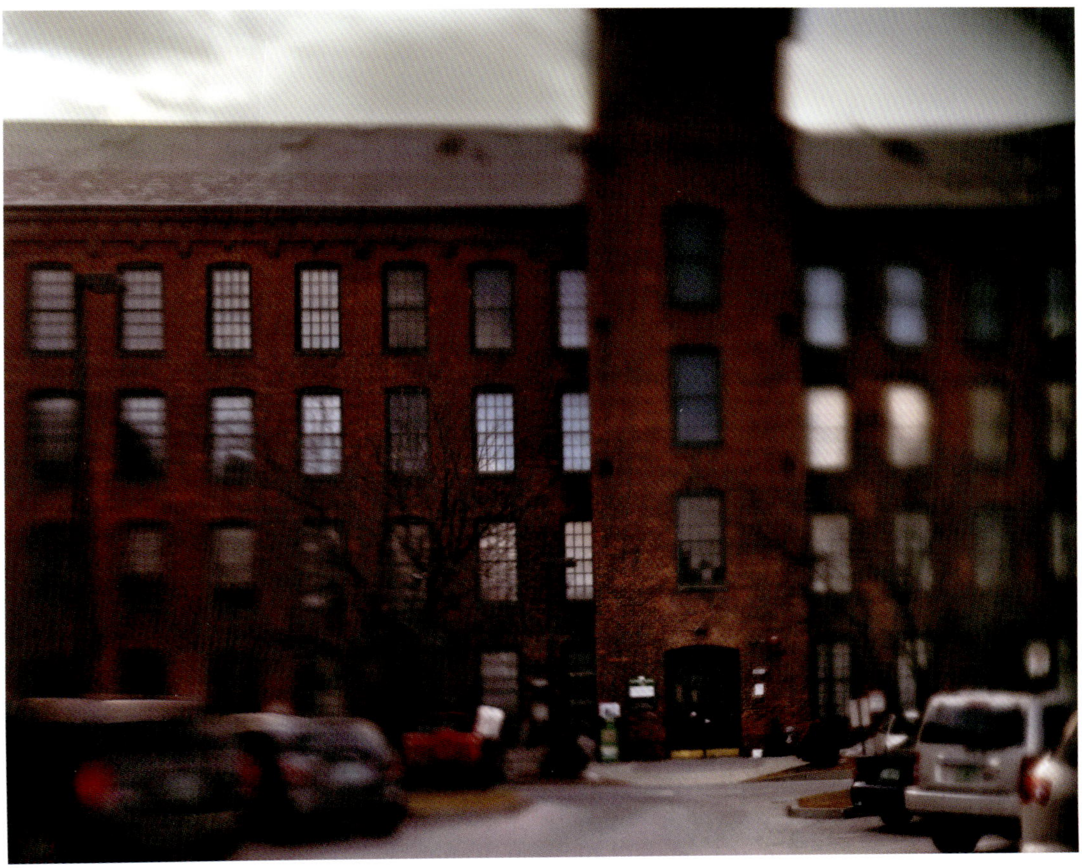

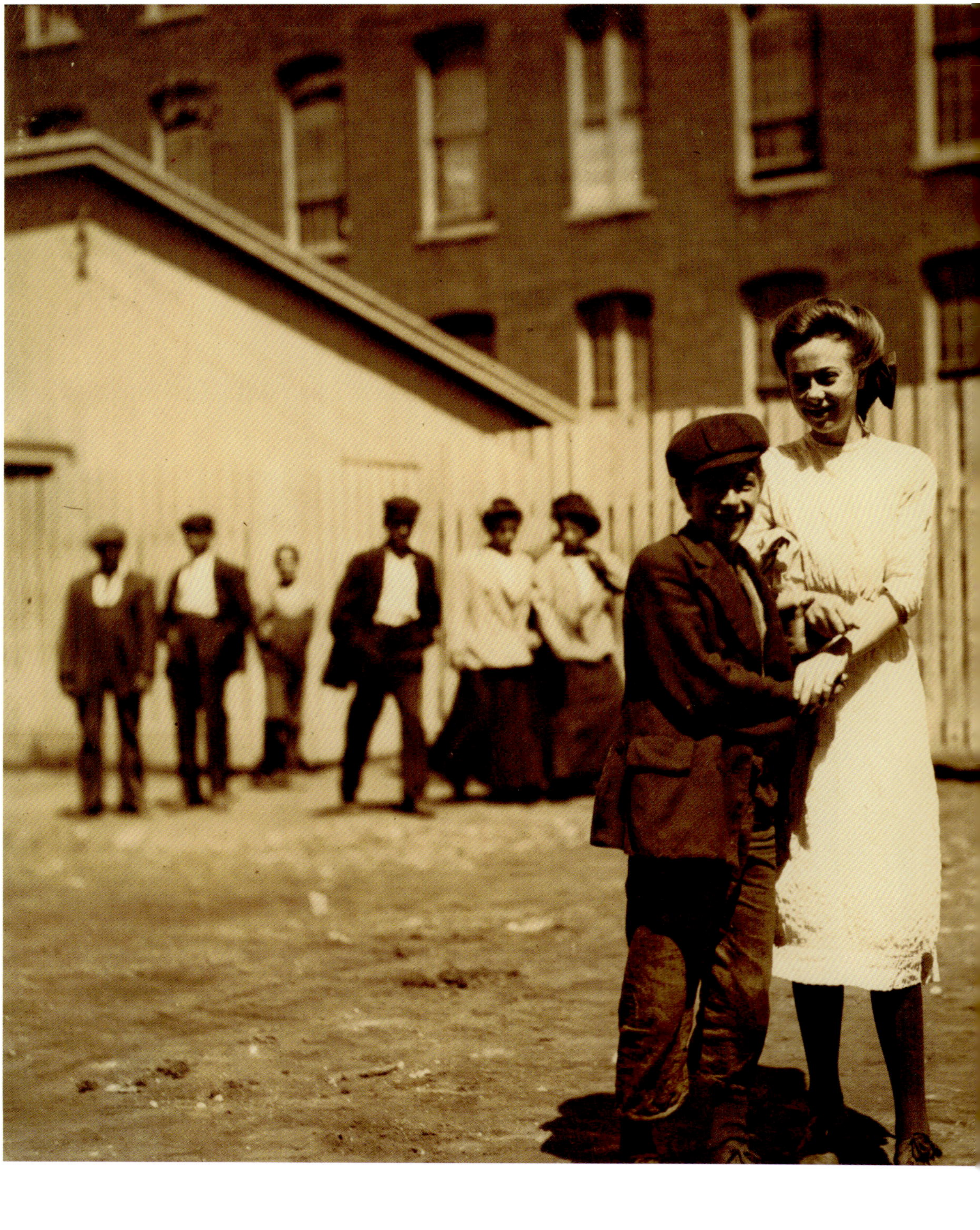

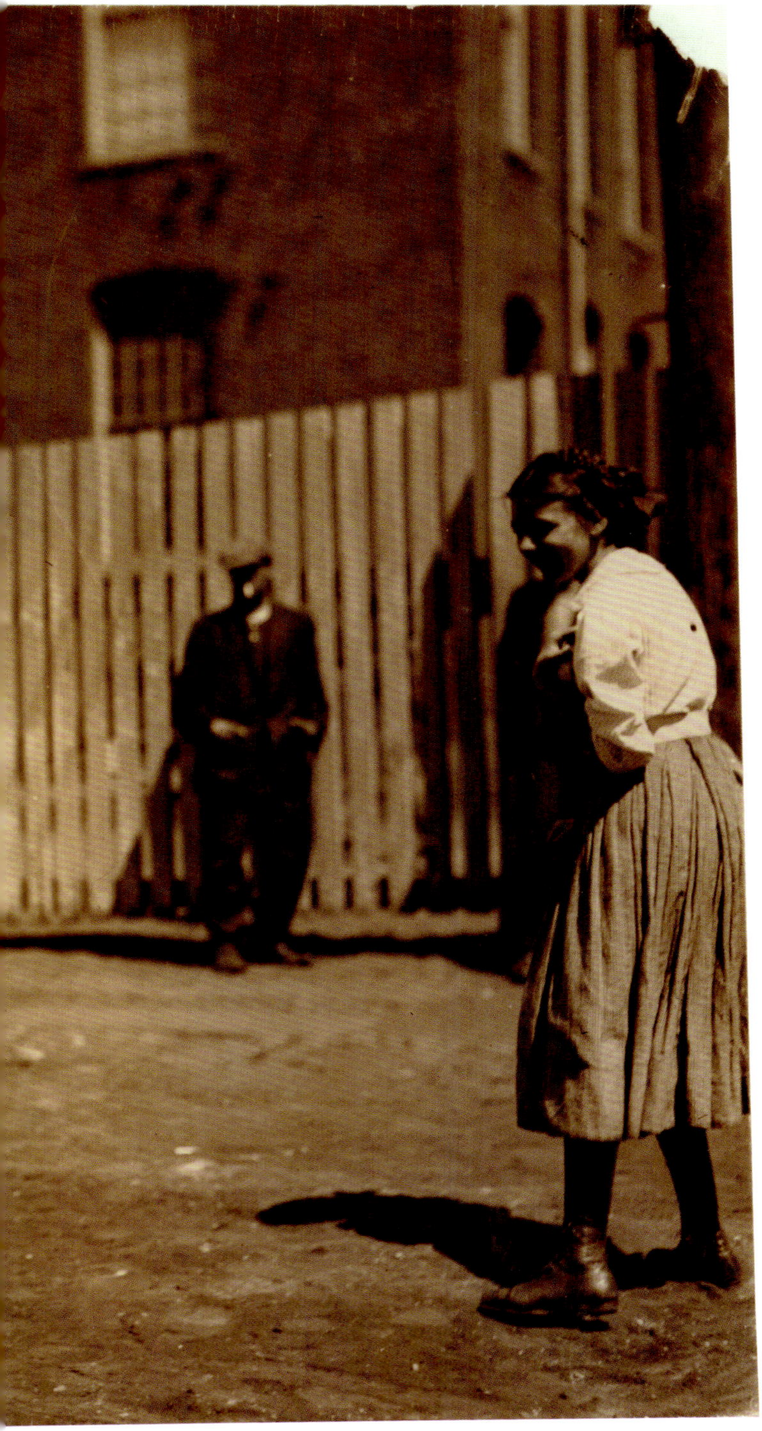

Fig. 111
Sarah Nelson, County Street, (over grocery store) Arthur Sarasin. Sarah is 14 years old. New Bedford, Massachusetts. August 1911.

not somehow structure our relation to the past. If the fantasy is redemptive—if it savors of rescue—it is only an echo of Hine's. He too did it for love.

At New Bedford, Massachusetts, in August 1911, Hine photographed fourteen-year-old Sarah Nelson as she stood next to a younger boy, Arthur Sarasin (fig. 111). Sarah in her white dress points with her right hand toward Hine and rests her left hand in Sarasin's. It is a kind of betrothal, unusual in Hine's photographs: she in white, he in dark, her shining hair swept back, the two children coming together in a vow of flirtation. Let no man keep apart this couple, child bride and groom, the girl tall and thin like the fence, the shadows of her fingers falling on her white wrist.

Nor are the couple the only ones in the romance. To one side, a girl in a white blouse smiles at the boy and girl posing for the little wedding photographer. Hand on her hip, her body swiveling slightly (her left foot raised off the ground), the girl looks jilted or jealous. Gathering one of her hands to her chest, she seems affronted or wounded in the way that people who smile sometimes do. Off at the edge, she is a spurned suitor, rejected both by the boy and the photographer who perhaps unbeknownst to her photographs her anyway. And maybe it is she who most fascinates him, as if the ceremony of the couple's pose were just a pretense to see what energies would spin to the sides of the official clasp of hands. That foolish goofy wallflower charges the empty space between her and Sarah Nelson with a strong blankness that the lounging man matter-of-factly smoking a cigarette against the fence cannot begin to detect. And if her swivel-hipped pose is that of someone precisely in the moment—who cannot think of anything other than what is happening at that time, pregnant with all that it means—she nonetheless spins from herself a whirling energy that is more than the sum of her disappointment. Sherwood Anderson called his 1932 novel of a strike at a textile mill *Beyond Desire*—he meant going beyond love and passion to causes of political righteousness. But I am not sure that Hine wanted to go beyond desire.

At the site now, Jason photographs a place like the one where Sarah Nelson, Arthur Sarasin, and the other girl stood (fig. 112). The blur of the tree is maybe where the past gets tangled, lost in leafless deficits. Or maybe it is in the abraded brick or the dirty melting snow. The blurry wet pavement makes a good choice. So do the boarded-up windows, the steep stairs, the cheap railings. The scene offers so much forlornness that the difficulty is finding the place where the past is *not* there.

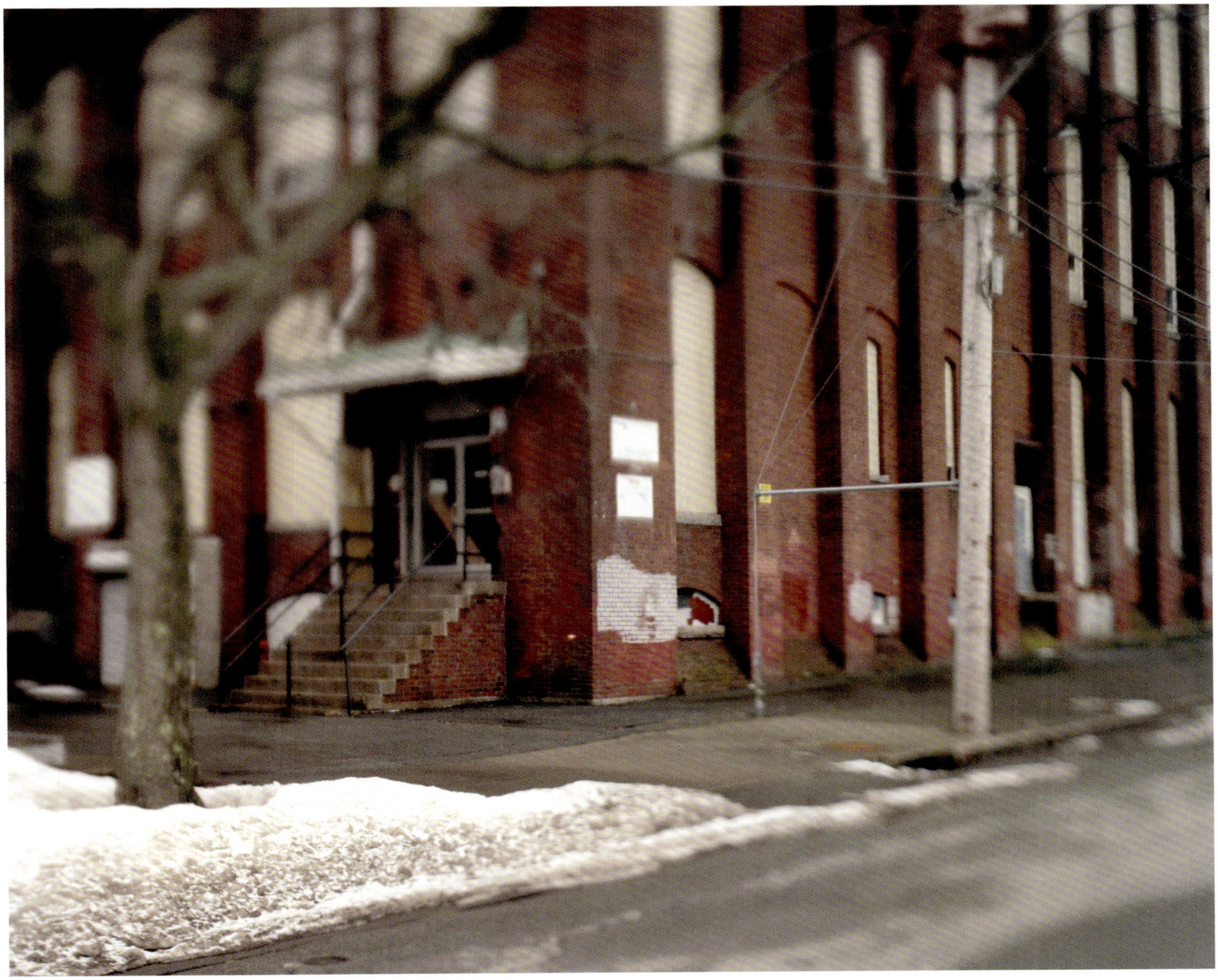

Its photogenic blankness is even glamorous. No wonder that *Beyond the Ruins* is the title of a recent book about the postindustrial landscape of America. The melancholy is too seductive. It is everywhere. One must resist. The sadness is just sentimental mysticism. Spare us the silent ordination, the formalities, visitations, and ceremonies. Don't go there. Yes, beyond melancholy. And beyond love. *Beyond the Ruins*. *Beyond Desire*.

Fig. 112
Jason Francisco, *The north gate of the former Butler Mills, New Bedford, Massachusetts*, March 2015.

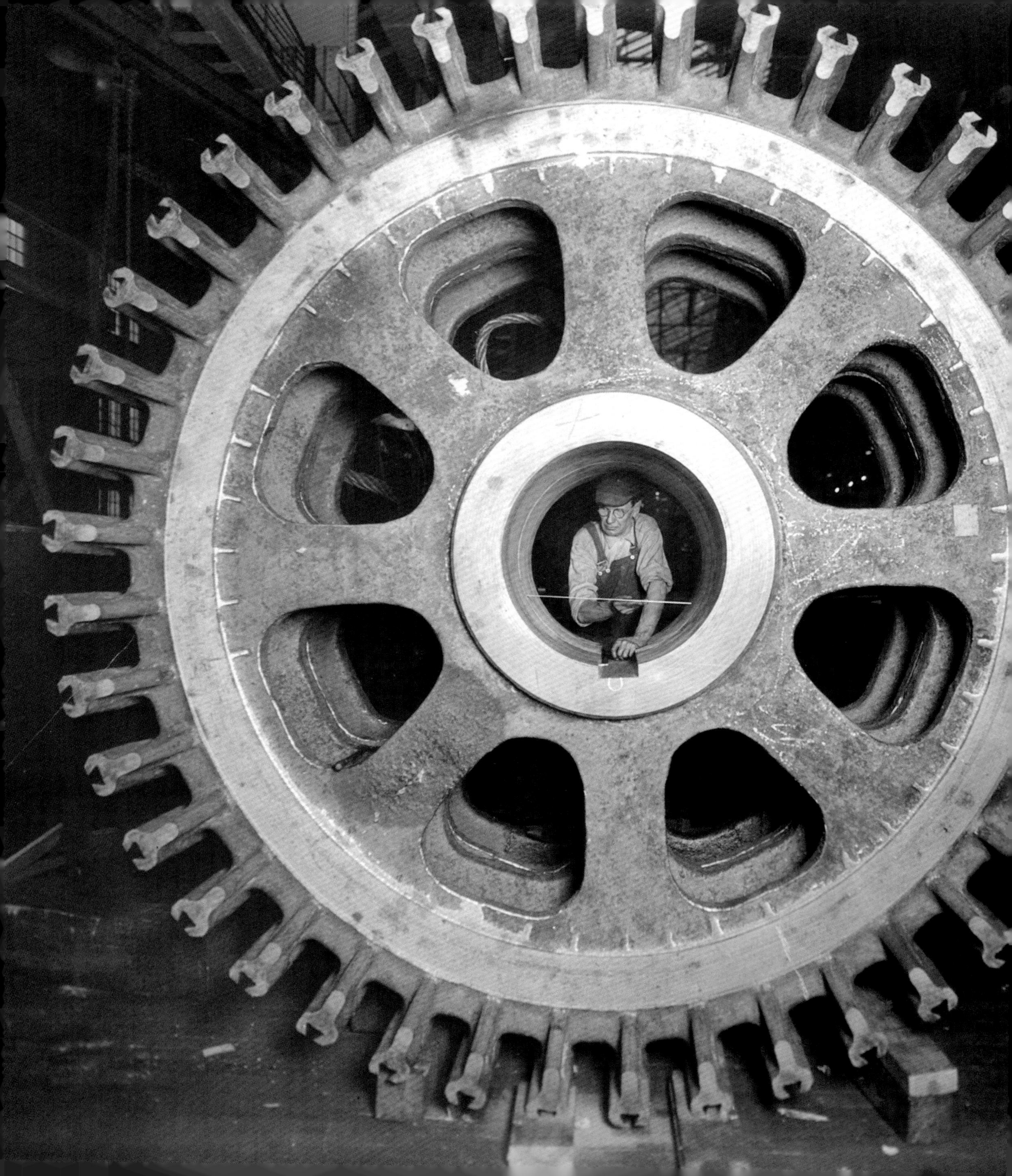

6 WE WORK IN THE DARK

Opposite the dedication page of Hine's 1932 book *Men at Work* is a photograph of a man at the center of a great gear wheel (fig. 113). His sleeves rolled up, wearing overalls, cap, and glasses, the anonymous man concentrates on the task at hand. Across the page is Hine's dedication: "To my friend Frank A. Manny," then a quotation from William James's "The Moral Equivalent of War," then acknowledgments. The photograph of the spectacled man in the cap, identity unknown, enshrines his labor. It also enshrines Hine.

There at the center of it all, precious like some coiffed Roman emperor on a centuries-old piece of bronze, the man is the coin of Hine's realm. *Men at Work* puts human toil at the center of things—no matter how dwarfed by machines the worker may be, he is the turning point, gleaming in his cameo. With modesty he makes the wheel go round, and if he is a martyr to his labor—Ixion strapped to his spoked disc—we do not see his tragedy but rather the mint of his worth. Oliver Wendell Holmes once likened photography to money—a new-struck currency back then when it was new—and Hine's book, made for children, tells the tale of laborers as pennies from heaven.

Hine also is ensconced in this medallion. By 1932 his portrayals of child labor were long past. He had moved to other projects—notably the photographs he made in Europe immediately after World War I—but he had not achieved any great recognition. "The drama of Hine's life," Elizabeth McCausland wrote in 1938, "is that history's rapid tempo has carried us beyond what he originally did and that in the haste of living, the younger generation does not have time even to know its spiritual progenitors, let alone appreciate them."

Berenice Abbott's photograph of Hine, taken also in 1938, shows him as the little man on a rocking chair in his house outside New York (fig. 114). He is smaller than life, a "genuinely simple and sturdy soul," in Abbott's friend McCausland's

Fig. 113
Huge casting for a big electric transformer. Ca. 1925.

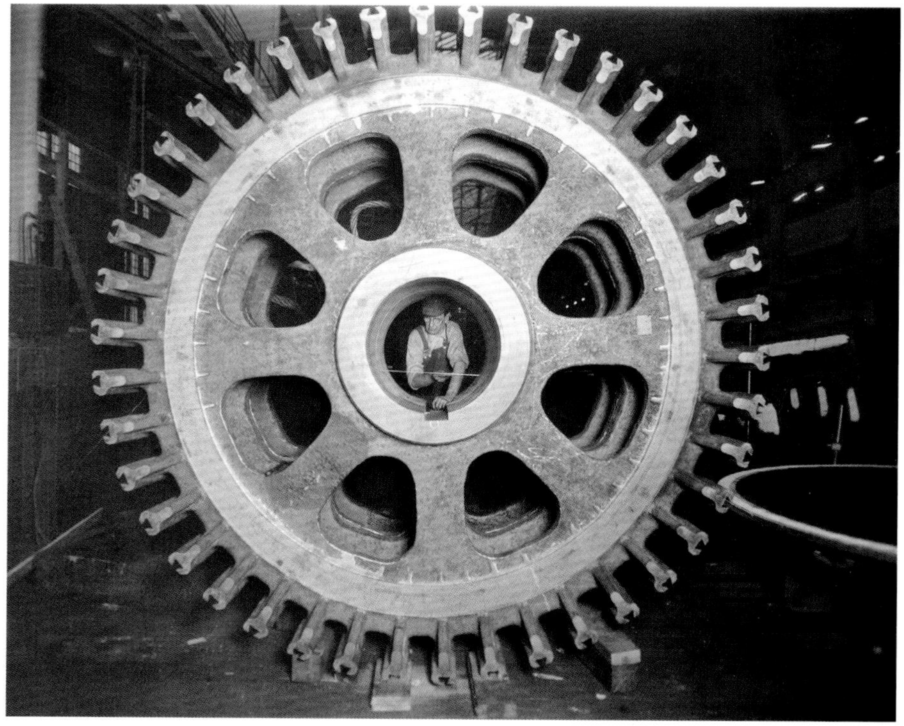

words, whose "innocence, naiveté and simplicity saved him when a more complicated nature might have gone under during years of neglect and lack of recognition." In Abbott's photograph the simple man is camera-less, there in that domestic and Victorian setting, dignified and quiet amid rugs and books and potted plants. He appears a "tired radical" in the sense defined by the progressive historian Walter Weyl: a man weary of the struggle who now wishes to tend quietly to his own garden. "He looked like an old schoolteacher in a Victorian film," recalled Walter Rosenblum, another person who knew Hine in those years. Rosenblum's story of watching a little man climb the stairs to the third floor of the Photo Students League building, of that man sitting down and looking silently out at the world, a man who turned out to be Hine, fits Abbott's conception of an ego-less and perhaps weary artist.

But Hine had other ideas of who he was, and what he had done. The worker at the center of the wheel is a Thor hammering his own shield, wielding the tong of his own sun, an armor blazing with wrenches at the radius. True, this god is small, protected, even here in his mightiness. In the eye of the storm, he is in that

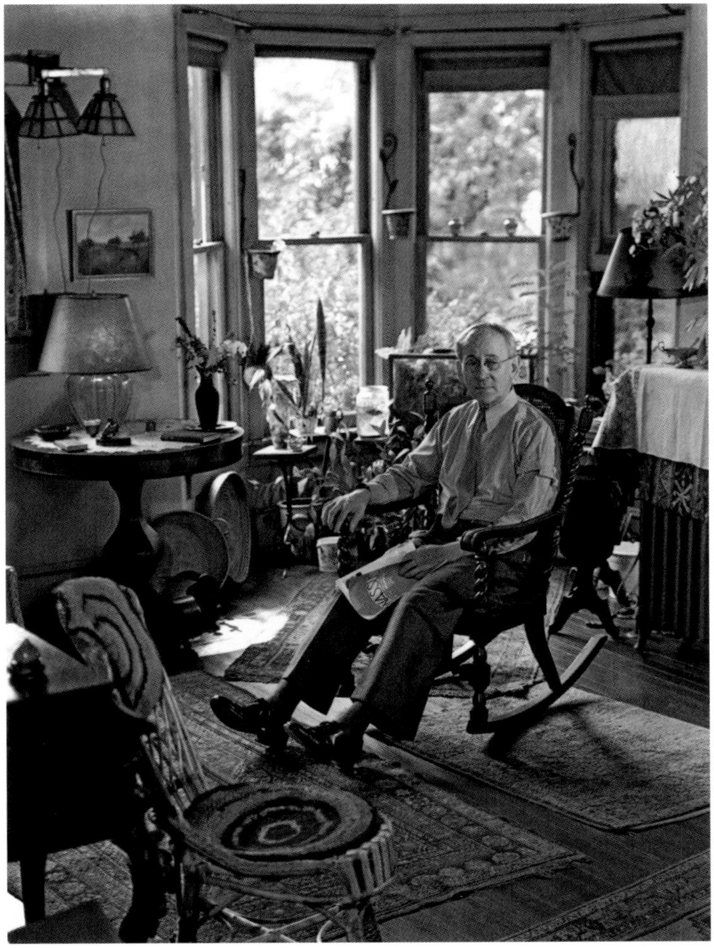

Fig. 114
Berenice Abbott, *Lewis Hine, Dobbs Ferry, New York*, 1938.

calm safe place that McCausland felt had preserved Hine amid the great whirring turbine energies of history that dwarfed him. Being innocent of destructive power is what made Hine a "male Cinderella," in McCausland's phrase—a man protected from all-around crushing pressure and lethal stings by the charm of an essential goodness and decency. So there at the center of the hive he is the honey maker scooping bravely from the bees. The guy Abbott photographed in his rocking chair is the superhero in his civvies. The worker at the center of the wheel is Hine's alter ego—a man of power.

Hine invented that herculean myth of himself because no one else did. Not even McCausland and Abbott, or the photography curator Beaumont Newhall, another of his admirers in the 1930s. They could praise what he had done, but the praise was belittling—"Hine is as American as the 'Oshkosh B-Gosh' from which he hails," he is a "Yankee genius." They could not know what it was to have made one of those child-labor photographs—really to have been there in Bennington or Knoxville or wherever the case may be. The man at the center of the wheel is Hine's dream of who he was.

Not that Hine was right. Resorting to hagiography, he devised a myth of authorship that makes him too heroic. That big wheel is the sum of a thousand complexities we do not see. The centripetal energies drawing down upon the man falsely exclude the million contingencies that Hine's child labor work was so good at portraying. The waywardness of incident, the swish-dressed sass and forlorn brick of a moment in time, strung together along gleaming railway tracks playing the makeshift role of an infinite depth—these are the chances Hine made his pictures from. But now at the center of the greatest lens ever seen—a flourish of self-representation like the mirror at the back of Jan van Eyck's *Arnolfini Portrait*—Hine gives us a glimpse of his art. The lens turned magically upon the man with the camera, the photograph celebrates the soulmaker because no one else will.

But Hine came too late to the game of self-promotion. The time to have done it was back in his heyday, when he was alighting in those little towns to make pictures to surpass them all. If he had looked around, and if he had had the temperament, he would have seen that his fellow socialists did not lack the esteem of self-promotion, that in fact Jack London was setting standards for vainglory. London's character Martin Eden, reading the poem of a socialist friend, extols a creative power that could only be London's own:

> It was terrific, impossible; and yet there it was, scrawled in black ink across the sheets of paper. It dealt with man and his soul-gropings in their ultimate terms, plumbing the abysses of space for the testimony of remotest suns and rainbow spectrums. It was a mad orgy of imagination, wassailing in the skull of a dying man who half sobbed under his breath and was quick with the wild flutter of fading heart-beats. The poem swung in majestic rhythm to the cool tumult of interstellar conflict, to the onset of starry hosts, to the impact of cold suns and the flaming up of nebulae in the darkened void; and through it all, unceasing and faint, like a silver shuttle, ran the frail, piping voice of man, a querulous chirp amid the screaming of planets and the crash of systems.

When Hine finally came up with his own glorious self-promotion, the terms he found were not convincing. "I am overwhelmed, crushed," Eden says after reading his friend's poem, but try as he might, Hine could not believe that the over-

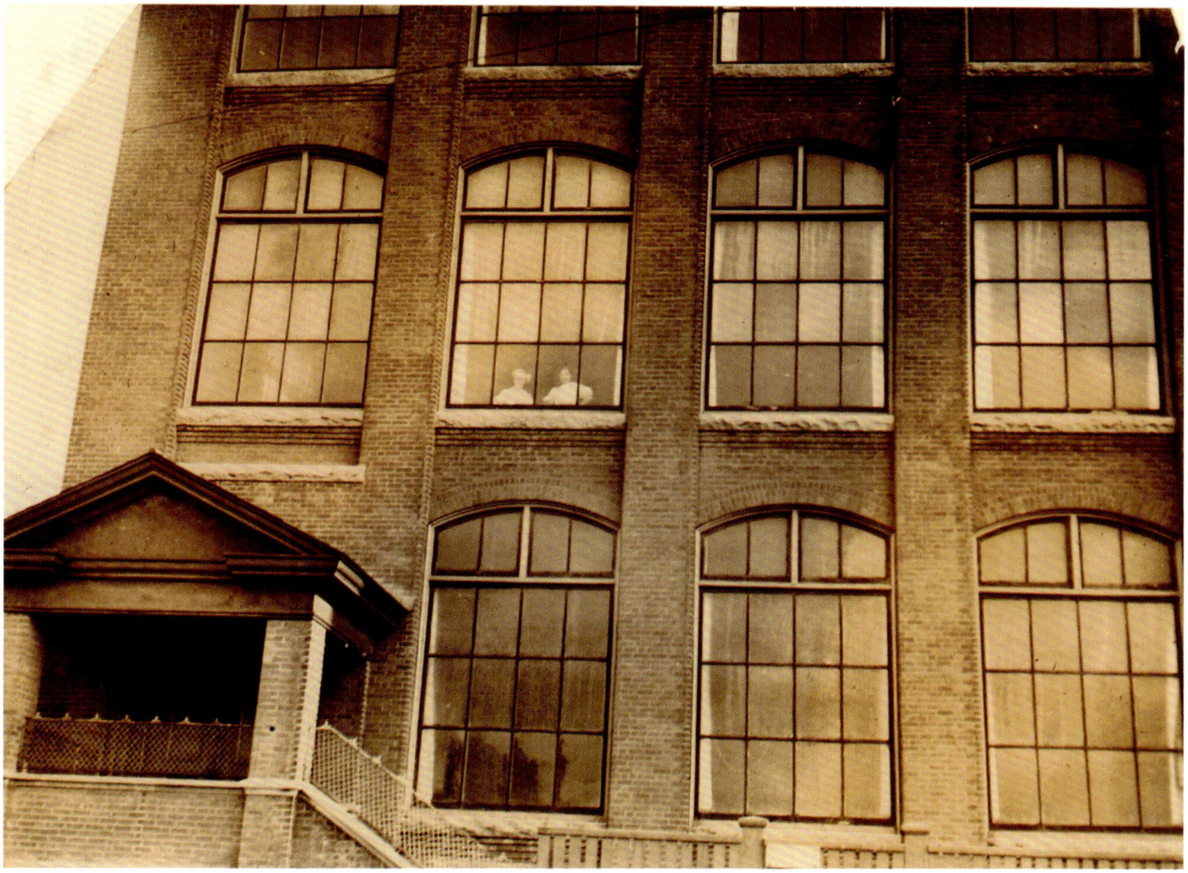

Fig. 115
Girls flirting through window of Manomet Mill. New Bedford, Massachusetts. January 1912.

whelming and crushing power of his work could be extolled in such heroic and self-aggrandizing terms. At best, the photograph of the man at the center of the gear wheel is a diagram of forces, a map of the terrain—of the consciousness of the person who negotiated the territory—recalled many years after the fact.

How different it was when Hine was intuiting his greatness in the most humble terms. In a photograph he took in January 1912, two girls stare at him from a second-story mill window in New Bedford (fig. 115). No detail is wanting in showing the girls' diminution and his remoteness from them. The fragile strangeness of the scene makes itself felt in both his rush to record the evidence of their employment—there they are, two of them, in that window—and in his reticence to make that document, to be the creator of who they were at that moment, who they forever will be, whoever they are.

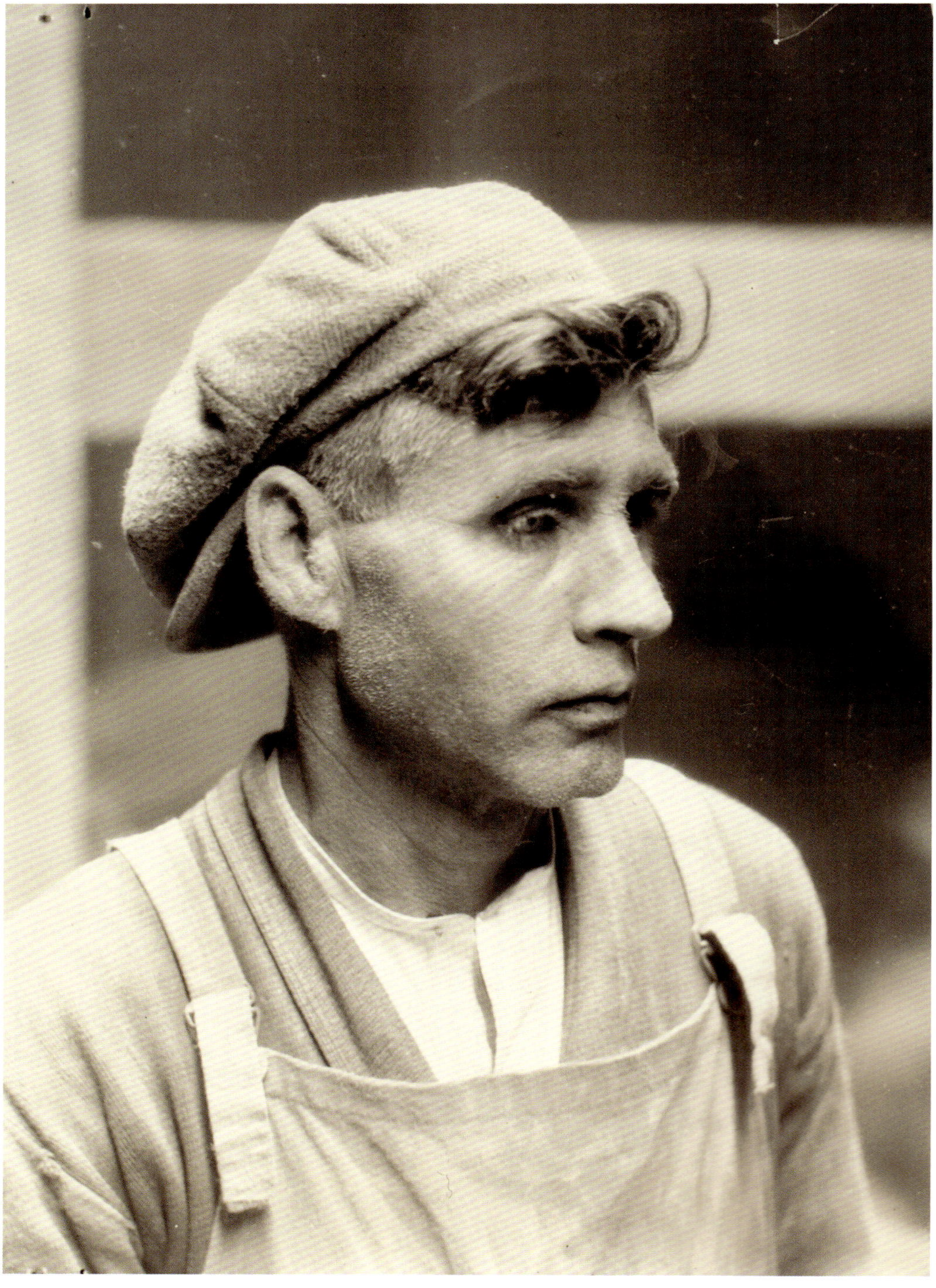

The nameless gallery of frosted windows is a factory that no diagram could teach a person to draw or operate. "I'm afraid, Mr. Hine, that you haven't the broad sociological background required," he was told when he initially sought employment as a labor photographer. But Hine's lack of training turns out to be only one of the many missing things that allowed him to make the pictures he did. His mill is a church of pasted visions, bleak in panels of brick and glass. It is a ship weighted and tilting to the right, the heavy porch at lower left an anchor, keeping the whole building in that seafaring town from toppling, from capsizing, from sinking. Yet it does start to keel over. The girls in the window are like last passengers gazing peacefully from the doomed vessel, staring at a would-be rescuer that they and he know is powerless to save them. The *Titanic* of child labor, there in 1912, a few months before the ocean liner went down—and the *Titanic* of time, the moment itself capsizing out of view: who is to know, least of all their maker, how such visions come to be?

Fig. 116
Portrait of Worker. Ca. 1931.

But in the 1930s Hine had a vision of what he had done and no lack of opportunities to portray it. The majority of the photographs in *Men at Work* show the construction of the Empire State Building, and the making of the new skyscraper in 1930–31 gave him a chance to imagine his own life's mighty achievement. Those 5,300 photographs of child laborers over a ten-year period, he now saw, were the equivalent of creating a building rising more than twelve hundred feet in the air. Let the curators gawk and let the citizens of the street stare upward in awe, because the monument of one man's oeuvre now topped them all.

It started from the ground up. The first spread of photo pages in *Men at Work* is called "Foundation Men." The photograph on the left-hand page shows one of these men, a pensive rock driller staring to the right (fig. 116). Below him a caption says that this man is a modest artist—he has "received an award for craftsmanship"—and that such men "work in a haze of rock dust which they know will shorten their lives." Labor of this kind takes a lot out of the quiet craftsman at the base of things.

The building starts to go up. A surveyor inspects the steel structure to make sure everything is correct (fig. 117). Called "Checking Up," the double-page spread in *Men at Work* emphasizes accuracy: "The work is checked continually to make the building 'true,'" reads the caption. The man at the surveyor's instrument is photographer-like, his left hand held in the air pointing to the distant Chrysler Building, yes, but also as if signaling to his fellow workers that he is about to take a picture.

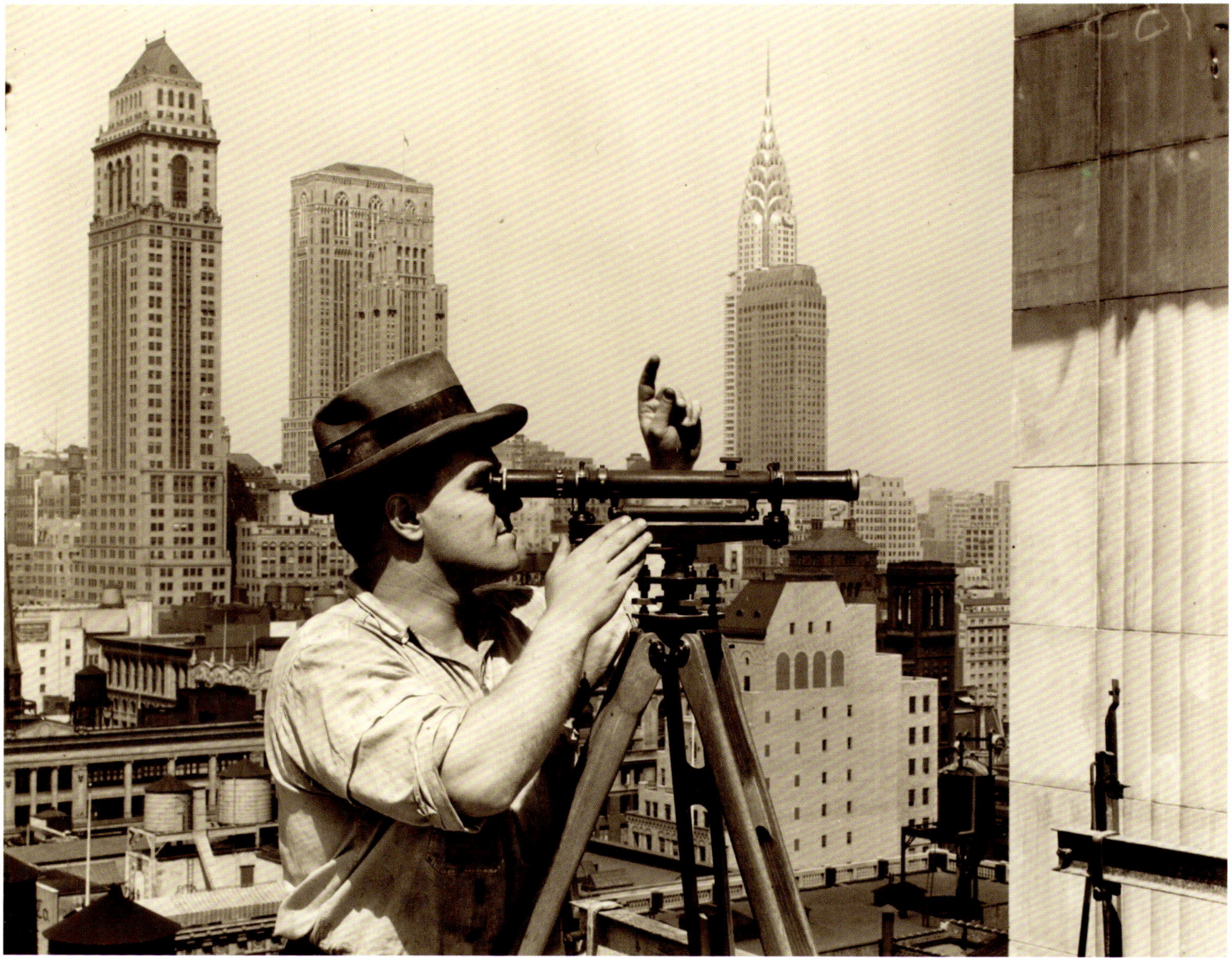

Fig. 117
Engineer with Level. Ca. 1931.

The man's steady gaze and scrupulous accuracy establish the simple faithfulness of his worthy and unsung pursuit. He will get it right. As the era of documentary photography emerged in the 1930s, Hine recasts his photo-interpretations as true. Having worked for *The Survey*, and having surveyed the state of child labor, Hine imagines himself in the guise of a surveyor because no one else can guess the heroism of his task and because in his own explicit self-portrayals, for Abbott and others, he fell back upon his "oh gosh" self-deprecation. But in his mind he was something else.

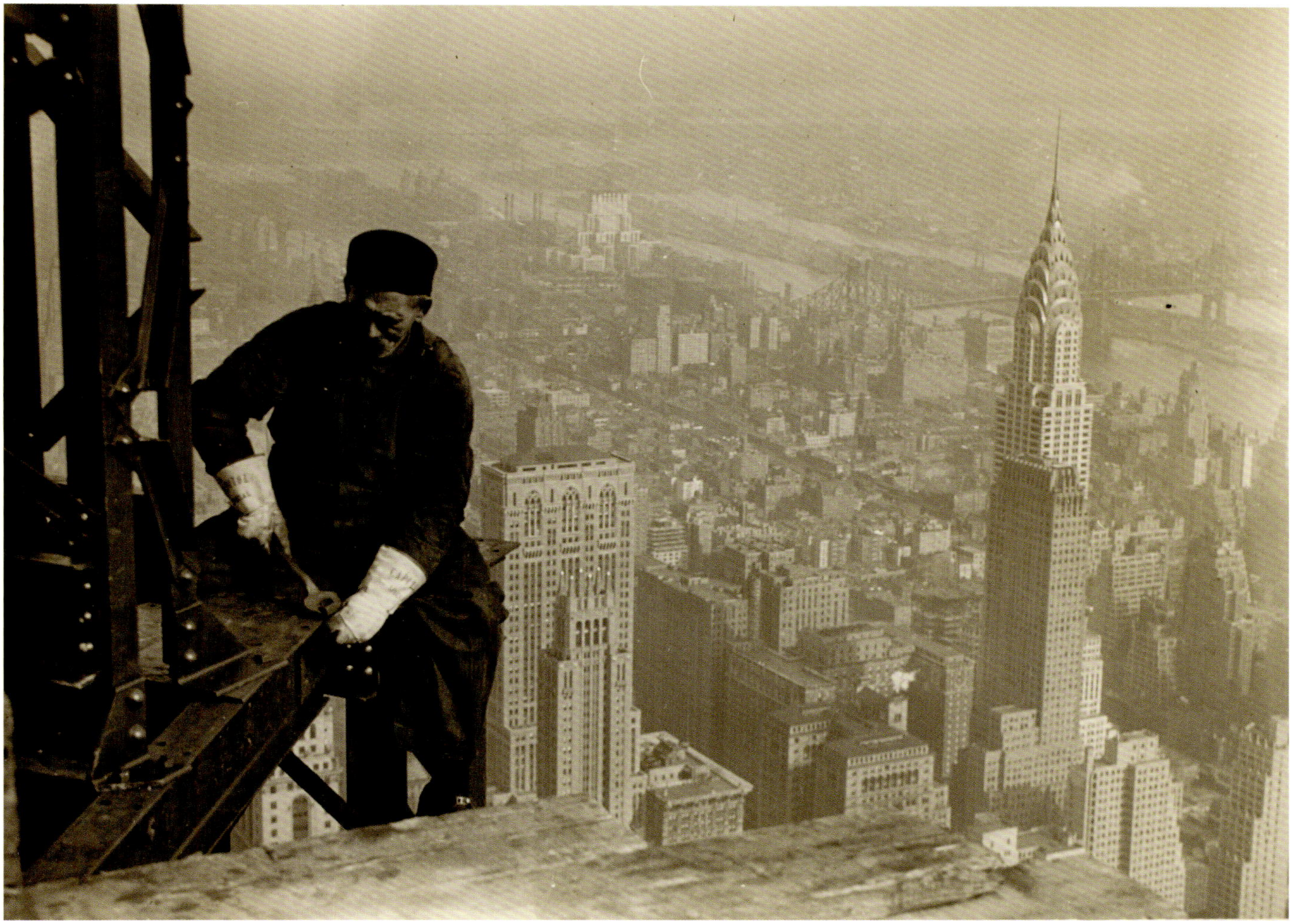

Up higher we meet the bolt boy "with a bag of bolts" "who "begins at eighteen." It is a fairy tale, this page, a reminder that *Men at Work* is a book for child readers. With its alliterations—"The bolt boy with a bag of bolts begins at eighteen"—the reader half expects to see a big letter *B* alongside the photographs, as if the page were part of a children's alphabet. The bolt boy travels in the air but his journey is as folkloric as the dirt road down which some grubby farmer lad travels as he seeks to make his way in the world. "He will have to take good care of himself, if he is to stay on the job as long as the old bolter above"—a wizened figure steadily at his task (fig. 118).

Fig. 118
Old-time steel worker on Empire State Building. Ca. 1931.

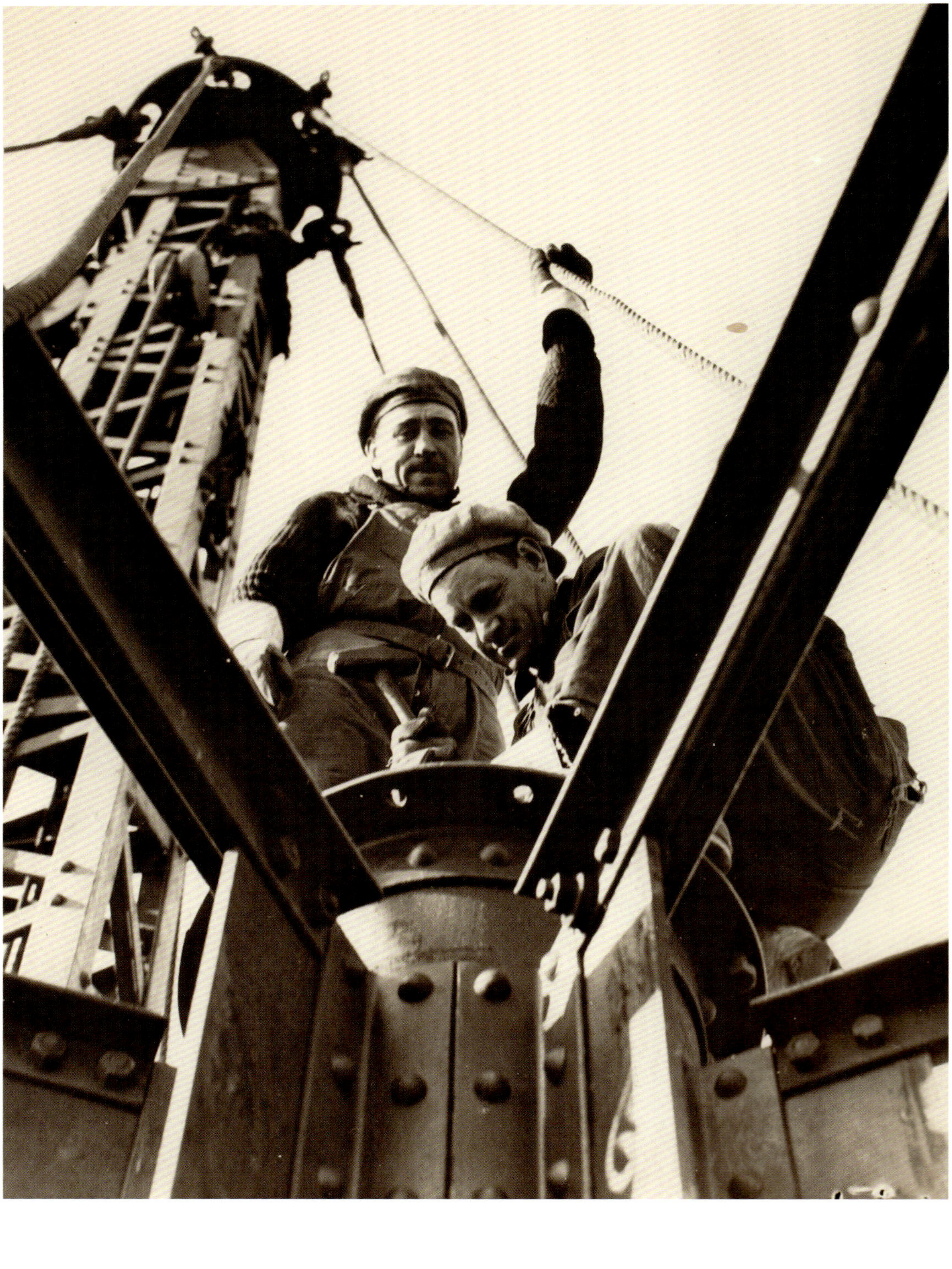

A bildungsroman, the page is a résumé, not unlike the life history Hine wrote in 1940 as part of a Guggenheim Foundation application, or the biographical articles that McCausland and Newhall were writing of Hine in the 1930s. "Thirty years of work," McCausland summarized in 1938, "led Lew Hine into southern cotton mills" and "finally out into the perilous ether about the Empire State Building where construction workers dangled on steel chains and the photographer teetered on a girder." Newhall wrote in 1938 that among the Empire State Building photographs "there is not one of Hine himself perched high above the city"—an astute point highlighting Hine's typical modesty—and yet each of the workmen he photographed was a kind of self-portrait as Hine mulled, and invented, what his own heroism had been. As a retrospective creation, the "life" looks like the pictures on that page: a boy starts out and rises all the way to the top.

Turning the page we see a spread titled "Finishing Up the Job," the last in *Men at Work* devoted to the Empire State Building (fig. 119). The men in the photograph work on the tip of the mooring mast, "the highest point yet reached on a man-made structure, a quarter of a mile up in the clouds." For McCausland, Hine was a "pioneer," his work providing a mark for the "newer generation of photographers—and public—who are growing up in the documentary ideal." These men who "finish the job" are like a younger generation of hardy photographers occupying the heights along with Hine. Progenitor and mighty sons alike cluster in the clouds, a steroidal pantheon of bulk-muscled masculinity, strung of hammers, wire, and steel. Meanwhile back down on the ground, little Lew Hine rocked in his rocker.

Back above—swinging far out there—is "The Sky Boy," hero of the photograph Hine chose to place opposite the title page of *Men at Work* (fig. 120). "One of the first men to swing out a quarter of a mile above New York City, helping to build a skyscraper," reads the full caption. An adventurous lad, the sky boy sets out alone, on a journey like no one else's. Free of constraints, of "real-world" requirements and obligations, he floats in some aerie of private exploration, the biographical ideal of the sovereign self in full flight, lifted like Lindbergh in ecstatic solitude. Some thirty years after Hine left Oshkosh, the Sky Boy is another *Solution of the Aerial Problem*, swinging on his twisting wire like Hine's girl-traveler floats in her tendril-pulled leaf-chariot (fig. 121). But the delicate rescue of the old days has now become only heroism. A few pages later, two men ride a hoisting ball to

Fig. 119
Putting its cap on. The highest point ever reached on a man-made structure. Ca. 1931.

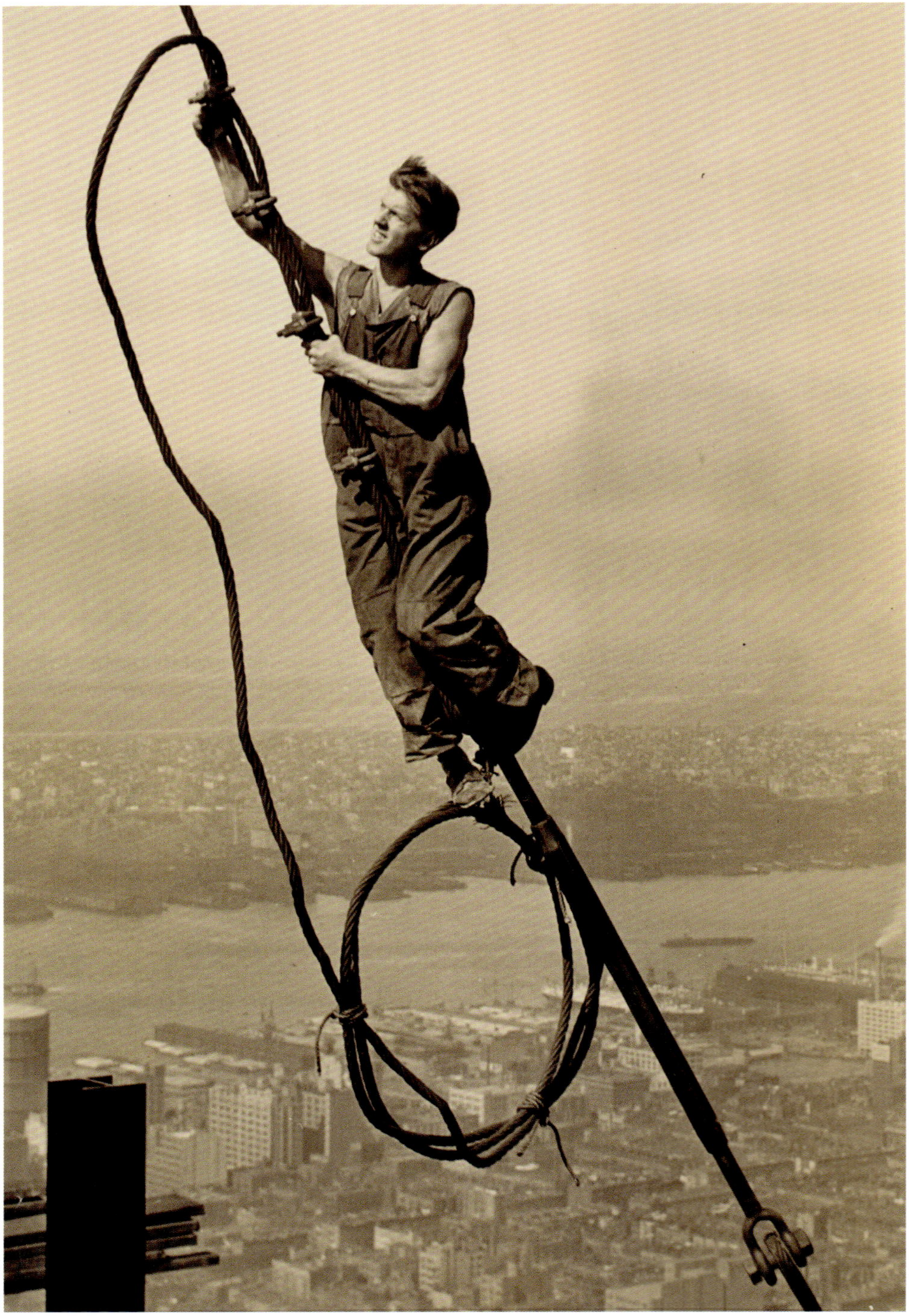

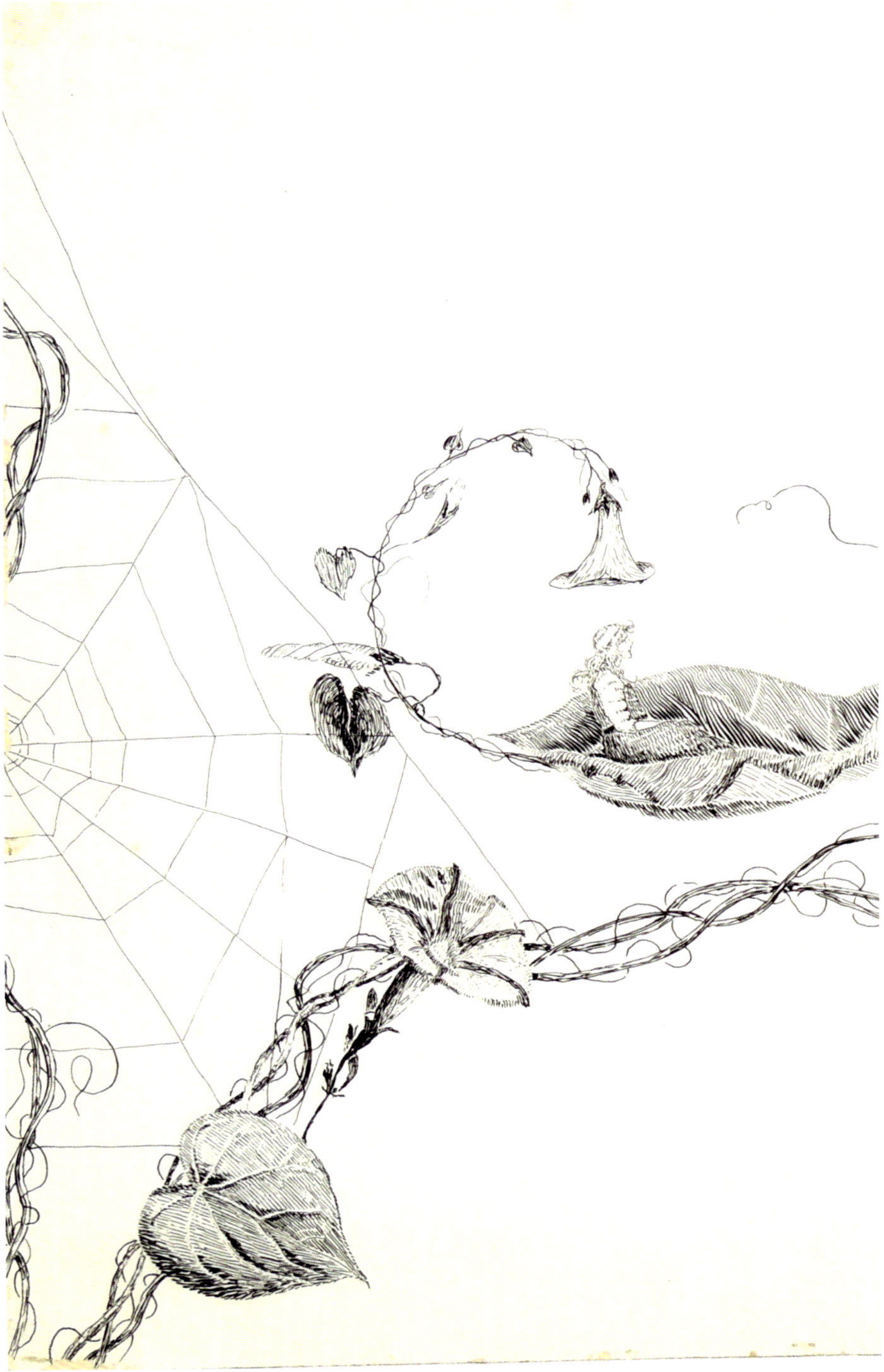

Fig. 120 (opposite)
The Sky Boy. 1931.

Fig. 121
The Solution of the Aerial Problem (detail).

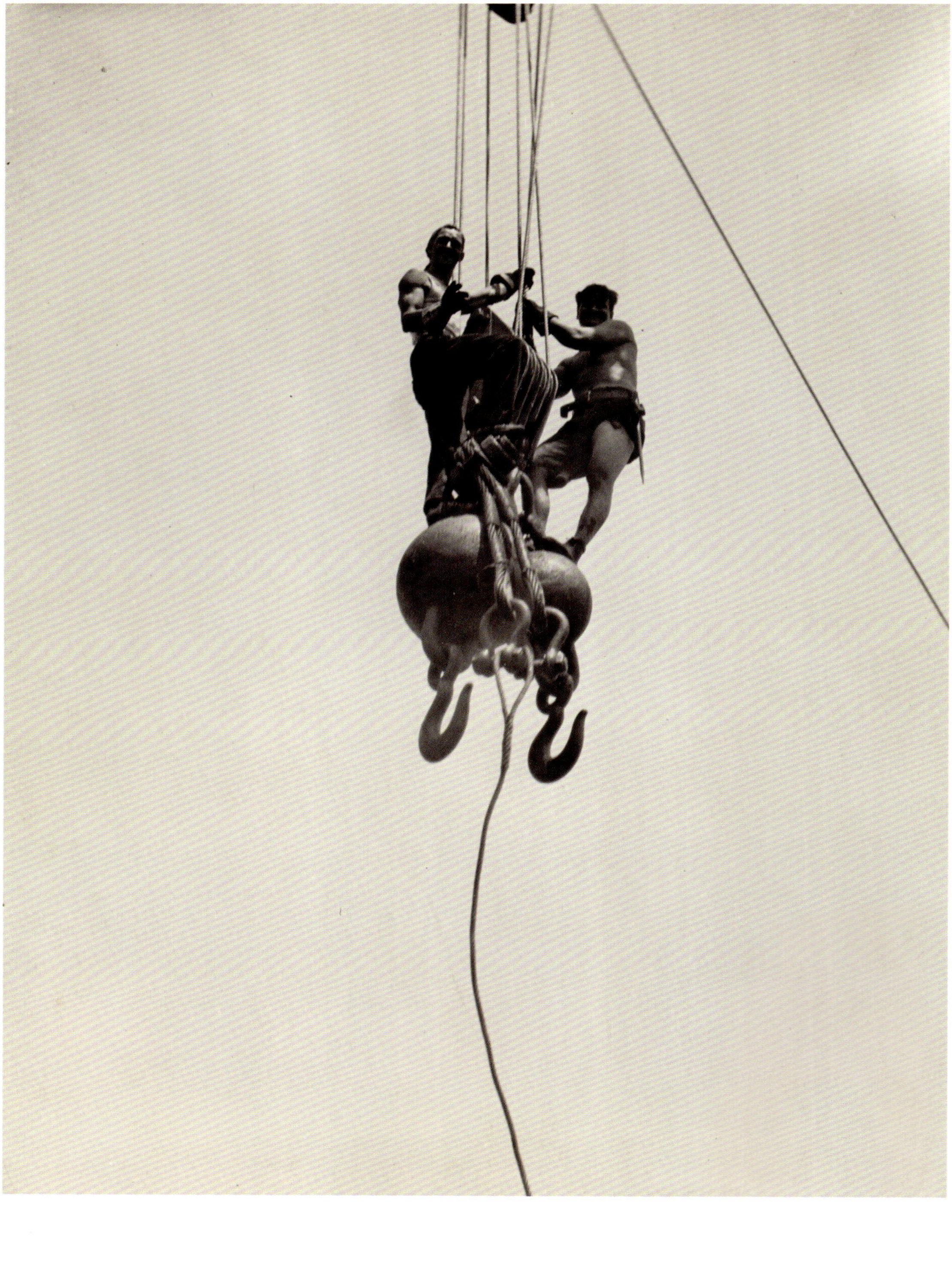

the next level "like spiders spinning a fabric of steel against the sky" (fig. 122). The masculine power of work, all balls, replaces the delicate spinners of the past—the two Knoxville girls, the two in New Bedford. And even as they go up and up, the great men are weighed down by their strength.

Fig. 122
"Riding the Ball" on Empire State. Like spiders spinning a fabric of steel against the sky. Ca. 1931.

In the prime of life Hine imagined his passion differently. In December 1908, soon after he started working for the National Child Labor Committee, he made a photograph of a mill running at night in Whitnel, North Carolina—the same mill where Cora Lee Griffin worked (fig. 123). Hine made it and several others like it to document the all-night operations of the mills in which children worked. The photograph glows also with the intensity Hine brought to the task.

It is a question of fire. One of Hine's favorite essays—he later called it his "credo" and used a quotation from it as the epigraph to *Men at Work*—was William James's "The Moral Equivalent of War," published in 1910. James wrote that if you want to advocate a just and humane society, you cannot be soft and sentimental. You must advance your cause with martial bravery, a sense that life is hard, that challenges must be faced, and that a keen and fair character is forged in surmounting these difficulties. For James, this righteousness demanded "spiritual energy" and "a certain intensity." A passion so inflamed would then ignite society, making it "only a question of blowing on the spark till the whole population gets incandescent." A martial resolve to do good was the moral equivalent of war.

Hine's *Mill Running at Night* is a moral equivalent, much more so than anything in *Men at Work*. The glow of the mill's interior illuminates the rows of windows, making the place a furnace of banked and structured fires, a dense and architectonic concentration of energy, a resonant storehouse of flame. Hine's photograph shows not only a factory operating at night but the glowing force of righteousness, itself working feverishly around the clock, to ensure the abolition of all it decries as unjust. For the next ten years Hine would be such a factory, churning out pictures, expending energy to the point of exhaustion. "Light!" Hine liked to quote Victor Hugo. "Light in floods!" Only such light would relieve "the great social peril" of "darkness and ignorance." The factory is illuminated all night, and so is Hine. He would burn out so that he might light the darkness.

The progressives of the time spent themselves in ferocious displays of righteous passion. In 1908 Eugene Debs gave speeches on sixty-eight consecutive days on his national presidential campaign tour. By September 15, he had made 187 speeches in the previous twenty-five days: "such a fire as burns in him," wrote Carl

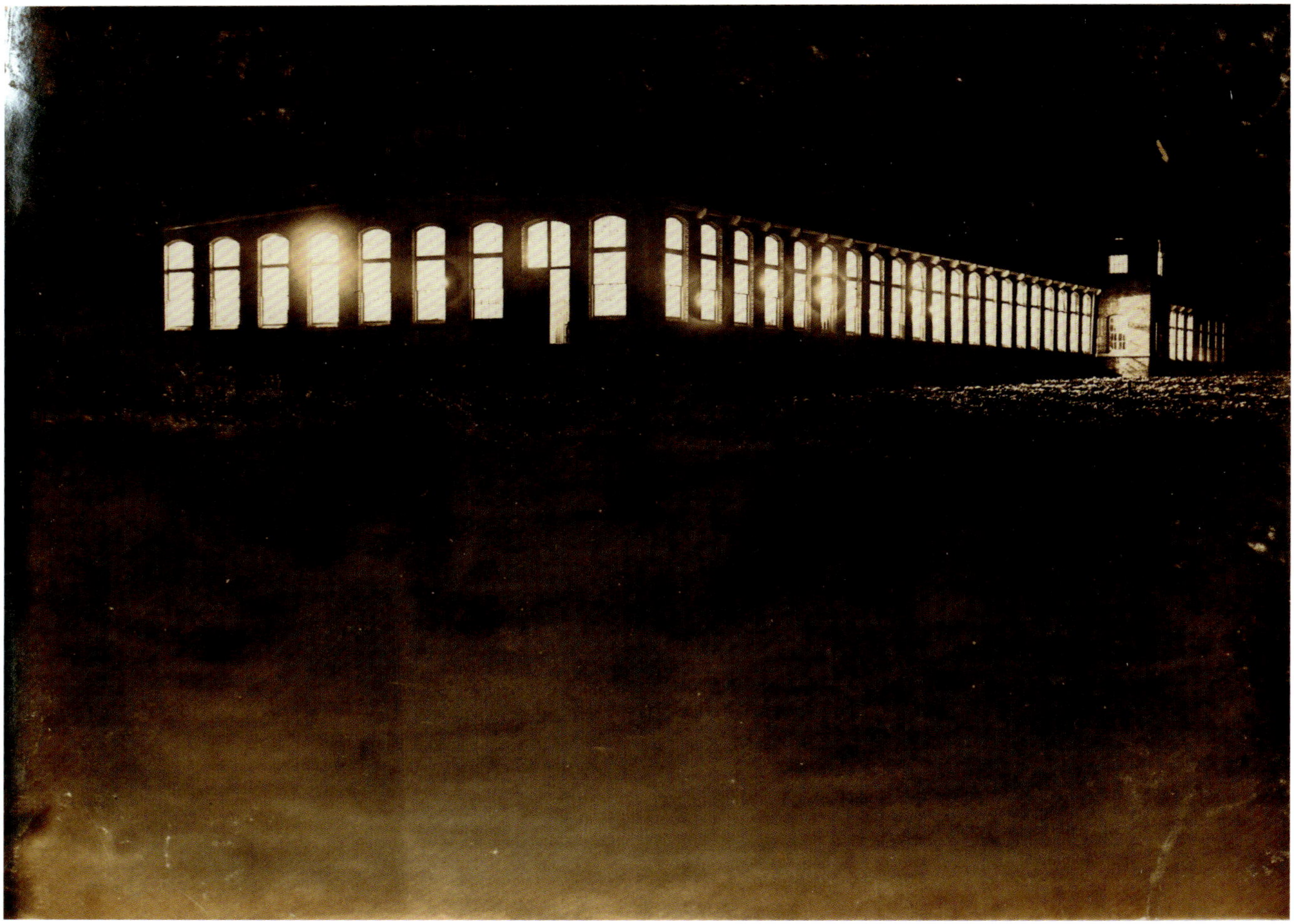

Fig. 123
Whitnel Cotton Mfg. Co., Whitnel, N.C. Running at night. Out of 50 employees there, 10 were about 12 years old, and some surely under that. December 1908.

Sandburg. Also that year Wisconsin senator Robert La Follette spoke on the senate floor for eighteen hours in an all-night filibuster—just a few months before Hine made his Whitnel photograph. Opposing the adoption of the Aldrich-Vreeland Currency bill—legislation that would make the rich richer—the progressive champion La Follette rose from his chair at 12:40 p.m. on the afternoon of May 30, saying "he was prepared to talk until his strength gave out," and spoke until 7:03 a.m. the next morning. When he began to run out of direct commentary on the bill, nothing daunted, La Follette proclaimed his intention to read the entire contents of "Poor's *Manual of Railroads*" into the record. When he finished speaking just after 7 a.m. on May 31, he still had energy to spare. "It looked," noted a reporter, "as though he could have gone on for some time." That December, *Mill Running at Night* proclaimed Hine's own righteous endurance.

The fire in such cases was not entirely his own. The concentric circles of light emanating from within the mill—the internal lamps lighting the mill floor—gleam like the pulsar-souls Hine would save. The children from within, trapped in the bastion, appeal to him as the voices inside his own words. As Spargo spoke the bitter cry of the children, as Albert Beveridge quoted Spargo quoting the children, as Debs implored his listeners so forcefully that he seemed to grow gaunter as he spoke, these impassioned orators, like Hine, burned brightest when they channeled the souls of others.

It meant not being blind. Describing travels through the mountainous western North Carolina areas Hine was to visit, William James noted how little he understood the ways of the people there. He came to realize, however, that his ignorance demonstrated "a certain blindness in human beings"—a failure to appreciate the special beliefs that govern a stranger's life. Perceiving his ignorance, James came to believe that every person has a guarded and idiosyncratic soul, inexpressible to others but perceptible all the same. That soul for James is not an ineffable thing but a lantern of private feeling. He quoted Robert Louis Stevenson's boyhood memory of walking about at night with a lantern hidden beneath his coat, of displaying this luminary to childhood fellows who likewise did the same, as an apt metaphor for the odd inward glow each person holds dear. Kept "deep down in the privacy of your fool's heart," the soul is a superstitious communiqué. Hine's photograph of the mill running at night corrects the certain blindness in human beings by imagining—there in the mountains of western North Carolina—the lantern glow of people different from himself. From within the mill the souls glow as otherworldly signals to the man who burns.

This man conducts a lonely vigil doubtful of success. The solitary figure is a brilliant light, firing to a bright intensity, but he leaves the world nearly as dark as it would have been had not a single one of these fires ever burned. His work changes nothing with its fiery beauty. The first page of Hine's Oshkosh poem book quotes the Scottish poet Robert Burns, closing with lines that feel prophetic of Hine's photography: "Perhaps, it may turn out a sang, / Perhaps, turn out a sermon" (fig. 124). Perhaps Hine will sing, perhaps he will preach. Maybe he will do both. But Burns, the poet, burns where he is—burning is the question of being an artist, no matter if what the artist says is sermon or song. The artist's life means being

Fig. 124
"Perhaps, it may turn out a sang." Lewis Hine Poem Book. 1898.

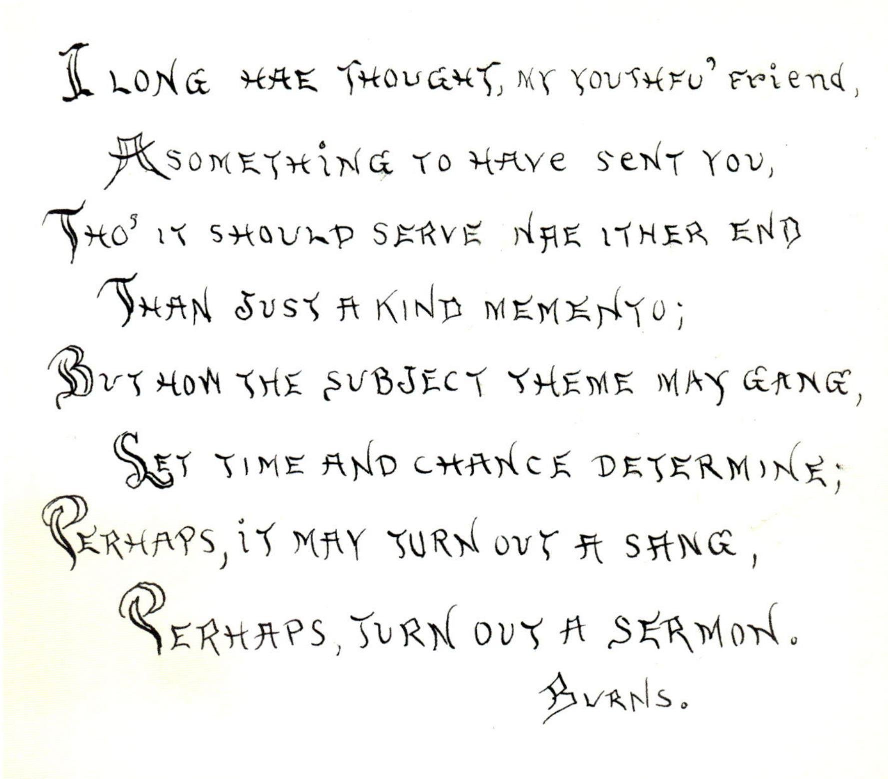
I long hae thought, my youthfu' friend,
A something to have sent you,
Tho' it should serve nae ither end
Than just a kind memento;
But how the subject theme may gang,
Let time and chance determine;
Perhaps, it may turn out a sang,
Perhaps, turn out a sermon.
Burns.

consumed by a fire all in one place, an energy that takes the light of others and consumes it as one's own. For the artist in thrall to the euphoric chant, the screams of the outside world burn in the incantation of the visible. The Whitnel mill is like a penitentiary outside of which a lone vigilant keeps sentinel to an execution, praying for the condemned, only to discover that the mill is actually keeping vigil on him and that it is he—rather than long-lived Cora Lee Griffin—who is to die that night. To observe his own destruction is Hine's lyric rapture.

Oblivion is the name of the game, the flash of the omen writ large and bright. It is an exhilaration to be called out, to be chosen, but also a fate to glow like this. It is a fiery vision of the kind saints behold, where the mill becomes a nimbus floating in space, a holy apparition that's glorious but hardly as uplifting as the hill it sits upon. The calling is so private that no Empire State Building dream of who one was could ever explain it. Even the artist himself, looking back, cannot really understand what it was to have been that much younger person who stood outside the Whitnel mill. That person was alive in the dark, subject to visions, thrall to life ecstatic and blown to otherworldly degrees, prescient and fantastic, flaring as bright as any disaster. If this be the summons, how could anyone ever know what it would be to make the work envisioned under such a burning sign?

"We work in the dark," William's brother Henry James wrote. That was in "The Middle Years," Henry's short story about a novelist named Dencombe who is dying in middle age. Regretting all that he has not accomplished, regretting that he did not bring everything he had to his work when he had the chance, Dencombe defines the artist's calling: "We work in the dark—we do what we can—we give what we have. Our doubt is our passion and our passion is our task. The rest is the madness of art."

Hine worked in the dark. His photographs glow in visionary moments set against the burnout of all time. The biggest of all Oshkosh fires, an ever-present one, consumes even the quasar-glimpses of human flame that stand out as lights within this all-immolating light. To see the souls in the ever-widening devastation that crawls and moves and torches everything is to glimpse a vision that all the Empire State Buildings ever photographed cannot rise above.

The dream of newness is a false sky. The real dawn is the din of the mill breaking and splitting apart at the seams. The vision of the burning building is a curse and a crown, a mixed gift Hine feels it is his calling to portray. That he could not know that this is exactly what he was doing is the saving grace, the Cinderella protection, that only the guileless possess. It is the charm granting him passage across and through the wastes, another of the ways Hine so beautifully worked in the dark. But moving blindly he was never far from his obsession.

"The world is on fire," says one of Sherwood Anderson's characters in *Winesburg, Ohio*. "This sidewalk here and this feed store, the trees down the street there—they're all on fire. They're burning up. Decay you see is always going on. It don't stop. Water and paint can't stop it. If a thing is iron, then what? It rusts, you see. That's fire, too. The world is on fire. Start your pieces in the paper that way. Just say in big letters *'The World Is On Fire.'* That will make 'em look up."

BIBLIOGRAPHIC NOTES

Spinner, Whitnel, North Carolina, December 1908. "To free the wage-worker": John Spargo, *The Spiritual Significance of Modern Socialism* (New York: B. W. Huebsch, 1908), 62–63; Spargo, *The Bitter Cry of the Children* (New York: Macmillan, 1906); Hine received "much encouragement" from Spargo (Hine, "Biographical Notes," in *Photo Story: Selected Letters and Photographs of Lewis W. Hine*, ed. Daile Kaplan [Washington, DC: Smithsonian Institution Press, 1992], 178); "Thousands of separate threads": Sherwood Anderson, *Beyond Desire* (New York: Liveright, 1961), 84; "At the mills, children over 12 years old": August Kohn, *The Cotton Mills of South Carolina* (Columbia: South Carolina Department of Agriculture, Commerce and Immigration, 1907), 30; "will experience the repetition itself with true satisfaction": Hugo Münsterberg, *Psychology and Industrial Efficiency* (New York: Arno Press, 1973), 204; "the whirling machines": Jack London, "The Apostate," in London, *To Build a Fire and Other Stories* (New York: Bantam, 1988), 214; "for ten or eleven hours a day": Spargo, *The Bitter Cry of the Children*, quoted in H. G. Wells, *The Future in America: A Search after Realities* (New York: Harper and Brothers, 1906), 112–13; "an infinitude of splash and hurry," Wells, *The Future in America*, 53; fairy tales: Felix Adler, "The Use of Fairy Tales," in *The Moral Instruction of Children* (New York: D. Appleton, 1908), 67, 94; The name Cora Lee Griffin: see Joe Manning, "Lewis Hine Project," on the *Mornings on Maple Street* website http://www.morningsonmaplestreet.com/; "a temporality specific to affect": Fredric Jameson, "The Twin Sources of Realism: Affect, or the Body's Present," in *The Antimonies of Realism* (London: Verso, 2013), 42; "I have come to think that the true history of life": Sherwood Anderson, quoted in Alfred Kazin, *On Native Grounds: An Interpretation of Modern American Prose Literature* (New York: Harcourt, Brace, 1942), 213; "did not merely live for the special 'moments' in experience": Kazin, *On Native Grounds*, 215; "The epiphanies": Anderson, "Nobody Knows," "Hands," "A Man of Ideas," in *Winesburg, Ohio* (New York: Penguin, 1992), 61, 34, 107; "left-handed mysticism": Kazin, *On Native Grounds*, 210, 212; "Life was a dream to him": Kazin, *On Native Grounds*, 211; "The insouciance with which he came into a town he did not know, into a factory he did not know": For a history of the rise of the mills and the potential benefits to poor whites, see Broadus Mitchell, *The Rise of Cotton Mills in the South* (1921), introduction by David Carlton (Columbia: University of South Carolina Press, 2001); for the historiography of the mills, see Carlton's excellent introduction, which discusses C. Vann Woodward's *Origins of the New South* (Baton Rouge: Louisiana State University Press, 1951) as the corrective to Mitchell's praise of New Southern entrepreneurship; for recent scholarship on mill workers' lives—the newest and richest turn in mill historiography—see for example Carlton's own *Mill and Town in South Carolina, 1880–1920* (Baton Rouge: Louisiana State University Press, 1982); for a period defense of child labor in the mills, see Kohn, *Cotton Mills of South Carolina*. "The depreciation of our racial stock": Alexander McKelway, "The Awakening of the South against Child Labor," in *Child Labor and the Republic* (New York: National Child Labor Committee, 1907), 16; "*White* children": Albert J. Beveridge, "Child Labor," in *The Meaning of the Times and Other Speeches* (Indianapolis: Bobbs-Merrill, 1908), 317, 340. Robin Bernstein points out the racial ideology of a Hine photograph—"Hine's image protests the use of an innocent white child as labor"—in her book *Racial Innocence: Performing American Childhood from Slavery to Civil Rights* (New York: New York University Press, 2011), 32–33. For an account that thoughtfully faults Hine—taking him to task for the bias and incoherence of his ideological project—see George Dimock, "Children of the Mills: Re-Reading Lewis Hine's Child-Labour Photographs," *Oxford Art Journal* 16 (1993): 37–54.

Addie Card, North Pownal, Vermont, August 1910. Manning, "Addie Card, the Search for an Anemic Little Spinner," "Lewis Hine Project," *Mornings on Maple Street*; Maxfield Parrish and Susan Lewin: Alma Gilbert, *The Make Believe World of Maxfield Parrish and Sue Lewin* (San Francisco: Pomegranate Art Books, 1990).

Marshall Knox, Rochester, New York, February 1910. "No man has been more richly and warmly loved": Spargo, "Eugene V. Debs, Incarnate Spirit of Revolt," in *Debs: His Life, Writings, and Speeches, with a Department of Appreciations* (Chicago: Charles H. Kerr, 1908), 505–6. "Break the shins of the people he hated": Walter Weyl, "Tired Radicals," in *Tired Radicals, and Other Papers* (New York: B. W. Huebsch, 1921), 9; "In the old days love was a cruel and proprietary thing": Wells, *In the Days of the Comet* (New York: Charles Scribner's Sons, 1923), 370; "Christianity bases all human relations on love": Walter Rauschenbusch, *Christianity and the Social Crisis* (New York: Macmillan, 1907), 312, 315; Hine against Stieglitz: Allan Sekula, "On the Invention of Photographic Meaning," reprinted in *Photography against the Grain: Essays and Photo Works, 1973–1983* (Halifax: The Press of the Nova Scotia College of Art and Design, 1984), 3–23, esp. 20; a "forecast," a "horoscope," for child labor: Wells, *Future in America*, 115.

Sadie Kelly, Port St. Louis, Mississippi, March 1911. "The Awakening": Wells, *In the Days of the Comet*, 252ff.

The Solution of the Aerial Problem. Spargo's ego: Hine, letter to Frank, February 18, 1921, Manuscripts Division, New York Public Library; he "seemed a rather unlikely person": Seville Osborn, quoted in Judith Mara Gutman, *Lewis Hine and the American Social Conscience* (New York: Walker, 1967), 15; "Try to get him to pose for a photograph": Elizabeth McCausland, "Portrait of a Photographer," *Survey Graphic* 27 (October 1938): 502; Bert Smallways: H. G. Wells, *The War in the Air* (London: Penguin, 2005). One recent good book on Houdini is Brooke Kamin Rapaport et al., *Houdini: Art and Magic* (New Haven, CT: Yale University Press, 2010).

Oshkosh. The Catskills: Lewis Hine, "A Tramp through the Historic Realm of Rip Van Winkle," Oshkosh *Daily Northwestern*, October 3, 1903; "Our hope for a deeper enjoyment": Frank Manny, "Types of School Festivals,"

Elementary School Teacher 7 (March 1907): 411; "gracelessness," "Dewey's theory of experience": Kazin, *On Native Grounds*, 146; "beyond being sociological tracts": for an opposite view, one that measures the success of Hine's work based on its ability to illustrate philosophical and sociological viewpoints, see Kate Sampsell Willmann, "Lewis Hine, Ellis Island, and Pragmatism as Lived Experience," *Journal of the Gilded Age and Progressive Era* 7 (April 2008): 221–52, expanded in her book, *Lewis Hine as Social Critic* (Jackson: University of Mississippi Press, 2009).

Knoxville. "The nozzles were variously set": James Agee, *Knoxville: Summer 1915*, in *A Death in the Family*, in *Let Us Now Praise Famous Men, A Death in the Family, and Shorter Fiction* (New York: Library of America, 2005), 469–73; "a delicate yet powerful odor of wetness": Agee and Walker Evans, *Let Us Now Praise Famous Men* (Boston: Houghton Mifflin, 2001), 113–14; "Here at the creek mouth," "rivers of shit," "At the far end of the warehouse": Cormac McCarthy, *Suttree* (New York: Vintage International, 1992), 4, 270, 64; "thirty-six thousan' moves a day": London, "The Apostate," 218.

Emerson. "Not the sun or the summer / alone": Hine, Poem Book, Oshkosh Public Museum, Oshkosh, Wisconsin; "A person who attended the lecture": "Ralph Waldo Emerson: The First Centenary of His Birth Is to Be Celebrated—His Visit to Oshkosh in 1867—Suggestions," Oshkosh *Daily Northwestern*, May 23, 1903. The text of Emerson's lecture does not exist. The notes for it, on which I rely, are in the Houghton Library, Harvard University. Emerson's sleigh ride: Ralph Waldo Emerson, *Topical Notebooks of Ralph Waldo Emerson*, vol. 3, ed. Glen M. Johnson (Columbia: University of Missouri Press, 1994), 324. "United the world of Emerson and the world of Zola": Kazin, *On Native Grounds*, 46; "A perception of the unity of all things under the sun": Howells, *Annie Kilburn*, in *William Dean Howells: Novels, 1886–1888* (New York: Library of America, 1989), 858.

Knoxville Knitting Works, Knoxville, Tennessee, December 1910. The Appalachian Exposition of 1910: see *Appalachian Exposition to Be Held at Knoxville, Tennessee from September 12th to October 12th, 1910: The Great Industrial Event of the Year, Premium List and Prospectus* (Knoxville: S. B. Newman, 1910), Special Collections, University of Tennessee Library, 28, 31, 27, 4. The Battle of the Clouds: see *Appalachian Exposition*, 4, and "Appalachian Exposition," *Hopkinsville, Kentuckian*, September 20, 1910, 5 (Chronicling America, Library of Congress, chroniclingamerica.loc.gov/lccn/sn86069395/1910-09-20/.../seq-5/. An "allegory of the future": quoted in Robert D. Lukens, "The New South on Display: The Appalachian Expositions of 1910 and 1911," *Journal of East Tennessee History* 69 (1997): 10. Further materials about the Appalachian Exposition, including the aerial entertainments, is drawn from Special Collections, University of Tennessee Library, Knoxville, and from the McClung Historical Collection, East Tennessee History Center, Knoxville.

Doffer Boys in Knoxville Cotton Mills, December 1910. "A growing uneasiness": Hamlin Garland, *A Son of the Middle Border* (Minneapolis: Borealis, 2007), 88; "In 1892 Hine's father accidentally shot himself": "Death of D. H. Hine, Shot While Busily at Work," Oshkosh *Daily Northwestern*, November 11, 1892, 1; bound up with this sense of loss: Hine's sense of the pleasures and melancholy of childhood rivals Charles Dickens's. "No one, at any rate no English writer, has written about childhood better than Dickens," wrote George Orwell. "No novelist has shown the same power of entering into the child's point of view" (George Orwell, "Charles Dickens," in *A Collection of Essays* [New York: Harvest, 1981], 60). Hine is an American Dickens, not just by virtue of his subject matter—his Knoxville doffers are recognizably Dickensian, latter-day Tennessee variations on Mealy Potatoes and the other child workers, including David himself, in the brief child-labor section of *David Copperfield*: "I became, at ten years old, a little laboring hind in the service of Murdstone and Grinby" (Dickens, *David Copperfield* [New York: Vintage, 2012], 153). Hine's politics, however, were far more radical—Dickens, as Orwell notes, hardly disapproved of child labor as such, only child labor as it pertained to sensitive children such as the autobiographical Copperfield himself.

Noon Hour, Singer Manufacturing Company, South Bend, Indiana, October 1908. For the strike at the Singer Works at Clydebank, see Ishbel Ballantine et al., *The Singer Strike,*

Clydebank, 1911 (Glasgow: Clydeside Press, 1989). For the Singer operations at South Bend, see David Hounshell, *From the American System to Mass Production, 1800–1932: The Development of Manufacturing Technology in the United States* (Baltimore: Johns Hopkins University Press, 1985), 132–44. "The cry of the Disinherited": Spargo, "Eugene V. Debs, Incarnate Spirit of Revolt," 509; the accident of Charles Schmalzreid: Leighton Pine, letter to Singer Manufacturing Company, New York, April 20, 1901; Singer Manufacturing Co. Cabinet Factory, South Bend, Ind., Papers, Wisconsin Historical Society, Madison. The accident of Walenty Kloska: Pine, letter to Singer Manufacturing Company, March 12, 1901, Singer Papers, Wisconsin Historical Society; "The agitators are silenced": Pine, letter to F. G. Bourne, April 7, 1900, Singer Papers, Wisconsin Historical Society. For an overview of the Oshkosh woodworker strike, including the entire text of Clarence Darrow's argument in defense of the union leaders charged with conspiring against the Paine Lumber Company, see Lee Baxandall, "Fur, Logs, and Human Lives: The Great Oshkosh Woodworker Strike of 1898," *Green Mountain Quarterly* 3 (May 1976): 1–113. For a study of the cranberry bog photographs, see Nicholas P. Ciotola, "From Philadelphia to the Pinelands: The New Jersey Photographs of Lewis W. Hine," *Pennsylvania Magazine of History and Biography* 137 (April 2013): 179–90.

Coming out of Amoskeag Mfg. Co., Manchester, New Hampshire, May 1909. "We were proud we were weavers": quoted in Tamara K. Hareven, *Family Time and Industrial Time: The Relationship between the Family and Work in a New England Industrial Community* (Cambridge: Cambridge University Press, 1982), 72; the ringing of the factory bells in Manchester: the *Manchester Mirror*, June 15, 1907, quoted in Hareven, *Family Time and Industrial Time*, epigraph, 13; Napoleon Camire: see Manning, "Lewis Hine Project," *Mornings on Maple Street*.

Noon Hour, Holden-Leonard Co., Bennington, Vermont, August 1910. The bell "ruled the daily lives of hundred of workers": Joe Colliano, "Remembers the Bell and a More Gentle Time," Bennington *Banner*, April 1987, n.p., Holden-Leonard files, Bennington Museum, Bennington, Vermont; Spargo wrote a book about the monument: Spargo, *The Bennington Battle Monument* (Rutland, VT: Tuttle, 1925); for Mary Robinson Sanford, see Anthony Marro, "The Two Worlds of Mary Sanford," *Walloomsack Review* 1 (October 2008): 16–29; the fate of the Holden-Leonard building and the disappearance of the bell: "Once-Ailing Ben-Mont Now Reports Big Upswing," Bennington *Banner*, May 8, 1969, 1; Tordis Ilg Isselhardt, "Destroyed Bell Should Heighten Historic Awareness," Bennington *Banner*, undated clipping, Holden-Leonard files, Bennington Museum.

The Octopus. "the "anticipatory habit": H. G. Wells, *Future in America*, 11; The architects of the future," "the ensnaring and illusive vision of things": Coburn, quoted in Giles Edgerton, "Photography as One of the Fine Arts: The Camera Pictures of Alvin Langdon Coburn," *Craftsman* 11 (July 1907): 403; the rally in Madison Square Park and the bombs bursting on New York: H. G. Wells, *War in the Air*, 128–50, esp. 131, 148–49.

Opelika, October 1914. For a reading of de Chirico's piazzas, see Hal Foster, *Compulsive Beauty* (Cambridge, MA: MIT Press, 1993), 61–73. For legislation and statistics concerning child labor and school attendance in Alabama, see Eva Joffe, "Rural School Attendance," in Edward N. Clopper, *Child Welfare in Alabama* (New York: National Child Labor Committee, 1918), 101–24; and Elizabeth H. Davidson, *Child Labor Legislation in the Southern Textile States* (Chapel Hill: University of North Carolina Press, 1939), 215–37.

St. Louis, May 1910. "The riffraff, catching the smell of corruption": Lincoln Steffens, *The Shame of the Cities* (New York: McClure, Phillips, 1904), 21. The demolition of Havlin's Theater: "Picturesque Havlin's Theater Being Torn Down for Garage," St. Louis *Globe-Democrat*, July 27, 1924.

Newsboys and Supply Men, Cincinnati, Ohio, August 1908. "The boys get rough treatment": Hine and Edward N. Clopper, caption on back of photograph, Lewis Hine, National Child Labor Photographs, Special Collections, University of Maryland–Baltimore County Library. "The great majority of the supply men": Maurice B. Hexter, "The Newsboys of Cincinnati," *Studies from the Helen S. Trounstine Foundation* 1 (January 15, 1919): 115–16, 149–50. "Army Officer Facing Chair," "Slain While in Her Bed," "Grand Jury Probes Riot," *Cincinnati Post*, August 17,

1908, 1, 3. "The House of Dreams": Jane Addams, *The Spirit of Youth and the City Streets* (New York: Macmillan, 1911), 78–79.

Vance, A Trapper Boy, 15 years old, West Virginia, September 1908. "You see, once again I positively maintain that this peculiar quality exists in much of mankind—this love of torturing children": Fyodor Dostoevsky, *The Brothers Karamazov*, trans. Richard Pevear and Larissa Volokhonsky (New York: Farrar, Straus and Giroux, 1990), 241.

Spinner, Lancaster, South Carolina, December 1908. Annunciation: for Hine's religious iconography—especially the way early in his career he deliberately modeled his photographs on Renaissance Madonnas—see Tom Beck, "Duality in Lewis Hine's Child Labor Photographs," in *Priceless Children: American Photographs, 1890–1925* (Greensboro, NC: Weatherspoon Art Museum, 2001), 25–26. A "Change": Wells, *In the Days of the Comet*, 233. Pregnancy and the Factory: London, "The Apostate," 206; Herman Melville, "The Tartarus of Maids," in *The Complete Short Stories of Herman Melville* (New York: Random House, 1949), 195–211; Spargo, *Bitter Cry of the Children*, 45–53. For the fear of pregnancy at Amoskeag, see Hareven, *Family Time and Industrial Time*, 76. Upton Sinclair writes that at a Chicago meat factory sausages were "miraculously born from the machine" (Sinclair, *The Jungle* [New York: Penguin, 1985], 160).

Photo of newspaper advertisement, calling for workers on hair-brushes, New York, March 1912. "To the range of advertising there is no limit," "I wonder, sometimes": Lewis Hine, quoted in Alan Trachtenberg, ed., *Classic Essays in Photography* (New Haven, CT: Leete's Island Books, 1980), 110. On the formation of modern advertising in the period 1880–1930, see Raymond Williams, "Advertising: The Magic System," in Williams, *Culture and Materialism* (London: Verso, 2005), 170–95, esp. 177–81. Three and a half million pieces of mail sent out: Ira Kipnis, *The American Socialist Movement, 1897–1912* (1952; Chicago: Haymarket Books, 2004), 246.

Howard Williams, Shreveport, Louisiana, November 1913. "Sent out to place bets": Spargo, *Bitter Cry of the Children*, 185–86. "Learnt, not how to ascertain what the public wanted": John Drinkwater, *The Life and Adventures of Carl Laemmle* (New York: G. P. Putnam's Sons, 1931), 55, 61.

Leon Valcourt, Lawrence, Massachusetts, November 1910. One of the nation's largest manufacturers of wool and cotton products: Noel Perrin and Kenneth Breisch, *Mills and Factories of New England: Photographs by Serge Hambourg* (New York: Harry Abrams, 1988), 71. "The meaning of the times": Beveridge, *Meaning of the Times*, 420, 423. For the death of Valcourt, see Joe Manning's stunning research on the topic in Lewis Hine Project, *Mornings on Maple Street*.

Mery Horn, Hartford, Connecticut, March 1909. Addams, *Spirit of Youth and the City Streets*, 10. The look on her face is hard to know, "unnamable sensation": Fredric Jameson, "The Twin Sources of Realism: The Narrative Impulse," in *Antimonies of Realism*, 34; for the relation of changeable and unnameable affect to the everyday, see also Jameson's discussion of Erich Auerbach's essay "On the Serious Imitation of the Everyday" (Jameson, "Realism and the Dissolution of Genre," in *Antimonies of Realism*, 142–43). Auerbach's essay is in Gustave Flaubert, *Madame Bovary*, ed. Margaret Cohen (New York: Norton Critical Editions, 2005). "Her vision of this vision of his": Henry James, *What Maisie Knew* (London: Penguin, 2010), 135. "Small children have many more perceptions . . .": James, "Preface to the New York Edition, Volume IX," 1908, in *What Maisie Knew*, 294.

Two Young Girls, Worcester, Massachusetts, November 1912. "Make the story run a little hotter": Willa Cather, letter to Harrison G. Dwight, October 9, 1906, quoted in Andrew Janell and Janis Stout, eds., *The Selected Letters of Willa Cather* (New York: Alfred A. Knopf, 2013), 98. Eugene Debs, in Worcester to give a speech on his presidential campaign, "though I cannot remember a single word," "There was something about Debs's delivery," Debs's suit and the "well-fed and genial" Roosevelt and Taft: S. N. Behrman, "Debs on Yom Kippur," in *The Worcester Account* (New York: Random House, 1955), 91–102, 98, 99, 99, 100–101. Two girls go into a garden to look for playmates who are not there: Josephine Daskam Bacon, "The Children," *Harper's* (August 1909): 327–39. "The illusion of nearness": Edward N. Clopper, *Child Labor in City Streets* (New York: Macmillan, 1912), v. Clopper refers to newsboys, bootblacks, and peddlers.

Jason Francisco. For Francisco's vast photographic works and accompanying writings, see jasonfrancisco.net. Quotations are taken from Francisco's "A Dialogue with Lewis Hine" and "An Unfinished Memory." See also on the website the many photographs of *Alive and Destroyed*, which Francisco describes as "gestural and intuitive and not aligned with claims of knowledge" and as sharing "a similar spirit and visual vocabulary" with his work on Hine (Francisco, e-mail communication with the author, July 8, 2015).

One of the Young Girls, Richmond Hosiery Co., Rossville, Georgia, December 1910. For the hosiery industry in the South—including the revolutionary change from "crude 'leg-bag' hosiery to more refined silk stockings, see Milton N. Gross, *History of Hosiery* (New York: Fairchild, 1956). For a "Brief History of Richmond Hosiery Mills," see James Alfred Sartain, *History of Walker County Georgia*, vol. 1 (Dalton, GA: A. J. Showalter, 1932), 312.

6:15 P.M., Going Home from the Arkwright Mills, Spartanburg, S.C. May 1912. For the popularity of Coleman Blease in Spartanburg, see David Carlton, *Mill and Town in South Carolina 1880–1920* (Baton Rouge and London: Louisiana State University Press, 1982), 217.

Young Helper, Muscogee Mills, Columbus, Georgia, April 1913. For a lucid essay on the amnesia of postindustrial commemorations of the past, see Kirk Savage, "Monuments of a Lost Cause: The Postindustrial Campaign to Commemorate Steel," in *Beyond the Ruins: The Meanings of Deindustrialization*, ed. Jefferson Cowie and Joseph Heathcott (Ithaca, NY: ILR Press, 2003), 237–56. I have also found helpful Pamela Lee's discussion of Andreas Gursky's photography in relation to that of his teachers, Bernd and Hilla Becher, in Pamela M. Lee, *Forgetting the Art World* (Cambridge, MA: MIT Press, 2012), 77–86.

Huge casting for a big electric transformer. For a facsimile of Hine's book, *Men at Work: Photographic Studies of Modern Men and Machines* (New York: Macmillan, 1932), see *Lewis Hine: From the Collections of George Eastman House, International Museum of Photography and Film* (New York: D.A.P., 2012). "The drama of Hine's life," "a genuinely simple and sturdy soul," "the 'Oshkosh B-Gosh' from which he hails," "I'm afraid, Mr. Hine, that you haven't the broad sociological background required," "So began thirty years of work," "a pioneer": McCausland, "Portrait of a Photographer": 502–3. Tired radical: Walter Weyl, "Tired Radicals," 9–15. "Victorian film"; "An elderly man slowly climbed": Walter Rosenblum, foreword to *America and Lewis Hine: Photographs, 1904–1940* (New York: *Aperture*, 1977), 9. "It was terrific, impossible," It is true, man, every line of it": Jack London, *Martin Eden* (New York: Penguin, 1984), 364–65.

Foundation Man, Checking Up, Bolt Boy. "There is not one of Hine himself": Beaumont Newhall, "Lewis W. Hine," *Magazine of Art* 31 (November 1938): 637.

Mill running at night, Whitnel, North Carolina, December 1908. "Spiritual energy," "a certain intensity": William James, "The Moral Equivalent of War," in *The Heart of William James*, ed. Robert Richardson (Cambridge, MA: Harvard University Press, 2010), 301–13, esp. 311. "Light! Light in floods!": quoted in Gutman, *Lewis Hine and the American Social Conscience*, 19. La Follette's filibuster: "La Follette Breaks Senate Talk Record," New York *Times*, May 30, 1908. Debs's public speaking in the 1908 campaign, "such a fire as burns in him": Bernard J. Brommel, *Eugene V. Debs: Spokesman for Labor and Socialism* (Chicago: Charles H. Kerr, 1978), 98. Stevenson's boyhood memory: William James, "On a Certain Blindness in Human Beings," in *The Heart of William James*, 145–63, esp. 149–51. "We work in the dark": Henry James, "The Middle Years," in *The Figure in the Carpet and Other Stories* (Harmondsworth, Middlesex, England: Penguin, 1986), 258. "The world is on fire": Anderson, "A Man of Ideas," *Winesburg, Ohio*, 106.

INDEX

Page numbers in *italic type* indicate illustrations or photographs.

PHOTO CREDITS

Bennington Museum, Bennington, Vermont: fig. 53

C. A. Wayland Collection, McClung Historical Collection, Knox County Public Library, Knoxville, Tennessee: figs. 31–34

George Eastman House: figs. 39, 114, 117–21, 123

Jason Francisco: figs. 92, 94, 99, 101–2, 104–6, 108–11, 113

Lewis Hine Collection, Special Collections, Albin O. Kuhn Library and Gallery, University of Maryland–Baltimore County: figs. 72–73

Library of Congress, Prints and Photographs Division: figs. 1, 3–5, 7, 10–16, 18–19, 21–23, 26–27, 38, 40–44, 46–48, 50–51, 58, 60, 64–67, 69–71, 75–80, 83–91, 93, 96–98, 103, 107, 112, 116, 124

Maxfield Parrish Family, LLC / Licensed by VAGA, New York: figs. 8–9

Metropolitan Museum of Art / Art Resource: figs. 49, 54

Metropolitan Museum of Art / Getty Images: fig. 115

Munch Museum / Art Resource / Photo: Erich Lessing: fig. 6

The Museum of Modern Art / SCALA / Art Resource: figs. 55–56

Oshkosh Public Museum: figs. 20, 24–25, 28, 35–37, 45, 68, 122, 125

Österreichische Galerie Belvedere, Vienna: fig. 62

The Philadelphia Museum of Art, Gift of The Estate of Paul Strand / Art Resource: fig. 57

The Seattle Art Museum, Gift of Mrs. John C. Atwood, Jr., 55.210. Photo: Paul Macapia: fig. 59

Spartanburg Public Library, Spartanburg, South Carolina: fig. 100

Special Collections, Bailey-Howe Library, University of Vermont: fig. 52

Special Collections, Hodges Library, University of Tennessee: figs. 29–30

Spencer Museum of Art, University of Kansas: figs. 17, 81, 82

Stanford University Libraries: figs. 2, 61, 63, 74, 95